John McQuirk

Sermons and Discourses

Volume I.

John McQuirk

Sermons and Discourses
Volume I.

ISBN/EAN: 9783337159658

Printed in Europe, USA, Canada, Australia, Japan

Cover: Foto ©Lupo / pixelio.de

More available books at **www.hansebooks.com**

SERMONS AND DISCOURSES

BY

REV. JOHN McQUIRK, D.D., LL.D.

RECTOR OF ST. PAUL'S CHURCH
NEW YORK CITY

VOLUME I.

FR. PUSTET
PRINTER TO THE HOLY SEE AND THE S. CONGREGATION OF RITES

FR. PUSTET & CO.

NEW YORK	CINCINNATI
52 BARCLAY STREET	184 MAIN STREET
L.B. 1886	L.B. 738

1896

COPYRIGHT, 1896, BY
JOHN McQUIRK

All Rights Reserved

TROW DIRECTORY
PRINTING AND BOOK BINDING COMPANY
NEW YORK

To

The Memory

Of His

Father and Mother

This Volume

Is

Affectionately Inscribed

By

The Author

Imprimatur

MICHAEL AUGUSTINE
Archbishop of New York

PREFACE.

The Discourses contained in this Volume are a few of those preached by the Author in the course of his ministry. He publishes them, somewhat against his own judgment, in deference to the urgent request of some whose opinion is entitled to his regard. The reception accorded to a few of them, issued in pamphlet form, would seem to justify their advice.

These Sermons were not written before their original delivery, but carefully prepared as to thought and matter; the moment of speaking was trusted to for the language and manner of expression. They were afterward reduced to writing, although without any intention of publication, but only as a means of preserving what had been the fruit of much reflection and some research. They were written, as far as memory served, as spoken. They are published as then written, with such verbal corrections as were necessary. This will account for what may be defects, perhaps, in a book, but not always such in discourses meant to be spoken and heard. Faults in the one may be merits in the other.

It is hoped that the idea, borrowed from the custom of the Church at all times, and formerly more in vogue in religious books than at present, of impressing Divine truths and lessons by illustration, may be found acceptable.

Trusting that the Collection may further the end for which the Discourses were spoken, and that, with God's blessing, it may do good to many, I leave it in the hands of the reader

ST. PAUL'S CHURCH, NEW YORK,
FESTIVAL OF STS. PETER AND PAUL, 1896.

CONTENTS.

		PAGE
I.	Mortal Sin,	3
II.	Death,	19
III.	The Particular Judgment,	33
IV.	Heaven,	51
V.	The Punishment of Hell,	69
VI.	The Delay of Repentance,	85
VII.	The Last Judgment,	105
VIII.	On the Greatness of God,	123
IX.	Almsgiving,	139
X.	The Immortality of the Soul,	157
XI.	The Example of the Saints,	173
XII.	On Prayer,	191
XIII.	Motives to Humility,	207
XIV.	The Love of God our True Interest,	221
XV.	The Incarnation,	237
XVI.	The Birth of Christ,	251
XVII.	Love of our Neighbor,	265
XVIII.	The Forgiveness of Injuries,	277

		PAGE
XIX.	THE LOVE OF JESUS IN THE BLESSED SACRAMENT,	291
XX.	NECESSITY OF A TEACHER IN RELIGION,	313
XXI.	THE IMMACULATE CONCEPTION OF THE BLESSED VIRGIN MARY,	329
XXII.	THE HOLY GHOST IN OUR SOULS,	353
XXIII.	THE PASSION OF CHRIST—THE LESSONS OF THE CROSS,	379
XXIV.	THE PASSION OF CHRIST—*Continued*,	397
XXV.	THE EXISTENCE OF HELL,	417

THE NEW YORK
PUBLIC LIBRARY

ASTOR, LENOX AND
TILDEN FOUNT -

MORTAL SIN.

"And a great Battle was in Heaven: Michael and his angels fought with the dragon, and the dragon fought, and his angels, and they prevailed not, neither was their place found any more in Heaven, and that great dragon was cast out, the old serpent which is called the Devil, and Satan, that seduceth the whole world, and he was cast unto the earth, and His angels were cast forth with him. And I heard a great voice in Heaven saying, 'Now salvation is accomplished and strength and the kingdom of our God, and the power of His Christ, because the accuser of our brethren is cast out, who accused them before our God, day and night.'"—Apocalypse xii. 7-10.

"For if God spared not the angels who sinned, but with ropes cast them down into Hell and delivered them unto chains of darkness to be tormented, to be reserved to judgment; and spared not the old world, but preserved the eighth man, Noe, a preacher of justice, bringing in the flood on the world of the Impious."—II. Peter ii. 4-5.

To realize the nature and enormity of mortal sin, we have but to consider what it is in itself. It is rebellion against God; it is that which, if it were possible, would cause the Lord and Maker of all things to cease to be! It is the usurpation on the part of the creature of the right and rank of the Creator. Theologians tell us that to estimate the gravity of the offence we must consider the dignity of Him to whom the offence is offered and the condition of the offender.

A man who offends his fellow-man commits an

offence; but yet not so great one because they are of the same rank. A man who offends his superior commits a still greater offence, because of the greater importance of him offended. A man who offends a king, commits an offence which men will not hesitate to avenge by the taking of the life of the offender, because of the heinousness of affronting so exalted a personage; and so the gravity increases as the dignity of the offended personage increases. What then are we to think of the gravity, the enormity of an offence offered to the Lord of Lords; the King of Kings; the Maker and Ruler of all things, compared with whom all human dignity and majesty is as nothing; of an offence by which the creature usurps the throne of God and bids defiance to His divine authority.

The gravity of an offence is measured by the dignity of the offended and the condition of the offender.

Now as God is of infinite majesty, of infinite greatness, sin, which is an insult to Him, partakes of this infinite character, and becomes infinite in its malice. And who is man that presumes to offend God? As God is infinitely great, man is infinitely vile, a worm of the earth, the creature of an hour! Who then can comprehend the deadly hate, the intense malignity of mortal sin? God, boundless in His perfections, power, wisdom, justice, mercy, at whose awful presence the angels hide their face, and earth and heaven do flee away—God supreme in majesty, and unutterably to be adored, is insulted by a vile creature, the work of His hands, a worm of the earth, who has nothing he can call his own, and owes everything he possesses to the munificence of the Lord he offends, and whose mandates he tramples under foot!

In this the offence becomes aggravated—that in offending this God of infinite majesty, he rises against his Creator, and abandons his last end. It is God that created the sinner, drew him forth from inexistence, bestowed upon him life, body, soul, immortal hopes, all that he has. Had it not been for God, he would forever have remained in the state of possibility; never known what life is; never have beheld the splendors of creation; never have known the great gifts with which God has endowed him,—making him little less than the angels; never have known the glorious destiny which awaits him! When then he sins it is the creature rebelling against the Creator, the creature rebelling against the hand that fashioned it into being, striking the God who drew it forth from nothing, and the giver of all his gifts.

Ingratitude among men is held to be detestable; ingratitude to a friend unpardonable. What are we to think of the black ingratitude of the sinner to God, his first Author and sovereign Benefactor? We cannot fathom the wickedness and ingratitude of the creature when it says to the Creator, " I will not serve."

He departs from his last end. Man feels himself born for God; he feels himself transported, by an impulse he cannot resist, to perfect happiness. He seeks it in all he does. He is not free, not to seek it. He knows that God has implanted this desire in his soul to direct him to his last end. He feels that this happiness is not to be obtained here below; that it is in God alone it is to be found. When he commits mortal sin he knows that his eternal salvation is involved in the act, and for sake of a petty gratification that can last but a moment, he abandons the happiness for which he feels he has been created and which alone can satisfy his soul. He prefers the creature to the Creator, his passion to the law of God, a momentary pleasure to a happiness that endures forever. He spurns the eternal bliss God holds forth to him, and wise in all other things, he becomes a fool in that which supremely and eternally concerns him. What folly, what madness, what infatuation! How comes it that so thick a darkness should obscure the mind of God's noblest creature, and of one so prudent and painstaking in all that concerns the affairs of this perishable world.

No! we shall never understand the folly of man in preferring the vanities of life to the glorious destiny that revelation discloses. We shall never fathom the ingratitude of man in offending his Lord and Maker and Benefactor. We shall never comprehend the full nature, the deadly malice of mortal sin while in this life! It will need the eternal sun of justice to illuminate us on this subject. God is infinite; sin is therefore infinite in its malice. As we cannot comprehend God, neither can we comprehend sin; we cannot measure what is boundless; we cannot, therefore, grasp what is meant when sin is said to be of infinite malice. Never in this life shall we do it. Not until our disembodied spirits shall stand in the presence of God and there behold the limitless perfection and loveliness, and the dazzling splendor of the God-head—not until then shall we at all realize the intense malignity of mortal sin and the hatred that God bears it!

Let us then despair of forming any adequate conception of sin. Yet from this very difficulty, nay impossibility, of comprehending it, we can best understand what it must be. As it is from the very mysteriousness that surrounds the Godhead we derive our best idea of the infinity of God, so it is from the incomprehensibility of sin, we can best feel what it must be. It is so great that we cannot comprehend it; how great then must it not be! No consideration could give us a better idea of the inherent malice, the inconceivable deformity of mortal sin!

It is not alone from considering the nature of sin in itself that we can form some imperfect idea of its enormity. Revelation has disclosed to us certain facts from which better than from any reasoning we are permitted to know something of its dread character.

We are told that long before this world was made it pleased God to surround Himself with myriads of angels, pure spirits, who were to minister around His throne. They were superior intelligences endowed with wondrous gifts. Their knowledge was greater by far than that which any creature has since possessed. They were

God's own handiwork. He poured upon them a profusion of His choicest gifts and graces. They were in the closest communion with God. It was their privilege to sing His praises, to glorify His name. They were created to last forever.

Yet a time came, a temptation came, and through pride they rebelled against God. It was but a thought of pride, and in that instant they were cast down from their high estate to bottomless perdition, there forever " to dwell in adamantine chains and penal fire." There was no time given for repentance, there was no ransom promised, there was no further trial, no awaiting of a second offence, no hope of any future alleviation or cessation of their misery. They sinned in thought, a mortal sin indeed, but yet only a sin of thought, and in that same moment " were cast down in darkness and everlasting chains until the day of judgment."

Here we have an awful illustration of the enormity of sin. God is a God of justice and of mercy. He loves all the works of His hands. He must have had a special love for the angels because of their sublime office, and the divine gifts of which He had made them the recipients. He could not inflict upon them a punishment out of proportion to their sin. What then are we to think of their sin? How are we to comprehend its magnitude? What must be this gigantic evil so loathsome to Almighty God, that for its punishment He condemns the noblest work of His hand, without a moment's warning, down to the lowest depths of hell, there to suffer everlasting torture, "unrespited, unreprieved, ages of hopeless end?"

But to come nearer ourselves. We read that God, to fill the void occasioned by the fall of the angels, created man. And in the gifts that He bestowed upon him made him but little less than the angels. He gave him not only a nature perfect in the natural order, but raised it to a supernatural plane, and assigned to it an immortal destiny—made it the heir of endless glory. There was no warring of the flesh against the spirit; there was no want of conformity between the will of man and that of God. Our inferior nature was held in subjection to reason, and reason in perfect harmony with the will of God, by the sovereign power of the grace with which man's soul was filled. There was no sorrow in the heart of man because he knew not sin. Pain, sickness, death, and all the other ills to which our poor flesh is heir, were exiled from man's happy state. He lived in God's holy pleasure and found the bliss which he has ever since sought in vain, and will forever seek in vain until he repossesses it in God, his beginning and final destiny. He was endowed with wondrous knowledge, with enlightenment of mind, and rectitude of will. Placed in the midst of a paradise, filled with every delight, given absolute dominion of all things, all nature was eager to do his bidding, all creatures acknowledged his authority. The world and all that God had made was for his use and benefit as means or instruments of his eternal good. He was created immortal, to be translated alive to the presence of God, if he remained faithful. There was but "one restraint, lord of the world beside." He could not be God's creature without owing submission to Him. God Himself could not create a creature without this necessary law of his being. It is an intrinsic necessity founded in the very nature of things. A thing created, from the very fact that it is created, can never, without sin, divest itself of the relation of subordination to its Creator.

Accordingly a restraint was imposed upon Adam to test his obedience. He was told that in whatever day he would eat the forbidden fruit, in that day he should die. He knew that on him depended the destiny of his posterity; that his fidelity would be meritorious for all; that his disobedience would entail the ruin of all.

Yet in an evil hour the woman was tempted, did eat, and gave to Adam, who did eat. In a moment all was lost; the glory of Paradise faded forever. "All nature gave sign through all her works that all was lost." Adam's past pleasure seemed but a dream. He was driven out of Paradise, the prospect of immortal happiness closed upon him; the certainty of unending woe stared him in the face. He was condemned, with all his posterity, to death and everlasting punishment. Thus we were all eternally lost.

It was from this estrangement from the Creator that has flowed all the evil and misery, sin and suffering, that has since afflicted our race. It was the sovereign power of the grace of God in man, that repressed his violent inclinations and harmonized his whole nature. This grace lost, his passions rebelled against reason; and reason obscured and weakened was no longer in accord with God. As it is the strong arm of the law that holds the discordant elements of society in subjection, and when this law is suspended, riot, bloodshed, tumult, and disorder prevail; so, when the grace of God was withdrawn from man, then pride, cruelty, envy, lust, and all evil passions burst forth, turning human society into that state so fearfully described by St. Paul as without God, and without hope. Soon man forgot God and his duties to Him, and gave to the creature the glory due to God. Yes, it is to Adam's fall, as its source and cause, are to be traced all the sin and misery, all the wars and pestilences, hunger, thirst, and nakedness, cruelty and licentiousness, discord, hate, and bloodshed,—all the physical pain and moral evil that has since deluged and afflicted humanity.

How dreadful then must be this evil of sin, which was capable not only of condemning our race to everlasting punishment, but also of entailing upon us all so many and such irremediable evils. Let us say again, that God is a God of Justice. He cannot inflict a punishment greater than the offence. What then must be the mysterious nature of sin, on whose account He condemns to everlasting death, not only those who had committed it, but us, their posterity, who had no personal participation in it, and inflicts upon all Adam's posterity all the temporal evils that man has ever suffered, is suffering, and will forever suffer! How infinitely displeasing to God must be sin when He visits upon it such condign, such inconceivable punishments! A whole race damned for *one sin;* for a sin committed thousands of years before our birth! Adam condemned to a temporal punishment of nine hundred years; the whole race involved in the misery and sin and suffering of which all history is but the record, and of which we ourselves have daily experience. What are we to think of that which brings with it such consequences?

From what has been said it is manifest that mortal sin must be a sovereign evil, unutterably offensive to God; of its own nature unpardonable and irremediable in its effects. The facility with which sin may be forgiven to those who have the required dispositions must not be regarded as due or belonging in any sense or by any right or necessity to sin itself. The remission is made possible by the redemption of Christ and by the merits of His blood applied to our souls. It is He who cancels our sins and takes upon Himself our transgressions. Without this ransom there had never been forgiveness for sin. Sin once committed is everlasting. Of its own nature it is irremissible. Nor can any valid reason be adduced to evince that God is bound to pardon the sinner, or to accept any atonement for sin, or be propitiated with any repentance. We see this in the case of the angels, whose sin was without remission.

As sin is in itself unpardonable, so its effects are of themselves irreparable. They have not yet ceased. They flow on from generation to generation, like wave after wave, to the remotest posterity. The effects of Adam's rebellion are still in our souls. His sin is renewed by all his children. Age succeeds age; it has the same story of human passion, misery, and iniquity to narrate. It is true that we have been redeemed with a wondrous, a copious, a superabundant redemption. Christ's blood was sufficient to atone for the sins of ten thousand worlds. But in spite of Redemption the effects of Adam's sin remain.

The sacrifice of Christ, all sufficient though it is, remains to be applied to individual souls. And how few are they who apply it! Not the indifferent, the sinful, and those who never think of salvation! What difficulties, what dangers in the salvation of everyone! What pains required, what diligence in the use of grace! What fidelity in avoiding sin! How many have never known the truth and salvation of Christ, or have abandoned it and fallen into heresy, indifference, or even infidelity. See the superstition, idolatry, immorality, skepticism, infidelity that prevail among men! What is human society but a seething mass of sin, unbelief, and corruption!

How great, how incomprehensible, I ask, must not sin be, which is capable of introducing into the world such horrid, intense, widespread, everlasting evils?—evils which endure after the shedding of the blood of the Incarnate God!—evils which shall only cease when He shall come to judge the world!

And now, my brethren, this is that with which we are so familiar; which we commit with so little scruple. Whatever may be said of the greater malice of sin, because of the greater knowledge of the angels and of Adam, yet in the light and understanding that comes from experience we know more of sin than they did. Had we then sinned but once we were far more guilty and more deserving of punishment than they. They had no previous experience of sin. But we have seen its enormity in the fall of the angels, in the fall of our first parents, nay, we even partook in that fall and still feel its effects. Seeing the irreparable ruin all around us caused by their sin and with its evil effects yet festering in our souls; seeing the wide and general devastation of that one withering sin; seeing that it brought death into the world with all our woe, seeing the millions that have been lost in consequence of it, seeing the plan of redemption that was had recourse to, to redeem us from it; seeing that in spite of this redemption these effects still remain; seeing that all this is the consequence of Adam's sin, what must be our guilt in renewing that sin even once? Have we not seen the sins of men washed away by a flood that destroyed all men with a few exceptions, have we not known of fire coming down from heaven and destroying cities on account of their sins. We then in the light of experience realize better than they the consequences of sin; and as a result we are far guiltier when we commit even one sin. Who can say that he has committed but one sin, how many hundreds, nay, how many thousands of mortal sins have many of you committed?

But what ought to make sin in a manner unpardonable in man is, that it is done after the shedding of Christ's blood; after the unutterable sacrifice offered on the cross for the cancelling of our sins and the salvation of our souls. It is committed in defiance of that priceless ransom; it re-crucifies the Son of God and makes a mockery of him. It grieves the Holy Spirit and puts Him to an open shame. Who then will describe the magnitude of sin? Who will conceive the black ingratitude of the sinner?

Better far than in the example of the angels, and in the fall of our first parents, are we taught the hatefulness and malignity of sin, when we estimate the price that was paid to redeem us from it and to restore us once again to God's favor. In the Incarnation, sufferings, and death of Christ, viewed as the necessary ransom of sin, can we comprehend its rank malice, the burning hate that God bears it; the injury it does our souls, and the woe and suffering and punishment it must entail upon us. Call to mind then that the Eternal God became man, lived a life of suffering, and died a death of shame and torment. Why? For sin. It was for the sins of men that he became man. It was the sins of men that made Him suffer; that nailed Him to the cross. " He was wounded for our iniquities, and bruised for our sins." Had He not died, we would have been all lost; irretrievably and forever lost. Man should suffer or some infinite satisfaction should be offered. We were all condemned in Adam. He had committed an offence of infinite malice. It was not in the capacity of his finite nature to atone for such a transgression. An infinite offence calls for an infinite satisfaction.

What could man, finite man, do to appease the anger of an infinite God. If an atonement was to be made, if a ransom was to be offered, that atonement should be of infinite merit, that ransom should be of priceless value. The Eternal God became incarnate and died for our sins. Verily are we bought with a great price.

If God, for the expiation of sin, had required the sacrifice of one man, it would have been a great ransom and would have made us conceive of sin as something of horrid deformity. If He had required the sacrifice of all men it had been an awful punishment; and yet it would have been insufficient to atone for sin. If he had required the incarnation, sufferings, and death of all the angels and archangels, it surely had been a sacrifice of incalculable value; and it would have taught us something of the gravity of sin, yet it would have been insufficient to exhaust its malice. But what are we to think when we know that God, for the expiation of sin, required the sacrifice of His only begotten Son; the figure of His substance and the splendor of His glory! What are we to think of the deep guilt, foul enormity, hell-dyed blackness of sin, which crucified the Eternal God. How are we to estimate the justice of God that was content with nothing less than the shedding of the blood of His Incarnate Son?

Yes, my brethren, it is here that we are to derive our best notion of mortal sin. It is in meditating on the awful agony of Christ in the Garden of Gethsemane, when the vision coming before Him of all the sins of men, past, present, and to come, overcome by their wickedness and black ingratitude, the blood burst from every pore; and His heart would have broken but for the greater sacrifice He had still to make; it is in contemplating the stern justice of the Father which permitted Him to drain the chalice of affliction to the dregs; it is in contemplating the excruciating torments, the untold agony of His passion; it is in beholding Him nailed to the cross for our sins; it is in the thorn-crowned head, the nail-pierced hands, the opened side, in the torrents of blood that drenched the hill of Calvary, which the sin-smitten earth, greedy for its ransom, drank up as they fell from His sacred wounds, it is in all this that we are to understand the true nature, the deadly malice of mortal sin, the hatred God bears it, and the eternal punishment with which, if unrepented, we may expect, it shall be visited in us.

How hateful must sin be to God when He punished it so awfully and so mysteriously in His only Son, hearkening not to the prayer uttered by Him in the dreadful agony in Gethsemane: "Father, if it be possible, let this chalice pass away," permitting all the horrors of the passion and crucifixion, suffering, without compassion, the awful cry to pierce the heavens, " Lord, God, why hast thou abandoned me?" And all this in whom there was neither sin nor the shadow of sin; but who was the heaven-ordained and accepted sacrifice for sin.

Oh, well may we despair of ever comprehending the nature of sin! Yet let us draw this lesson.

If God so punished His Son, how will He punish us? If He spared not His only Son, who was without sin, what will He do to us, covered " with as many sins as there are hairs on our heads; with as many iniquities as our hearts have conceived thoughts." If He has done so in the green wood, what will He not do in the dry?

Let us tremble at our peril. Let us tremble at the punishment that awaits us. Let us think what it is to fall into the hands of an angry God. If He spared not the angels, if He spared not Adam, if He spared not His only begotten Son, the figure of His substance and splendor of His glory! If He spared not the Creator infinitely great will He spare the creature infinitely vile?

If it were as easy to make men hate sin, and to deter them from it, as it is to convince them that sin is the greatest of evils, the preacher would not have so often to lament the fruitlessness of his ministry. But it is one thing to be convinced of a truth and quite another to act upon the conviction. We may be persuaded that sin is the greatest of evils, and yet cling to it. It needs the grace and light of God to enable us to overcome sin.

Pray then to the Giver of every good and perfect gift, that He may pierce your souls with a vivid perception, an intimate realization of sin. Pray Him to touch your hearts, and strengthen your wills, that you may rise without further delay from the grave of sin to a life of sinlessness and Christian virtue that will be a pledge of your eternal life hereafter.

DEATH.

A PRAYER OF MOSES THE MAN OF GOD.

LORD, thou hast been our refuge from generation to generation.

Before the mountains were made, or the earth and the world was formed; from eternity and to eternity thou art God.

Turn not man away to be brought low: and thou hast said: Be converted, O ye sons of men.

For a thousand years in thy sight *are* as yesterday, which is past.

And as a watch in the night, things that are counted nothing, shall their years be.

In the morning *man* shall grow up like grass, in the morning he shall flourish and pass away: in the evening he shall fall, grow dry and wither.

For in thy wrath we have fainted away and are troubled in thy indignation.

Thou hast set our iniquities before thy eyes: our life in the light of thy countenance.

For all our days are spent; and in thy wrath we have fainted away.

Our years shall be considered as a spider: the days of our years are three-score, and ten years.

But if in the strong *they be* fourscore years: and what is more of them is labor and sorrow.

For humiliation is come upon us: and we shall be corrected.

Who knoweth the power of thy anger, and for thy fear who can number thy wrath?

So make thy right hand known: and teach our heart wisdom.

Return, O Lord, how long? and be entreated in favor of thy servants.

We are filled in the morning with thy mercy: and we have rejoiced, and are delighted all our days.

We have rejoiced for the days in which Thou hast humbled us: for the years in which we have seen evils.

Look upon Thy servants and upon their works: and direct their children.

And let the brightness of the Lord our God be upon us: and direct Thou the works of our hands over us; yea, the work of our hands do Thou direct.—PSALM LXXXIX.

ALL nature is in a state of continual transition. Look where we may, everything is perpetually changing. The least of God's works is not any more exempt from change than the greatest. From the most contemptible insect that crawls the earth to the magnificent heavenly bodies, in all things above us, around us, and within us we see change, never-ceasing change, and perpetual renovation. And yet, in the midst of this universal and never-ending process, not one atom of matter is lost. Everything is endowed with an essential virtue, which preserves it through the multiform changes it undergoes.

If things are continually dying, they are continually coming to life again. If they are undergoing change, it is but assuming new forms of organization, new modes of being. Nations rise, flourish, and decay, and from their ruins spring new forms of government; one civilization contains within it the germs of a newer and higher advancement. The trees of the forest, the flowers that fill the earth with fragrance, the myriad forms of vegetable life, all in due time languish and perish and die; but they provide for their resurrection in the teeming abundance of seed which they cast upon the earth. The sun disappears to-day, to re-appear to-morrow; spring is overtaken by summer, dies in autumn, is buried in winter, and returns with undiminished freshness and beauty in April; so throughout the moral and physical world there is continual death and continual resurrection, unceasing dissolution, and yet continual permanence.

Is man any exception to this law of mortality written on all things? Does he escape the law of corruption to which all things are subject, and if he changes is he renewed as all things else?

Yes, my brethren, man changes, changes continually. When he begins to live he begins to die. With the principle of life, which sustains him in being, there is a principle of dissolution by which he dies daily, and to which he shall altogether eventually succumb. Generations of men rise, flourish, decay, die, and are forgotten with the regularity of the crops of the earth. Man is born, lives for a little while, is subject to much misery, and then dies; this is the life of every man. New beings are continually coming upon the stage of life, as others disappear to make way for them. Compare the world of to-day with the world of twenty or thirty years ago. How completely changed! New men, new events, new enterprises, new ambitions! The children of men pass with fearful rapidity from time to eternity. Others disappear to make way for us. We, too, shall disappear to make way for those who will come after us.

We are changing continually; we are dying continually. We are told that so universal and complete a change is unceasingly going on within us that but a few years serve for the entire renovation of our bodies; that nothing preserves their identity but the gradual nature of the change and the permanence of the soul, whose nature is unchanging.

Of the 1,500,000,000 of human beings that cover this habitable globe, we are told that not a moment passes but witnesses the death of some one. If men are continually coming into life, they are also continually going out of it. Even now while I speak some are dying; some, who in health, and while death was at a distance from them, thought as little of it as you do now. The world is indeed a stage on which we fret our busy hour, soon to make our exit and then die and be forgotten.

This life that we call time has been compared to a bridge connecting two great oceans—that of the eternity that preceded our birth, with that of the eternity that begins with death. If we could in imagination ascend some lofty eminence we would see the multitudes that are continually going out of life, falling through the trap-doors that fill this bridge, some at the very beginning of their career, some almost before they have touched the bridge, some in the middle, some further on; but all somewhere.

Yes, my brethren, we must die; nothing is more certain. "It is appointed for all men once to die." This is the solemn lesson I would teach you. You

DEATH.   23

must all one day die. Perhaps you smile at the
novelty of the news and ask me who ever doubted
it, who ever did not know it, is it not to be seen on
every side? Why proclaim with so much solemnity that trite saying so generally admitted and
so incontestable that no one has ever called it in
doubt? Yes, you know it, you have heard it a
thousand times, it is to be seen every day, it is
written on all God's works. But withal you know
it, notwithstanding you are taught by God Himself that " Dust thou art and into dust thou shalt
return," notwithstanding the abundant evidence
with which it is brought home to you daily, perhaps, by the loss of a father, or mother, or sister,
or brother, or dear friend, in spite of your intimate
persuasion and certain knowledge that you are all
one day to die, how many realize this belief, how
many infuse it into their actions, so as to make it
the governing principle of their lives? Our faith
is only a speculative one; we live as if we were
never to die; because we are not sure of the moment, we act as if it were not to come at all. The
uncertainty lulls us to sleep. We are standing on
the verge of a frightful precipice, all unconscious
of our danger; we only feel it when we miss our
foothold and are dashed into the terrific abyss that
lies yawning beneath.

We believe in God. How few act as if they
believed in Him! We acknowledge Christ, His
Church, His Sacraments. How little of this belief
is infused into our lives! Yes, my brethren, again
and again I say, we must die; and no more solemn lesson can be taught by the minister of Christ

than that, " It is appointed for all men once to die and after death be judged."

And what is it to die? Have you ever reflected on the agony that must accompany death? Remember death is the separation of soul and body. Who can measure the keenness of the pain this involves? How great must be the pain of the separation of soul and body bound together by a union so close and incomprehensible that not even the greatest philosophers have been able to understand it! Remember the soul is made for the individual body—" a body thou hast fitted to me," so that the soul of one man will not suit any body but its own. Imagine, then, the agony inseparable from such a sundering! It is true that this agony is not always manifested; that, however, is because the dying man has not strength enough to show it; the agony is yet felt; the body, worn by some long sickness, has not the energy to exhibit the throes of its separation from the soul. But see death approach the strong, well-built frame of a man struck down in his vigor, and behold the fearful agony of his dissolution! Even the saints trembled at the thought of the natural sundering of soul and body.

There is not one of us, even the bravest, who does not tremble at the thought of the pain of death. There may be those who can exclaim at the hour of death—the vision of God overcoming the intensity of the pain of dissolution—" O Grave, where is thy victory? O Death, where is thy sting?" But it is only the just who have died before death comes upon them; died to the world, died to the desires of the flesh; separated soul and body by continual mortification of the latter. It is only the just man who looks upon the body as a prison, who feels that his death will be the termination of his trials and temptations—the beginning of his reward and glory; it is only he who can exult at the approach of death; it is not the wicked, who at the hour of death, in addition to his bodily pain, is tortured at having to abandon those pleasures and vanities for which alone he has lived and in which he has placed his happiness, and with the awful thought that he is now about to receive his reward; that no sooner will that soul be separated from the body than it will be cast down into eternal misery and woe!

But the spirit has this moment fled, the lifeless corpse lies there before us. See what the body is without the soul! Approach and lay your hand upon that brow, cold in death. Feel the shudder that runs through you as your hand is met with the cold and clammy touch of death. See that head which but a short time since was filled with great enterprises of business, with maturing vast worldly speculations, or with plots and plans to circumvent his fellow-man in the affairs of life! Of what avail now is all that energy and duplicity shown in the world's affairs? See those eyes, closed with a darkness which will never be dispelled till the light of the judgment-day; then to open, perhaps only to behold the eternal loss of body as well as soul. See the tongue, but a little while ago so eloquent in defamation, so ingenious in calumny, and which was the cause of so much uncharitableness and sin! See the ears, which so recently drank in the sound of revelry and dissipation, deaf to the wailing and lamentations of sorrowing friends, standing around his corpse bemoaning their loss, commending his good qualities, and throwing the mantle of charity and forgetfulness over his evil ones! See that manly form, that vigorous frame, stiff and stark and cold in death—utterly helpless and beyond the reach of all human skill and assistance! Remember that it is but in the condition to which everyone of us shall one day come.

But the body must be clothed in the habiliments of the grave; shroud and coffin, costly as may be, must be had, to show proper respect to the departed; but more frequently to pander to a miserable vanity, which is not lost sight of even in the presence of death. The prayers of the Church are asked for the departed by those who never moved a step for the conversion of the dead man during his life, when mercy was obtainable. A few days pass, the funeral takes place, crowds of friends gather to partake in his obsequies, the body is placed in a vault or grave, the last look is taken, all return home, and resume their parts once more in the play of life.

Return to that vault in a few days; raise the lid from the coffin and behold the hideous spectacle that greets your eyes; endure, if you can, the horrid stench that issues forth from the remains of your friend! Approach and behold! Listen to the questions that rise spontaneously to the mind while contemplating that sight so suited to show forth in the most vivid manner the nothingness of man, the emptiness of life, the vanity of all things human! The eyes, so lately filled with lust, and which so often conveyed poison to the soul and to the souls of others, where are they? See the sockets filled with worms. The nose, where is it? The most delicate organ of the body has been the first to succumb to the terrors of the grave. The ears, what sound hear they now, or, could they hear, what would it be but the sound of gnawing rats? The mouth, see the hideous and mocking grin that it assumes! Where is the beauty of feature and grace of form of which you are so proud and which you seek so sinfully to decorate to the loss of untold souls? Where is it now? Lost in corruption. See how the muscles and bonds that hold the body together are relaxing, limb separating from limb, head dropping from the body, joint from joint, the whole frame in the process of disintegration and corruption! Where are those talents, that comprehensive mind that raised its owner among his fellows, giving him an influence and respect that he ought to have employed for the glory of God, but which he centred upon himself? Where are now those graces and accomplishments that made their possessor the ornament of society, the life of conversation, and the pride of his friends? Where is now the reputation he enjoyed, where is now that immense property, those blocks of houses that he acquired, the immense fortune he saved during those fifty years he lived? Have they followed him to the grave? Alas! all that he has is what covers his carcass—a coffin, a shroud, and a pocketless one too. This is all that he has been able to take with him from the untold wealth which he spent his life to accumulate.

Yes, my brethren, it is standing beside the fast corrupting remains of our departed friend that we can best understand how supremely contemptible man is! It is by looking down into the grave and pondering what we shall be, that we can best understand what we are; by feeling our misery and wretchedness, we best learn our real value. At the same time it is there, too, that we can best understand how supremely noble, how God-like in the destiny that awaits him, is man; for we know that from that mass of corruption, all hideous as it is, shall one day arise incorruption. From those ashes shall the just man one day come forth, all glorious and immortal, to enjoy God forevermore.

Death, too, is a separation from the world. When we look out upon the world and behold the marvellous energy that men exhibit in its pursuit, we are almost tempted to believe that they believe not in a future life; else why not show a fraction of the solicitude to attain that life which they show to obtain the goods of this.

But death reverses all this and shows us the truth of things. Ask the ambitious man at the point of death what now he thinks of all the honors which he enjoyed and aspired to, when he is about to enter that bourne where prince and subject, millionaire and beggar, pontiff and priest shall be reduced to the same common earth? Ask the proud man what now it avails him to have thought so well of himself, or to have been esteemed by others, when he is going before a judge who sees the secrets of hearts and judges all things justly? Ask the rich man what now he thinks of his riches, when he has to abandon all and be content with that which is not denied to the meanest beggar—six feet by two of mother earth? Ask the voluptuary what now he thinks of his past excesses and disorders, when he sees hell yawning to swallow him the moment the soul leaves his body? Ask, in general, the sinner at the last hour what he thinks, when he sees nothing in the past but the sins and the pleasures which he must now abandon, sees nothing in the present, but the agony of having to leave all that his heart craves, and in the future nothing but everlasting misery and despair! But ask the just man at the hour of death and he will tell you that he has little terror of death; for he long since died in the world; that he has accustomed himself to the thought of death; that he has long since prepared for it; that it is but the fulfilment of his hopes, the end of his trials, the beginning of his glory. Death then enlightens us as to the world and its delusions.

The time of death is uncertain. We know not the day nor the hour. This is what makes us thoughtless of death. The uncertainty lulls us to sleep. Because we know not when we shall die, we live as if we were never to die. As we advance in years, death seems as distant as in youth. While we all speculatively admit that we must die, we would seem, practically, to believe that we were never to die. It may come at any moment. Ten thousand causes are at work, within us and around us, that may in an instant bring on death. We are organized with a skill and delicacy which beggars the proudest efforts of human ingenuity. The slightest cause may derange, or destroy, this divine workmanship.

A blow on the head, touching the brain, is enough to send angelic reason into howling madness. A slight affection of the heart, stopping the pulsations of that faithful organ—and death at once ensues. A few days' pneumonia will bring the man of stalwart frame and giant strength to the bed of death. I forbear to speak of the uncounted accidents on water and land that in every conceivable and always unlooked-for way are continually befalling untold multitudes.

Death is abroad everywhere. We know not when we shall fall before it. Our only safety is to be prepared to meet it. Thus armed, we have no reason to fear. It cannot harm us. It can destroy only the life of the body; the soul it cannot reach; and even over the body its dominion is but temporary.

We know not where or when or how we shall die. We know that we shall remain forever in the state in which death will find us. Everyone expects to die the death of the righteous, even though he lives the life of the reprobate. He continually looks forward to a season of pardon and repentance, which he keeps before his mind, but which recedes as age advances, until at length he is struck down by death, when repentance is no longer possible, and justice begins its sway. The son follows in the footsteps of the father, looking forward to a repentance that never comes until he joins his father in misery. And so generation succeeds generation, age succeeds age, God's love and mercy are trampled on, thousands are daily plunging into everlasting misery, cursing, when too late, the recklessness and folly that made them delay their conversion.

We all would wish to know the kind of death we shall die; we know that it is to be followed by our eternal happiness or eternal misery. The fear of something after death, this it is that makes us tremble at the thought of death. Yet how few ever try to think of the kind of death they shall die? Would you know it? The question is of easy solution. Would you know how you shall die? The Scripture answers you, " As you live."

" As you live, so shall you die." Do you live a life of godliness? Your death shall correspond thereto. Do you live the life of the wicked? Such shall be your death.

There may be, there are exceptions; but you have no right to count yourself among them. The conversion of a soul from sin is as great a miracle as the raising to life of one dead. You who pass your life in contemning God's law and abusing His grace, have no right to expect this priceless mercy at the hour of death. " As you live, so shall you die;" that is the character of your death. You may say, that this being true, few shall be saved. I am not going to argue this question. Rash indeed would the man be, who would base his hope of salvation on the fact of his belonging to the majority, who, he thinks, must be saved because they are the majority. We are told that "Narrow is the way that leads to life, and few there are who find it;" that "Many are called, but few chosen;" that of six hundred thousand Hebrews, but two entered the Promised Land; that of the human family all perished in the deluge save Noah and his family. Reflect on all this and see if you see much to encourage you in the delusion of the most of men being saved! Let us not try to improve on the doctrine of Jesus Christ.

"As you live, so shall you die." The proper preparation, then, for a good death is a good life. How few believe this in their actions! How thick the darkness that obscures the mind! How strange the perversity of the heart of man! But no words of mine can do aught; it needs the light and grace of the Holy Ghost.

Deign then, O God, to illumine us with this light, to pour down upon us this grace. Grant us to think of death now, as we shall when Thou wilt be pleased to send it; grant us to know and perfectly to understand that we only live to learn to die, that we only live well, when we so live that we are always ready to die. Grant us to look upon earth and all things here below as we shall when, for the last time, we close our eyes upon them, to open them to those of eternity.

THE PARTICULAR JUDGMENT.

But why judgest thou thy brother; or thou, why dost thou despise thy brother? For we shall all stand before the judgment seat of Christ.

For it is written: *As I live*, saith the Lord, *every knee shall bow to me, and every tongue shall confess to God.*

Therefore every one of us shall render account to God for himself.

Let us not therefore judge one another any more. But judge this rather that you put not a stumbling-block or a scandal in your brother's way.—St. Paul's Epistle to the Romans, xiv. 10–13.

For Jesus is not entered into the holy places made with hands, the patterns of the true; but into heaven itself, that he may appear now in the presence of God for us.

Nor yet that he should offer himself often, as the high-priest entereth into the Holies, every year with the blood of others:

For then he ought to have suffered often from the beginning of the world: but now once at the end of ages, he hath appeared for the destruction of sin, by the sacrifice of himself.

And as it is appointed unto men once to die, and after this the judgment.

So also Christ was offered once to exhaust the sins of many; the second time he shall appear without sin to them that expect Him unto salvation.—St. Paul's Epistle to the Hebrews, ix. 24–28.

FROM Scripture and from our own experience we know that man's life upon earth is a warfare. The life of every one of us, from the cradle to the grave, is but the record of a conflict, severe and unceasing, of our virtuous with our sinful inclinations; of the struggle of the flesh on one hand, alluring us to sin, and the law of the mind on the other, forbidding it. The world is but a great battle-field, where all men are enrolled under either of two banners: that of Jesus Christ or that of the prince of darkness. And it must be owned that the greater part of men, avowedly or not, are fighting under the standard of the evil one. And, what is worse, it must be acknowledged, that, if the final issue of this terrible, deadly encounter going on between God and the devil is to be sought within the limits of this life, vice is victorious, the devil gets the better of it, and is to be proclaimed the victor.

But fortunately this battle ends not here below; its final triumph is not to be had within the narrow limits of this life. This life is but the scene of the conflict, the bloody arena where the heat and burden of the fight are to be sustained, where limb is to be maimed, and life lost, and blood shed, if it be needful, for the cause in which we are engaged; but it is in the great hereafter that we are to seek the laurel wreaths of victory.

Human life begins here, but ends not here. Have you ever thought what a great thing human life is? How infinite in its nature! How immortal in its duration! It seems a little thing for a man to be born into the world, and yet, every soul born into the world adds to God's creations something that shall never die. It begins in time, but shall pass through time to eternity, and

THE PARTICULAR JUDGMENT. 35

partake of the immortality of God Himself. The human soul once created is deathless forevermore; it shall inherit undying torture or unending bliss. Its history is divided into two great periods—one ending with death and the other beginning thereat. It is placed here in this life to prove its worthiness for an eternal one hereafter. At the hour of death a judgment shall be pronounced by its great Captain, on the way it shall have fought His fight, on the bravery and success with which it shall have defended His cause. " It is appointed for all men once to die, and after death be judged." If found worthy, we shall receive the reward due to the brave; if we shall have proved ourselves cowards and traitors, we cannot but expect their punishment.

It is my purpose to speak to you to-day of the particular judgment; as the general will be but the reaffirming of the first without change, except that the body will be consigned to the soul's punishment or made to share the soul's glory, the first is for all of us the more important as irrevocably decisive of our eternal condition.

As there is no alarm or apprehension concerning the death of the just; as he who judges himself God will not judge; as his whole life is a continued preparation for judgment spent in the mortification of the passions, in dying to the world to live to God, in the practice of every virtue, there can be no doubt that a holy confidence will fill his soul when he comes to judgment, as the judgment of the just will be but his entrance into the kingdom prepared for him—we shall confine our remarks to the consideration of the sinner brought before the tribunal of Christ the moment after death. Nor shall we take our sinner from among pagans and those who have not so much as heard of Christ, nor from heretics, who, perhaps, more from misfortune than fault, have not known the whole truth; but we shall take him from our everyday Catholics, born in the faith, reared in it, who have sometimes even received its sacraments, and, perhaps, regularly attended at the divine sacrifice; from those whom the world believes good, and who are even so regarded by their fellow-religionists.

But let us say a word about the life of this man. He is a man, who, although born in the true faith, lives not up to it. He is content with a dead, speculative faith. He lives for the world, not for the end for which he has been made. He is intent on accumulating a fortune, not on the sanctification of his soul. His life is one of pleasure and gratification, not of penance and self-denial. He is solicitous for the praise of men, not for the approval of his conscience. He makes little or no scruple of violating God's law, if it will serve his purpose. He seldom thinks of God or raises his thoughts heaven-ward. From his mode of life you would think he was to stay on earth forever. He regards it not as a battle-field, he feels not the conflict going on between man and the devil, because he makes no resistance to temptation; the attacks of the devil are not attacks to him, but embraces which he covets. He has already virtually abandoned the cross and made himself over to its enemy. He lives on in mortal sin without purpose of change; he seldom or never approaches the sacraments. Perhaps he goes to mass; if he does it is the sum of his piety. He does it because it is respectable, and because his wife goes, and he would otherwise lose caste with the world (which regards a little religion as respectable). He hears the priest utter the truths of religion, but they affect him not; he serves them out to his neighbor as inapplicable to himself. He stifles the voice of conscience calling him to repentance. He chokes the inspirations of God, or, most fatal of all delusions, he eases his conscience by promising himself that he will repent before he dies; that he must take his salvation into serious account at no distant day; but that *now* he has too much to do, that, of course, he could not think of being damned, and looks forward to a season of repentance, that, alas, never comes!

At length he is prostrated on what shall prove his death-bed. At first it is but a cold accompanied with a cough, a slight affection of the nerves or heart, or some other trifling ailment. By and by he grows weaker and weaker, blood comes from the lungs, his heart is still more painfully agitated; yet his friends and doctors assure him it is nothing, it will pass away in a few weeks, and he will be himself again. Ask him to have the priest. "The priest!" he will exclaim. "Why, no, there is no need! I am not going to die!" And of course, he does not want him until then. Time passes on, the disease ripens, weaker and weaker he becomes; he is dissatisfied with the doctors, others are consulted but with no better success. He begins to think that his ailment is really clinging to him a long time! Strange thoughts flash across his mind. Sometimes a light, as from the other world, illumines it, and he begins to look upon the world differently from ever before. It is but delirium, he thinks, the fever mounting to the brain. He checks the course of his thoughts, brings back his wandering imagination. He knows not what it is that brings such strange thoughts into his mind; he is sorely perplexed; he begins to feel that something is about to happen. Like Balthasser he knows the hand-writing on the wall portends some strange calamity, but knows not what it is. Or, if it should occur to him that the hand of death is upon him, and that it is the light of eternity breaking upon his soul that perplexes him, his friends are careful to remove so annoying a thought, by telling him of his greatly improved condition, and of the bright hopes the doctors have that he will soon be out of danger. Finally a few days pass away. Death shows itself by signs not to be mistaken; the death-rattle is heard in his throat, his breathing grows fainter and fainter, light vanishes from his eyes, his friends scarcely realize that he is dying; hastily the priest is sent for, and a mock repentance is gone through with—a mock one, I say, for how can the sinner then be reconciled to God by a true repentance when he is scarcely conscious, or, if conscious, convulsed as he is with the agony of death, he can think of nothing but his tortures.

He dies. The soul, separated from the body, hastens that moment before the tribunal of Christ. Although the sinner is judged the instant the soul leaves the body, yet we may imagine the soul to tarry for a little while, exhausted after the death agony, before being ushered into the presence of his judge, and to cast a glance back at where it has just left and forward to where it is just going.

The soul will at first glance at the body in which it has been so recently encased. There it is surrounded by bereaved and mourning relatives, who do their utmost to honor the lifeless clay. They speak the praise of the departed, the evil is not mentioned. He was a good father; he has left an ample provision for his wife and children (the less said about how it was gotten the better). All care must be given to his obsequies; a few masses are requested for him, and in a few days the body is consigned to the grave. The soul looks back on the fortune which he spent his life in accumulating, often with so little scruple as to the means, and with so evident a disregard of honesty and of the rights of his fellow-men. Of what avail is it to him now, trembling at the prospect of the examination he is about to undergo? The pleasures which he enjoyed in the body, with what remorse does he regard them as being the sins which give him the greatest anguish and torture, because he knows they will be the surest to call forth God's unsparing justice? His reputation or fame among men—of how little worth is it now that he is about to appear before Him who reads the heart, and who will see how little he deserved the good name he may have had on earth, who will see that all was filth and abomination where men thought all was pure and righteous? His companions, faithful to him at all times, ready to assist him in every emergency, where are they now? Can they assist him in the greatest of all his trials? now, when his eternal destiny is trembling in the balance? They are in the world pursuing, as he once pursued, their worldly objects, thinking little of the sad condition of their sometime friend and companion.

Will all these worldly conditions inspire him with confidence in that hour, or give him grounds to hope for mercy from the Lord who is about to judge him? Will they not rather confound him and drive him into despair, or consume him with withering fear, seeing that they have been the means of his damnation?

He looks forward. Before whom is he about to appear? Before an all-righteous God, who searches all hearts and knows all their secrets; before a God of infinite justice who has declared that we shall render an account of every idle word. But, you will add, before a God of boundless mercy too. No, I answer, no longer a God of infinite mercy. It is finished with mercy, the reign of justice has begun. Mercy was very suitable and much needed on earth, where the passions were strong, where the fascinations of the world were many, where the contest was hot, and there, it was to be had in abundance. Mercy extends over the whole period of human life: it ends at death, and then justice, severe and inexorable, begins its sway. It is no longer before Jesus, the mediator, but before Jesus, the judge and avenger, that the sinner seeks pardon. It is not before Jesus stretched upon the cross, with arms outstretched to embrace all men, with the streams of blood that wash away the sins of the world falling from His sacred wounds, that the sinner is to appear, but before Jesus sent into the world to execute justice, to wreak vengeance, to reject them who have rejected Him.

We may imagine how the conscience of the sinner will smite him in that hour! Those of you who know what remorse is, how it eats the soul, how it is intense in proportion to the good we have lost or the evil done, and to the difficulty or impossibility of remedy, may imagine how the sinner will be torn with its stings, seeing that he has lost his soul when he might have so easily saved it; how he has, for a pleasure that has ended, lost a happiness which will be eternal, and how his misfortune is utterly beyond remedy or hope of recovery. His misery will be heightened when he calls to mind how easily he might have avoided the dreadful state to which he has brought himself. Had he employed a thousandth part of the care for the salvation of his soul, had he employed a fraction of the energy in the service of God, which he employed in the service of the devil—in business enterprise, in accumulating money, in gratifying passion—he would not now be about to approach God, shivering and wasted with fear, knowing of his sure damnation; but filled with a holy confidence, because in the days of the flesh he performed the deeds of righteousness, he would now be about to receive his reward; because he had fought well and valiantly under his Master's standard in the day of conflict, he would now be about to receive the crown of victory which the Lord, the just Judge, will render in the day of retribution to his faithful followers.

He will consider what is at stake in the trial which he shall in a moment undergo. Eternal bliss or eternal woe hangs trembling in the balance of that scale which the Divine Judge will hold in His hands. The estate of his soul through never-ending ages—the loss of God, his Creator and Redeemer, his supreme felicity, and who should have been the final end of his heaven-destined soul. Condemnation to the pain and misery of hell, infinitely intense in its nature and everlasting in its duration, without hope of cessation or alleviation, unrespited, unreprieved, ages of hopeless end! A sorry exchange, he will think, to have bartered heaven for hell, God for the devil, eternity's happiness, pure and unalloyed, for time's sinful pleasures so unsatisfactory in themselves, so miserable and lamentably irreparable in their effects.

At length the soul puts an end to these woful and useless regrets, and is ushered into the presence of its Judge. He sees Him not as He is. The sinner is not permitted to look upon the glory of God. God is covered with indignation, in which the sinner reads his doom. His presence speaks terror to the soul and fills him with dismay.

THE PARTICULAR JUDGMENT.　43

We may suppose that his guardian angel will not desert him in that hour; but, as the faithful lawyer, who stands to his client, even to the last when there is no hope, except against hope, as he stands by to sustain him with his sympathy, when there is nothing else, when the sentence is to be pronounced against him—so the Angel Guardian will, with downcast look, betokening his despair, take his place by the side of the sinner. But he has no good inspirations for him now, no words of cheer. His gloom adds but another misery to the sinner, who sees that he who knows him best after God has no hope for his acquittal. Nor will his old friend, his former chieftain, under whose banner he fought so valiantly in the days of the flesh, to whose cause he brought so many raw recruits, be absent. No; the devil will be there to claim as his own the soul of his old soldier, scarred and blackened with wounds received in his service. Although the sinner may have never seen him visibly before, yet he will at once recognize him. The recognition will be mutual, although despairing to the sinner.

The trial begins. On what will the examination turn? What will be its subject-matter? Every thought, word, work, and omission; the whole history of his life from the first moments of reason to its last hour; sins of commission, sins of omission, benefits, spiritual and temporal, graces vouchsafed, inspirations neglected, talents given for God's honor turned to his dishonor, riches given for the poor perverted to wrong purposes, all gifts, natural and supernatural; his heart and mind will be turned inside out; nothing shall escape the all-seeing eye of God. " He shall render an account of every idle word."

A formidable inquiry and one that will take a long time, you may think. No, not for God who sees all things at a glance and to whom are open our most secret thoughts and actions.

This history of the sinner's life shall be in an instant immensely narrowed down; a great blank will suddenly cover and hide from view everything in his life that has not a bearing upon the question at issue; everything shall be expunged from that record, which concerns not the sinner's conduct as a soldier of Christ fighting against the devil for the salvation of his soul. The epochs of his life shall be his victories over hell—his baptism, communions, confirmation, confessions, temptations overcome, acts of self-denial, in a word, every duty which rested upon him as an armed soldier of the Lord Jesus. There will be no account of his business enterprises, of the fortunes he made, of the stations he filled, of the reputation he enjoyed, and of all those other vain pursuits in which men engage, and in which they seek to find their happiness. This will be contracting the sinner's life within very narrow limits, you may think. Yes, my brethren. The sinner will be examined only as to the manner in which he has fulfilled those orders which, as a soldier, his Divine Captain has given him to fulfil. What are these commands? "Thou shalt love the Lord, thy God, with thy whole heart, soul, mind, and strength." "Thou shalt love thy neighbor as thyself." These two commands include all our duties and obligations. The ten commandments are but a development of them. They include whatever is obligatory in the beatitudes and counsels which Christ has given us.

The questioning begins. "Hast thou loved the Lord thy God with thy whole heart, soul, and mind?" the sinner is asked. The devil smiles with a sarcastic jeer when he hears such a question put to his old follower. The sinner is convulsed with terror, and would fain wither away at the terrible earnestness of outraged justice with which the question is put. What will he answer? Let us answer for him. He love God! who never thought of God; who lived as if there was no God; who laughed at the thought of God's retributions; who ridiculed the fears of those who spoke of God. He may not have called in question the existence of God; he may not have been an atheist professedly; but he has been such practically. He lived as if he had no account to render, as if there was no hereafter, as if to enjoy himself and gratify his passions was the sole end of his being; he regarded not the world as a place of trial, but as his fixed and permanent abode. He may not have fallen into the worship of idols, but has he not made an idol of himself and his passions? What has he ever done but gratify himself—to seek riches, pleasures, honors, and whatever else might minister to his self-love? Has he not made himself the centre of all his thoughts, the object of all his solicitude, the final end of all his labors? He love God! whose holy name was continually on his lips, the emphasis of his language, the spice of his conversation; that name at which the angels bow their heads and hide their faces, which the Jews would not mention for reverence. He love God! who did not hesitate to perjure himself, to give false testimony when his interest seemed to require it, or when he could thereby accomplish some wicked purpose or secure some passing gain. He love God! who seldom or never, by frequent, devout, fervent prayer, acknowledged God's supreme dominion over him and all creatures, rendering Him thanks for His benefits, praising His holy name, asking for a deliverance from all evil; who failed to attend at the great meed of public worship on Sundays which God's Church accounts God's due. Or who, if he did attend, did so from human respect to accompany his wife, and who, while physically before the altar, in mind was engaged in worldly thoughts and sinful desires. Or perhaps he was of the multitude of those who make attendance at mass the sum of their religious duties, who never receive the sacraments, who spurn or neglect those great channels through which the blood of Christ is to be applied to the souls of men. He love God! indeed, who failed to have frequent recourse to the heavenly means of receiving pardon for sin and strength for amendment. He love God! What is it to love God? To prefer Him to all things, not with a speculative preference, but with an habitual resolution to lose all things, the world and all in it—to lay down life itself rather than once offend Him by mortal sin.

THE PARTICULAR JUDGMENT. 47

He love God! who was habitually in mortal sin, who sinned, in a manner, as often as he breathed, who sinned when he could obtain the least temporal advantage thereby.

But perhaps he will be able to give a better account when he is examined on the second count. "Thou shalt love thy neighbor as thyself." Hast thou assisted thy neighbor in his spiritual needs? Hast thou given him the edification and encouragement in the pursuit of virtue which every Christian should give another? It is not likely that the sinner, who has been so careless of his own salvation, has been at all anxious for that of his neighbor. Hast thou assisted him in his temporal needs? What use didst thou make of the superabundant means which I gave thee? Didst thou live sumptuously every day, while the poor were content with the crumbs that fell from thy table? Wast thou clothed in soft raiment, while you saw the poor in rags hanging at thy gate? Did'st thou see me hungry and not feed me, naked and not clothe me, in prison and not visit me? When did we see Thee hungry or naked or a prisoner? But didst thou do it to the poor who represented me? Didst thou cause my providence to be blasphemed by the impatient poor, who, seeing the unequal distribution of temporal goods—so much given to the wicked who deserve so little, and so little to the poor who deserve more—not infrequently cursed such a dispensation of my wisdom? Didst thou think that it was ever my intention that the rich should revel in affluence, while the poor should perish from in-diligence? Was I not their father as well as thine? Didst thou not know that I made thee the possessor of wealth only that thou shouldst give it to the poor; that you were its recipients only to be its almoners? Perhaps the sinner may be able to say that he has not been entirely wanting in this respect—he may have given an alms now and then. But what was thy motive? Human praise to sound a trumpet before thee? Amen, thou hast received thy reward; for your natural virtue, if such you had, you have received recompense in the temporal prosperity I sent you. Thou hast not murdered. But hast thou not wished the death of thy neighbor? Didst thou not wish great evil to befall him? Not only he commits murder who does it in act, but he that harbors the thought or cherishes the purpose. But hast thou not murdered his soul by scandal? by teaching him the sins of which he was ignorant? by counsel, command, or provocation? How many shall in that hour arise and demand their souls on your head. Didst thou not commit that most dreadful of crimes—sundering the bonds of the holiest of unions—the union of two hearts knit together by the closest ties and cemented by the blessing of Christ's Sacrament? Didst thou not ruin the good name, blast the hopes, and damn the souls of the young, the thoughtless, the confiding, the unsuspecting? A fearful account will many have to give on this score. Didst thou not calumniate and detract thy neighbor, injuring him in profit and in the esteem of his friends?

Found guilty on so many counts, on what will

the sinner rely? Has he nothing to offer in extenuation, nothing with which to appease the anger of God? May he not say that he had the faith, that he was born a Catholic! But this, far from improving his case, will only serve to make his sentence the surer—his damnation the deeper; for, having known better, he has not acted up to his knowledge. He has sinned against light. Less culpable is he who sins through ignorance than he who sins through malice. No; his being born in the faith will not avail him. Little thanks to him that he had the faith; he received it as a family inheritance; he was baptized, we may say, in spite of himself; for as soon as he could, he tried to render nugatory the promises made for him at the holy fount. If he had not been born in the faith, he would have been as careless for its acquirement as, born in it, he has been faithless to it. All precious is faith. Without it, it is impossible to please God. It is the beginning, the source of justification. Yet we must remember, that by it alone it is impossible to please God; that it is but the beginning, but the source of justification. The faith that God requires is faith animated by charity; a living faith that shows itself in the observance of God's law.

Nothing remains but to pronounce sentence. He has been weighed in the balance and found wanting. "Depart from me, your Creator and Redeemer, your first beginning, and your last end, into everlasting fire prepared for the devil and his angels!" What can the sinner do but curse himself; curse the day when he was born; curse the folly and blindness which has entailed upon him such misery and woe. The devil, mocking him, takes charge of him, glad that he has defrauded Christ of another soul bought with the shedding of his blood. He is received in hell with the shouts of derision of the damned rejoicing, that, if they must suffer, there is still another to suffer with them.

Think not, friends, that this picture is overdrawn, as it might seem to you from the detail with which we have dwelt upon it. This was necessary. Many words are required to describe what the eye, at a glance, takes in, or what may be but the work of an instant. This trial is continually going on—it follows every death.

I end as I began by assuring you that this life is a conflict; we must fight under either of two standards—that of Jesus or that of the prince of this world. Ever since the fall of the angels, the world is filled with them; the devil goes about like a roaring lion seeking whom he may devour. We contend with principalities and powers; the devil is called the prince of this world and the prince of darkness; he tempted Jesus Himself, he tempts us all. There are those who have no experience of this conflict; they are not tempted because the evil one is already sure of them; they know not what temptation is, for they yield at once and without resistance; yet if we could but penetrate into the invisible world, we would find a sharp line of demarcation drawn between those enrolled under the standard of Jesus and those under that of the prince of this world.

HEAVEN.

After this I saw a great multitude, which no man could number, of all nations, and tribes, and peoples, and tongues, standing before the throne, and in sight of the Lamb, clothed with white robes, and palms in their hands:
And they cried with a loud voice, saying: Salvation to our God, who sitteth upon the throne, and to the Lamb.
And all the Angels stood round about the throne, and about the ancients, and about the four living creatures; and they fell before the throne upon their faces, and adored God,
Saying: Amen. Benediction, and glory, and wisdom, and thanksgiving, honor, and power, and strength to our God for ever and ever. Amen.
And one of the ancients answered, and said to me: Who are these that are clothed in white robes? and whence are they come?
And I said to him: My lord, thou knowest. And he said to me: These are they who are come out of great tribulation, and have washed their robes, and have made them white in the blood of the Lamb.
Therefore they are before the throne of God, and serve him day and night in his temple; and he that sitteth on the throne shall dwell over them.
They shall not hunger nor thirst any more, neither shall the sun fall on them, nor any heat.
For the Lamb, which is in the midst of the throne, shall rule them, and shall lead them to the fountains of the waters of life, and God shall wipe away all tears from their eyes.— Apocalypse vii. 9–17.

WE all desire to be happy. We seek perfect happiness in all that we do. We are not free not to seek it. It is an inborn tendency of the soul implanted there by Almighty God. We may seek it under various forms, and in places where it is not to be found, yet seek it we always do. Free in all other things, man is not free to act against the irresistible impulse of his nature, and to resolve on his misery. Even in the commission of sin he seeks that which seems to him good or convenient in some respect. Of course he is mistaken; but that only proves the misdirection of his tendency, not that the tendency does not exist.

Consult your hearts; ask yourselves what desire is there uppermost? You will answer that it is the thirst of happiness, that there is nothing nearer, or dearer, or more natural to you, than the desire of something to satisfy the longings of your soul for perfect content; that for it you live, that for it you labor, and that for it you are ready to die. From the cradle to the grave, the life of man is but the record of labors undertaken, of sufferings endured, and of sacrifices made in the pursuit of happiness.

The student seeks happiness in the pursuit of knowledge, the scientist in the investigation of science, the politician in the intrigues of diplomacy, the rich in the accumulation of wealth, the lustful in the gratification of passion, the worldling in the fashions of life, the laboring man in his daily toil, the debauchee in his nightly revel. No matter how high or low, how cultured or illiterate, every one seeks to be happy. He tells you that he is urged to it by a necessity far above his control.

The life of nations, from the first moment of their existence to the last of their downfall, is but the record of unceasing efforts to advance in happiness. And those mighty revolutions that are continually taking place, overthrowing one government and substituting another, are but the fruit and manifestation of this tendency to its happiness which is inseparable from our nature. The history of the race itself is made up but of the conflicts, successes, and reverses, in search of the happiness for which it has been made, and to which it feels itself impelled with the whole energy of its nature.

Yes, we have been made for perfect happiness. Our hearts crave a felicity which knows no evil, which includes all good, and which we can never lose. Who enjoys it? Who has ever enjoyed it? Do nations enjoy it? Why, then, this continual endeavor to better themselves? If they have all they desire, why seek for more? Do individuals enjoy it? Answer for yourselves. Is there one of you so happy, that he seeks nothing more? Ask the rich man, if he is perfectly happy in the enjoyment of his wealth? He will tell you that his riches enkindle in him desires and needs which the poor man knows not of; that, even if he were happy, the thought of one day having to lose all, would itself be enough to destroy all true felicity. Ask the lustful man, if he finds the pleasure, pure and unalloyed, which his soul seeks, in the gratification of passions which bring on death and premature decay? Ask the student, if his mind is perfectly content with the researches he makes?

He will tell you that, the more he learns, the better he understands how little he knows, and that life is too short to learn all that he would fain know. Ask the king, the pontiff, the priest, the statesman, and they will all tell you that, though they may enjoy as much as anyone can expect of happiness in this life, yet there is something which they have not, and which they must have to be happy. Solomon, after the enjoyment of all that men hold to be necessary for happiness, exclaimed, " Vanity of vanities and all is vanity." No, my brethren, the goods of this life cannot satisfy the soul. They are the viands whose exquisite flavor may excite, but cannot quench the appetite. Our hearts seek a boundless happiness. Nothing limited can fill them. We pass our lives seeking to be happy, and it is only at the end of our days that we realize our mistake, and find that we have not possessed happiness, because we sought it not where alone it was to be found. We are continually picturing it to ourselves, in the distance, but no sooner does it seem within our grasp, than it eludes us; it fades at our approach; the nearer we come to it, the further it recedes from us, withering at our touch, like the apples of the Dead Sea. We are in the wilderness of this life, surrounded, as we imagine, with misery; and, discontented with our situation, we look ahead, and think we see happiness far in the future. We push on, straining every nerve, to find nothing but chagrin, disappointment, and misery, where we had promised ourselves a millennium. We look upon the past, and think we see happiness where before we had experienced but want and misery.

This is the life of man. Born for happiness, he never enjoys it, and dies, convinced that all is vanity and vexation of spirit. Why is this? Has not God implanted this desire in the heart of man? This desire is not like so many others that find their place within us,—lust, avarice, pride, and envy; but it is the principal and supreme tendency of man's rational nature. God could not have put it there, if it were never to be satisfied. He could not place before man the prospect of perfect happiness and urge him to it with an impulse which he cannot resist, if that desire were never to be realized. Why then are we not happy? It is, my friends, because we seek not happiness where alone it is to be found. If we would be happy, we must seek it in the heavenly Jerusalem—that happiness purchased for us by the blood of Jesus Christ. We seek an infinite and eternal happiness. God alone is infinite, God alone is eternal; in God alone, then, can our souls find rest. " Thou alone, O God, hast made our hearts, Thou alone canst fill them."

In vain will we seek to satisfy the spiritual cravings of our souls, with the material pleasures of life; but this is our mistake. We think to fulfil the desires of our souls, all spiritual, with pleasures all material. We are so gross and carnal, we are so immersed in the things of sense, that in them alone we seek our happiness. It is the soul alone that seeks happiness; all our other desires are but the outlets of this supreme tendency of our nature. As it is the soul alone that desires happiness, it is the soul alone that is capable of enjoying it, that is susceptible of the sensations of pleasures. Even gross pleasures must be experienced by the soul in order to give delight; they must be carried on through the senses and body to the seat of sensation and intelligence. As the soul must be the recipient of pleasure, it is the soul alone that seeks it. Our souls are spiritual. They cannot then be satisfied with material pleasures. Our souls know and desire and can only be satisfied with a pleasure suitable to their nature—spiritual, infinite, immortal. No gross material pleasure is of this kind. God alone can satisfy the cravings, and fill the boundless capacities of our souls. To be happy, then, it is the soul that we must satisfy. And God alone is capable of doing this, because it is for Him alone we have been made. In vain will we satisfy the inborn cravings of our soul with the perishable things of time—glory, honor, power, pleasure, magnificence—empty names. We must raise our hearts heavenward, and contemplate the celestial Jerusalem, that city of God, of which such glorious things are said. It is there that we can obtain the boundless happiness which we seek, and which earth does not contain; that uncreated happiness which contains all good, excludes all defect, and lasts forever. It is in beholding the ravishing beauty of God that our hearts shall be made happy. It is in beholding the illimitable perfections, the unfathomable abysses of divine loveliness, the dazzling splendors of the God-head, that we shall realize the happiness that we seek in vain here below. In that glorious sight, man shall be transported out of himself, and in the ecstasy of delight with which it shall fill his soul, he will forget his proper nature and become as God. "Ye shall be as God." As a cloud, transfused with the rays of the sun, becomes all luminous, so man's soul in the splendor of God shall be all glorious and like unto God Himself.

The angels and saints possess this glory now, and find in it bliss ineffable and joy supreme. They are so ravished with the all-absorbing beauty of God, they are so transported with the ever-increasing weight of glory which belongs to Him, that they find their only and eternal happiness in singing glory, honor, praise, and benediction to the God who liveth and reigneth forever;—not by word of mouth, not by empty sound, but filled to overflowing with the worship and pleasure and love and gratitude that His presence inspires,—by internal and heartfelt adoration!

It is hard for us to understand this, because, filled with the corrupt things of time, immersed in sense, we cannot lift our hearts to comprehend the unimaginable glory of God and the perfect happiness that His presence confers. We cannot understand what the beauty of God is. Let us try to get some glimpse of it. We admire the beauty of this world. Our spirits expand,—we are transported in feeling when we look upon the earth in springtime,—everything clothed in verdure and breathing freshness. Our eyes delight to look upon the crystal stream, or mighty cataract rushing down the mountain side, leaping from rock to rock, till it empties itself in the clear lake beneath. Our ears drink in the gladsome notes of the birds jubilant at the resurrection of all nature from the death of winter. Our nostrils are filled with the fragrance which the flowers are sending up, as an incense of praise to the great Creator. We ascend some lofty mountain when the sun casts its splendor upon the boundless ocean, and there before that vast expanse of water, lit up, as it were, with the glory of heaven, we are transported out of ourselves, and fall down in ecstatic homage to God, because we seem to catch a glimpse of His own glory. But what is all this to the uncreated glory of the Creator Himself? Contemplate nature in its most glorious aspect, what is it all to the glory of its Lord and Maker? The world is surely an awful manifestation of the beauty, greatness, and power of God, so illimitable that light, travelling as light only travels, sent to us untold ages ago, has not yet reached us; —so stupendous, so vast, so complicated, and yet so harmonious, that it bewilders the imagination and distorts the mental vision to try to comprehend even the most insignificant of God's works. And yet God could have created a world inconceivably more perfect and more worthy of Himself. He could have created a countless number of worlds, each incomparably more glorious than the other; and even then His power would not be exhausted.

What, then, must be the beauty of God Himself,

HEAVEN. 59

who is capable of communicating so much to His works! If we are so enraptured with the beauty of this world, what wonder that the angels are so enamoured of the beauty of God as to find their sole enjoyment in singing His praises, in glorifying His name, in casting themselves before Him in transports of love and homage.

Again; the angels have beheld God from their creation. They have been permitted close communion with Him. They have seen more of Him than we can imagine. Yet they have not begun to comprehend Him,—have not begun to know the limits of His glory.

The Blessed Virgin surely has seen more of God than all other created beings; yet even she has caught but the veriest glimpse of His beauty. Now put together all that angels and saints have perceived of God, add to it what the Blessed Virgin has beheld, multiply it ten thousand times, and even then God is as far beyond our comprehension as ever. You might multiply it an infinity of times, and you would be as far from reaching the limits of Divine Beauty as you were at the beginning. What wonder, then, that the happiness of the saints is the presence of God! What wonder that the happiness of heaven is the vision of God,—all beautiful and glorious!

Yes, my brethren, the happiness of heaven is not the beauty of the city, with the walls of ivory and gates of gold, paved with precious stones, watered with the crystal stream, brilliant as the sun, fair as the moon, or any of the other material representations under which the Scriptures seek to bring it home to us. The beauty of heaven and its happiness is the beauty of God. It is to see, love, and enjoy God forever.

Have you ever thought that God's perfection is so great that in the Divine Nature it is the origin of the Third Person? We are told that the Son is the image of the Father, the "Splendor of His glory and figure of His substance." The Father knows Himself. The expression of this knowledge is the Son. From the mutual love which is engendered by the Father for the Son, and by the Son for the Father, proceeds the Holy Ghost, the infinite and personal expression of the love of the God-head. God finds His own happiness in the contemplation of Himself. What wonder, then, that the happiness of heaven is the presence of God! If He is sufficient for His own happiness, if the contemplation of Himself satisfies the exigencies of His own infinite nature, will He not be able to satisfy ours? Will He not be able to fill the void in our finite hearts? Well might the Scripture say, "That which the eye hath not seen, nor the ear heard, nor hath it entered into the heart of man to conceive hath God prepared for those who love and serve Him."

Some may think that this pleasure arising from the beatific vision will be to them but little;—will not be that which their hearts at present desire. I can imagine the rich man, who places his happiness here below in the amassing of wealth, and who thinks that it alone can make him happy, will have but little appreciation for the glory that I have been attempting to place before you. I can imagine the lustful man, who tries to make himself believe that his sovereign happiness consists in the gratification of passion, will have but little taste for the joy, pure and holy, which comes from serving God. There may be those among you who think that they would be happier, in the enjoyment of this world's goods. But this arises from what I have already alluded to. We are made up of soul and body. The soul would soar heavenward; but the body with its concupiscence drags it down to earth. We are so immersed with things of sense, that we can scarcely imagine our happiness outside of them. We can scarcely realize a happiness in which they will have no part. We place our happiness in them here below, because, here below we see no other, because they agree with our present conditions as gifted with material bodies and material sense; we cannot rise to the lofty vision of God. We understand not His marvellous fascination. This obstacle will be removed when our souls are separated from our bodies. Then they will seek their happiness in a different sphere and among different objects. Our souls then freed from their bodies of corruption, will aspire to God, their last end, and in Whom alone they will then feel that their perfect happiness can be found. As the steel freed from restraint, flies to the magnet, so shall our souls, freed from the restraint of body, fly to God, their eternal attraction and their final happiness.

These passions which we call pride, lust, avarice, and all other desires, are but the outlets of our inborn appetite for felicity, are but the means we employ to gratify that one great, supreme, and dominant tendency for perfect happiness, which fills our souls and absorbs all our faculties. Almighty God will gratify all these passions. How? By filling the soul, their source and fountain, with the fullest happiness, by pouring into it such a torrent of delight, by so inebriating it with His love, that it can know no other or greater, and desire no other or greater happiness. Thus shall God satisfy the unconquerable thirst of the human soul. Absolutely one in Himself, He is manifold in the fecundity with which He communicates Himself to His creatures. This truth may be put in another way. We look upon a picture, say of the Blessed Virgin, by one of the great masters. In beholding this picture we are so enraptured with the heavenly purity and mildness and holiness to be seen in every feature, that every unworthy feeling dies within us, every unbecoming thought goes out. We are lifted above earth and absorbed in heavenly thoughts. So shall it be when our disembodied spirits will stand in the presence of God. The happiness of this life will be forgotten; all thoughts of riches, honors, and human pleasures, will perplex the soul no more, because it shall already have been made happy by the enjoyment of the beatific vision. The apostles, surrounded with the glory of Divinity on Tabor, wished to return no more to the world, but to build three tabernacles and dwell there forevermore.

What is necessary to make man supremely happy, but to satisfy fully all his faculties? What is the happiness of any faculty or creature but the attainment of its end. God has made everything for an end. He has endowed it with capacity and virtue to reach this end. It can never rest till it attains it. It receives from God an impulse which it must obey, and which only ceases when its end has been reached. When, then, man and all his faculties shall have attained their ends, they will be happy and at rest. What are man's faculties? Intellect, heart, and will. What are their objects? Truth, content, love.

Truth is the object of the intellect. The possession of truth, then, will constitute its beatitude. So long as the intellect possesses not truth, or but imperfectly, it cannot be happy. In this life it can never possess truth fully, hence it is never fully happy. Although capable of knowing truth, yet outside of that which has been revealed, how little do we know! How the human mind seeks truth, and how happy it is when it comes by it, only those can tell who, born in ignorance of it, have afterward, by the grace of God and their own efforts, obtained it in the Church! But in God we shall see the truth and our intellects will be in perfect rest. We shall understand clearly and perfectly what now at best we know but darkly. We shall be forever rid of the bondage of ignorance. We shall indeed know the truth, and the truth shall make us free.

The object of our hearts is contentment. Their beatitude will be found in its attainment. Here below we cannot find true content. It was on earth before Adam sinned. Since that time it has been exiled from earth. Some little may, perhaps, yet be found left to make life bearable; but of how few is it the portion, and with how much alloy is it mixed? In heaven our hearts will be in perfect peace. None of the ills that we are subject to at present will then afflict us. Pain and sorrow shall be no more. Death shall be no more. The vanities of life will no longer obscure the intellect and perplex the will. All these evils shall be banished forevermore. All the good that we enjoy here below, we shall possess there in a more eminent degree. Whatever joy there is on earth is but a foretaste of the joy of heaven.

The object of the will is love. Its beatitude will be in possessing an object which it can love with an infinite love. We love a thing because it seems to us good. The more of its goodness we see the better we love it. An infinite love we can have only for something whose goodness is infinite. Nothing infinite exists outside of God. This is why we never perfectly love anything. We know the strength of love, the strongest passion of the soul, capable of great good or great evil. No wonder we are unhappy here below, since we have no object to fix this passion upon, or if we love, it is but for a while; we soon see the defects of the object of our love; its goodness is at an end, and we love no more. But in heaven we shall love God with a boundless and undying love. We shall see a good, boundless in perfection, whose loveliness will be as infinite for us throughout eternity, as it was in the beginning; and for whom, accordingly, our love can never wane, and shall be as strong at the end of untold ages, as at the moment of its entrance into heaven. As the Father, contemplating His infinite perfection and beauty mirrored forth in the Son, loves this Son with an infinite and immortal love, so shall we, in some analogous way, contemplating the ineffable beauty and majesty of God, be inflamed with a love as intense as our souls can endure, and as undying as the God that excites it.

But are we all called to this happiness of heaven? We are. Only one condition is required, namely, sanctity, the keeping of God's law. Are we on the road that leads thither—that narrow road that so few find? Or are we pursuing the beaten path that most pursue? The road that leads to heaven, is the road of suffering—the royal road of the Cross. Are we leading lives of sacrifice and self-denial? If not, in vain do we hope to enter heaven. Jesus as man purchased the right to enter heaven by His sufferings and death. "It behooved Him to suffer and so enter into His glory;" and He thought not the sacrifice too great to purchase the glory of heaven. The martyrs shed their blood, and sacrificed life itself to purchase heaven; and they did not esteem the price an exorbitant one. Holy hermits and religious abandoned the world, and gave themselves up to incessant prayer and mortification among the beasts of the desert, far removed from the abodes of men; and they thought the exchange an advantageous one. Are we unwilling to buy heaven by the keeping of God's commandments? Are we unable to deny the flesh and its concupiscence to the extent of keeping within God's law? We are the children of the saints. But are we worthy of them? Do we walk in their footsteps? Are we but living on their great name? Have their merits only come down to us as a family inheritance, unincreased by any addition of our own? I fear it; I fear it.

We love to think of the martyrs; we are moved with compassion in reading of their sufferings for Christ and His Gospel; and we say that, had we lived in those days, we would have done the same. We condemn with no measured bitterness the recreancy and baseness of those who in persecution abandoned Christ. But, are we imitating the martyrs or the apostates? The contest in which they spilled their blood has not yet ended; it continues from age to age; it is going on to-day. The conflict of right and wrong, of God and the devil, is as hot to-day as in former times; it never ceases; it was scarcely more visible then than it is now. Are we then doing now what we say we would have done in those times? I fear not. There were many in those days for whom the fascination of the pagan world was too great. There were those who thought that Christ required too much: who abandoned His standard and enlisted under His enemy; who enjoyed the world, and were lost. We have the same among us to-day: those who are overcome by the allurements of the age and by the threefold concupiscence of the world, and who deliver themselves to sin and Satan and unbridled passion. Is it not so? Look around you! See the votaries of the world on every side; see them even among Christians, Catholics!

Who is in earnest about salvation? who shows the slightest concern for his soul? It is not by saying Lord, Lord, that we shall enter heaven. If we are to be saved, we have a work to do, a duty to perform. If we are faithless now, we would have been faithless in the beginning and would have betrayed Christ. The saints gave themselves no repose until they secured heaven. We expect it as a matter of course. But God is as just now as He ever was. He exacts as much from those who would enter into life. He does not widen His mercy as iniquity increases. "Nothing defiled can enter heaven." "He who does not take up his cross and follow me, is not worthy of me."

All the expressions of Scripture denouncing woe against the sinner, and declaring the fewness of the elect and the difficulty of salvation, are as true to-day as they were when uttered.

Some do not aspire to a very high place in heaven. Such will scarcely enter it at all. He who would run along the brink of a precipice must allow himself some margin lest he stumble and fall into the chasm. He who would keep God's law must allow himself some vantage-ground, must make allowances for the wear and tear of the conflict, for the power of temptation, for his own weakness, for the inroads that sin makes upon the best of us; he must aim at avoiding all deliberate sin. He who proposes avoiding mortal sin, yet committing venial with impunity, will ultimately fall. The marksman aims high that he may strike the mark. He who wishes to be saved must aim at a high rank in heaven in order that he may secure an ordinary place, or even enter at all.

THE PUNISHMENT OF HELL.

" And I saw the dead, the great and the small, standing before the throne, and the books were opened, and another book was opened, which is of life, and the dead were judged by these things which were written in the books, according to their works. And the sea gave up the dead that were in it, and death and hell gave up their dead that were in them: and they were judged everyone according to their works. And hell and death were cast into the lake of fire, this is the second death. And whosoever was not found written in the book of life was cast into the lake of fire."—Apocalypse xx. 12-15.

" But for the fearful, and unbelieving, and abominable, and for murderers, and debauchees, and sorcerers, and idolaters, and all liars, their portion shall be in the lake burning with fire and brimstone, which is the second death."—Apocalypse xxi. 8.

THE punishment of hell is revealed to us as fire, " The vengeance on the flesh of the ungodly is fire and worms," Ecclesiastes, vii. " So shall it be at the end of the world: the angels shall come forth and separate the wicked from the just. And shall cast them into the furnace of fire: there shall be weeping and gnashing of teeth," Matthew, xiii. 49-50. " And if thy hand scandalize thee, cut it off: it is better for thee to enter into life maimed, than, having two hands, to go into hell, into unquenchable fire, where the worm dieth not and the fire is not extinguished. And if thy foot scandalize thee, cut it off: it is better for thee to enter lame into life everlasting, than, having two feet, to be cast into hell, into unquenchable fire, where the worm dieth not, and the fire is not extinguished. And if thine eye scandalize thee, pluck it out: it is better for thee with one eye to enter into the kingdom of God, than, having two eyes, to be cast into hell fire, where the worm dieth not and the fire is not extinguished, for everyone shall be tortured with fire, and every offering shall be salted with salt," Mark, ix. 42–48. "Depart from me, you cursed, into everlasting fire, prepared for the devil and his angels," Matthew, xxv. 41.

Every word of the sentence to be pronounced on the damned, indicates the awful nature of the punishment inflicted. The command to leave Him of whom they are not worthy, and to go to their due abode, the curse, upon which follows, as an effect, everlasting punishment, the specifying of the punishment, namely, that inflicted upon the devil and his angels—all this sufficiently manifests that it is fire, and everlasting fire. A judge does not make use of tropes or figures when inflicting the gravest penalty known to the law. Our Lord speaks literal language when He pronounces sentence on the most momentous of trials. When He awards eternal happiness to the just, He speaks literally. Why should He speak a metaphor, when He completes the sentence by condemning the wicked to their just punishment? He speaks a verity, when He bids the elect enter into the bliss prepared for them from the beginning. Does He utter a falsehood, when He bids the reprobate enter into the fire which, He adds, was prepared for the devil and his angels?—and not alone for these; but for you who, by your works, have made yourselves his slaves and servants.

Everywhere in the Scriptures, new and old, is the punishment of the damned spoken of as fire. If this were but a figure, the figure would at times betray itself, and we would learn its literal meaning. But universally are the sufferings of the damned spoken of as fire, and as such torments as preclude the possibility of tropes and figures. Was it a figurative fire that was prepared for, and which the devil and his angels are still enduring? The fire of the fallen angels, is the fire of the reprobate souls of men. During life those souls found their delight, to the contempt of God, in pleasures forbidden by His holy law. They now endure pain and sorrow and torture, even hell fire for their forbidden delights, and thus their contempt of God is avenged and serves to show His justice. Human souls endowed with the sovereign gift of free will, may defeat God's purpose of mercy in their regard, and refuse to be saved, and thus to be eternally happy, but they cannot frustrate the general purpose of the manifestation of His glory for which He made all things.

The real fire of hell is proclaimed in "the lake burning with fire and brimstone," in "the everlasting fire prepared for the devil and his angels," in "the fire that is not extinguished," in "the flame in which the damned suffer," in the "which of you can dwell in everlasting fire?" in "the fire taking vengeance on those who have not known God," and in so many other places. The very name of Gehenna, being the valley in which children were burned to death as holocausts to Moloch, "horrid king, besmeared with blood of human sacrifice and parents' tears," and which may be taken as a figure of hell, intimates the character of hell fire. The visitation of fire upon Sodom and Gomorrah may be regarded as a foretaste of hell fire.

Because hell fire may differ in many respects from that with which we are familiar, it does not cease to be a real fire. We have no means of knowing that it is the same as that of this life. But it is real, since it produces in the soul the burning and torture of ordinary fire. Fire in this life proceeds from physical nature, and serves the purpose for which it is ordained. There is no reason why we should make this one identical with hell fire, which is called forth by God, and serves a purpose in the supernatural order. As we need not hell fire for our physical well-being, so we need not physical fire for hell's punishment of sin and the sinner. The fire of hell is not figurative or ideal, but actual and an instrument of torture.

If we are permitted to use the words of the great poet, who, in language not unworthy the subject, has lamented the fall of the race, hell may be described as "A dungeon, horrible on all sides round, as one great furnace flamed, yet from those flames no light, but rather darkness visible served only to discover sights of woe, regions of sorrow, doleful shades, where peace and rest can never dwell; hope never comes that comes to all, but torture without end still urges, and a fiery deluge, fed with ever-burning sulphur unconsumed."

The fire of hell will be endowed with the virtue of reaching even the soul directly, and not through the body only. It shall also preserve the body while it tortures it; "It shall be salted so as by fire." Other fires destroy; hell fire will preserve and yet torture, will preserve forever, that its torture may last forever; "The smoke of their torment ascended forever and ever;" it shall suffer no diminution or extinction. Which of you can dwell with devouring fire? The rich glutton calls it a place of torments. We cannot endure material fire even for a moment; what if God, in His indignation, should blow it into tenfold rage? We cannot touch fire, cannot endure the too scorching heat of the sun. No wonder the saints have declared the pains of hell to be incomparably greater than all the torments we can imagine. Job says that, "Hell is a land which is dark, and covered with the mist of death, a land of misery and darkness, where the shadow of death and no order but everlasting horror dwells." St. Augustine says: "The bare sight of the devils excites sufficient terror to cause the death of all the damned, if they were capable of dying." There will be no light save what suffices to torment the damned by the sight of their associates and the devils.

Think of the pain of thirst; all the waters of the earth would not be sufficient to quench the pains of the damned, yet they shall not have even a drop. The rich glutton cried out, "Father Abraham, have pity on me, and send Lazarus that he may dip the tip of his finger in water to cool my tongue, for I am tormented in this fire." And Abraham said to him: "Child, remember that thou didst receive good things in thy lifetime, and Lazarus, in like manner, evil things; but now he is here comforted, and thou art tormented."

Consider the company of the reprobate in hell. They would constitute a hell, even without fire; what shall be the misery of the damned when they will have to endure such companionship, not for a limited time, but for eternity, without hope, without chance of possible liberation, condemned to dwell in the congregation of all the wicked, and to converse forever with everlasting groans, "unrespited, unpitied, unreprieved, ages of hopeless end." If a man were to give way to the bad passions within him, if pride, lust, cruelty, envy, and all the other evil instincts of the human heart were to obtain freedom and mastery in him, what a hell would run riot in his soul? If human society were to cast aside all restraining influences, the fear of punishment, the hope of reward, if it were to act as if there were no God, to what a hell would human society be reduced? Yet this is the state of the damned. God being eternally lost to them, no longer hope, no longer fear, nothing but blank despair stares them in the face. Even here in this life, with all the restraints of future retribution, the laws of society, the esteem of men, the fear of shame, the sacredness of holy obligations, the suggestions of natural sympathy, the dictates of friendship and love, yet society is, in a manner, but a hell; virtue is everywhere trampled under foot; iniquity is exalted to high places; there is nothing but deceit, duplicity, hypocrisy, among men. Society is seething in corruption, flooded with unmentionable crimes; all flesh has corrupted its ways; there is no fear of God under heaven. What then will be the misery, intense and universal, of all the reprobate spirits gathered together in hell? Could we endure such companionship for a moment? How suffer it for eternity?

Remorse. Who has not felt its power? Who is ignorant of how it preys upon the mind, of how it consumes the soul? It sets men mad. It is the greatest misery of the soul. If not a hell in itself, it is a foretaste of hell. So true is this that you will sometimes hear denied the existence of a future hell, and maintained that hell is to be found in the conscience of the sinner, in the anguish with which he is filled, in the self-reproach with which he is tortured. The poet says, "The mind is its own place, and in itself can make a hell of heaven, a heaven of hell." "The children of the kingdom shall be cast out into exterior darkness, there shall be weeping and gnashing of teeth, where the worm dieth not, and the fire is not quenched."

Whether the reprobate looks back upon the past and considers how easily he could have saved his soul, or looks up to heaven possessed by his friends where he, too, might so easily be, or looks forward to the future with the prospect of unending misery, he finds nothing to console or encourage him, but everything to make him miserable and to fill him with blank despair.

He looks back upon the past; he remembers the opportunities he had of saving his soul, the many good inspirations he received, the good intentions he formed, the sermons he listened to, the occasions of well-doing which he allowed to pass away unimproved. How easily he could have mortified his passions and restrained his sinful habits, how little effort he ever made to observe the commandments! St. Thomas says that, "The damned soul will find its greatest misery in the thought that it is lost for nothing; it could so easily have been saved." This will constitute a supreme agony. He will remember the tepidity and listlessness with which he heard the word of God, that word which admonished him in time of his present misery, and which, if followed, would have saved him from irreparable ruin. Still he must do himself the justice that he never purposed to go to hell, that nothing was farther from his mind; he intended to repent; he did not look for so sudden a taking off; he had made up his mind to restore those ill-gotten goods which his children are now enjoying, and to make good the reputation of his neighbor, who is still suffering, among men, from the effects of his calumny. It never entered his mind to leave the world without approaching the sacraments and making his peace with Almighty God. He always intended to die the death of the righteous; he shuddered when he thought of the death of the unrepentant; he was, in a word, full of good intentions. He has received their reward; hell is paved with them. There is not a damned soul that intended to be damned.

He looks up to heaven, which, he remembers, was his inheritance; he sees it possessed by friends and associates. St. Peter Chrysologus says, "To the damned the voluntary loss of paradise is a greater torment than the very pains of hell." The sinner considers its never-ending joys, its supreme felicity, the presence of God, the society of angels and saints; he beholds his companions now in the enjoyment of the reward due to a few years of virtue; he feels that even out of hell the loss of heaven would itself be a hell; he remembers that so little was required to put him among the elect. Conscious that the fault is all his own, he upbraids himself and turns upon himself; willingly would he annihilate himself, as the just punishment of his folly and the only escape from his misery. But he is held in existence in spite of himself. He looks to the future; he reflects upon the eternity through which he must live and suffer, without hope or prospect of alleviation or cessation of his misery. Who will describe, who can imagine the anguish of his soul?

Loss of God. In this life we understand not what it is to lose God; we are darkened by sin; we are held down by earthly affections; we are dominated by objects of sense. We are made for God and for infinite happiness. Man, free in all things else, is not free not to choose what he esteems good. He may be mistaken in what or where he places it. Yet in all that he does he seeks his happiness. In this life we are engrossed with the sensible world around us, we try to satisfy our souls with the small reflex of God's beauty which creatures possess. As breathing is a vital necessity to the body, union with God is a vital necessity to the soul. "Thou alone, O Lord, has made us, in Thee alone can we find rest." The soul is made for God. A being can only be sovereignly happy in the attainment of its end; everything has been made for God, and tends to Him in a manner proportionate to its nature. The soul has an inborn inclination, an inherent and invincible tendency to be united to God. He is its last end, as well as its first beginning. As the steel turns to the magnet, as the eye is made to see, as the arrow makes for the mark, as the exile longs for home, as the lover sighs for the object of his love, as the son seeks the embrace of his mother, as the law of gravitation draws all things to the earth, so by the very nature and law of our being does the soul aspire to be united to God. In that union, and in that union alone, shall it find its true happiness and final glory. Outside of that union, even in time, it is unhappy; in eternity, it must be forever miserable. In this life we feel not this loss of God. His place is, in a manner, taken, and our hearts, in a degree, filled by the objects of life which we are forever seeking, and in which we fain would place our contentment. If we could see God, we should no longer seek the

THE PUNISHMENT OF HELL.

sensible world around us and the objects that fill it. If we were not encased in a body of sense, we should seek higher and holier and diviner objects. Nothing less than God Himself would satisfy us.

But when these veils of sense will be withdrawn, when the earth will sink beneath our feet, when our spirits will be emancipated from these bodies, then shall our souls rush with all the energy of their nature, with every fibre of their being, to God, their final end and supreme beatitude. But the damned soul shall be repelled by Almighty God forever, and cast down to hell. Infinite purity and holiness cannot unite with defilement and sin. Eternally drawn to God and eternally repelled—this will be the hell of the soul. It is this disappointment of the soul's aspirations, this loss of the soul's glory, this deprivation of God, this exile from heaven, this forfeiture of its inheritance, this sacrifice of its last end; it is all this that constitutes the supreme misery of the soul, and the most essential pain of hell. Damnation is the loss of all the joys of the elect augmented by all the pains of sense. The soul will become demoniac by its bitter hate of God and dire despair. St. Thomas says, "The pain of the damned is infinite because it is the loss of the infinite good." The greatest agony of the sinner will arise, not from the fire, nor the remorse, nor the company, but from the loss of God. The greatest torments could not equal the loss the soul feels in being deprived of Him. Consider the keenness of our pain when rejected by one we love; how if the object of our love were one of infinite beauty and loveliness, how if we were created for no other purpose than to eternally love that object, and yet to be eternally repelled. St. Antonine says, "The soul separated from the body understands that God is its sovereign good and that it has been created for him." St. Augustine says that, "If the damned saw the beauty of God, they should feel no pain and hell itself should be converted into a paradise." Let the heart place its bliss and content in any object; what suspense and anxiety till it reach it, what suffering, if it be forever precluded from it. Such disappointment is known to make men mad.

God of the soul! its maker and final destiny, its only bliss, whose loss is eternal misery! Never to behold the glory of the God-head! Never to know the wisdom of the Son! Never to share the love of the Holy Ghost! To be separated, and forever, from union with God, from the company of angels, and spirits, and the elect of the sons of men! To be excluded forever from the enjoyment of heaven! To endure forever this privation made even more dreadful by the physical torments of hell! To hunger and thirst for the Supreme Good, and never to be satiated! To pass eternity in self-reproach and soul-piercing regrets! To be forever the victim of unavailing remorse and withering despair! Annihilation would be a boon.

As no happiness is infinite but what is everlasting, so no punishment is as great as it can be, unless eternal. Hell would not be so frightful, if its horrors were one day to end. It is the duration of hell that gives its tortures the character of infinity. We may submit to a painful operation, because we know it will soon be over, and we will enjoy good health. It is the continuance of pain that makes it unbearable; the continuance of even pleasure becomes painful; to lie in the same posture for a long time becomes excruciating. Yet the damned must suffer forever the same fire, the same company, the same remorse, the same privation of God; willingly would they die; death would be a mercy; annihilation would be a paradise beyond comprehension. "And in these days men shall seek death and shall not find it; they shall desire to die and death shall flee from them."

We cannot comprehend eternity — duration without beginning, without end; we are overpowered in trying to measure it. In it, better than in any other attribute, can we obtain an idea of the impenetrable mysteries of God's nature; if one divine perfection could be greater than another, his eternity would be the greatest. Reason reels, the imagination is bewildered, in its efforts to comprehend eternity. Time and space are among the most inexplicable of the mysteries that surround us, and of which we have the least adequate comprehension, but in the effort to comprehend eternity all our faculties collapse, and we fall prostrate to the earth. If the damned soul knew that when its tears formed an ocean, that if at the end of as many ages as there are stars in heaven, as there are atoms in the earth, or drops in the sea, there would be an end of his sufferings, he would still have hope. If he thought that when the echoes of his sighs would have travelled through infinite spaces and untold ages, and returned to him, there would be hope of salvation, he would feel consoled. Take the years of human life or the years of a century—but what are they?—take five hundred years, or one thousand years, the measure is yet small; take the years that have passed since Christ, the years that elapsed from Christ to the flood, from the flood to creation, let it be six or sixty or six hundred thousand years, it is yet but a brief measure for eternity; multiply it till the power of numbers is exhausted, and you have not yet a unit with which to count the days of eternity. Let this world of ours, so great and yet so small; so great when viewed by our intelligence; so small when viewed in the light of a loftier being; let this universe of worlds be unbuilt at the rate of the removal of one particle every ten thousand years, and then be rebuilt from its foundation at the rate of one particle every ten thousand years. This process of destruction and construction would have continued through ages, which human calculation cannot declare, before you would have realized one hour, nay, one moment of eternity. Let the vast mighty ages, which geologists tell us were necessary for the development of physical nature from its primal germs, be multiplied by immeasurable periods throughout incalculable times, and you have not yet begun to count the days of eternity; you have not yet lighted upon the first moment of that infinite duration; you have not yet begun to know the meaning of eternity. Who can stand an hour's agony, who can stand an hour's burning, who could lie for a week in the same posture without feeling as if it would never end? A night spent in a fever seems interminable, and to the sufferer the light of day would seem to never come; hours become days, days become years to him who bears the fearful pains of some dreadful malady. How if these torments, unrelieved by death, were to last for years, for centuries, till the end of the world! But we sink beneath the thought of suffering even such pains as this life can inflict, for eternity. And yet these pains are not to be compared with the torments of the damned. When shall all this be? Perhaps this very year, perhaps this very week, perhaps this very day, nay, my God! it may be this very hour. We know not when; we may be even this moment upon the very brink of hell.

Eternity! Eternity! Be thy thought ever with us to remind us that this human life is but a point, compared with the eternal duration that follows it. Eternity of pleasure, be thou ever present to the mind of the saint as an incentive to his perseverance in virtue. Eternity of suffering, be thou never absent from the mind of the sinner to intimidate him from sin and to lead him back to the path of pardon. Eternal hell, be thy remembrance ever with us to remind us of divine justice when less constraining motives shall have lost their effect.

If, then, we would escape the vengeance of an angry God, let us seek Him while He may be found, and call upon Him while He is near. Do now what the damned soul would do if it could return to life. You may imagine what such a soul would do; the innocent life it would lead; the anxiety with which it would avoid sin; the penance it would practice to blot out its former transgressions; the vigilance it would employ in shunning sin and its occasions; the frequency and assiduity with which it would approach the sacraments; how, in a word, it would avoid even the shadow of sin; how the thought of salvation would be ever present in its mind. Do ye now the same. You have received even a greater grace than the damned soul would in being allowed to return to life from hell. To be saved entirely from an evil is greater goodness than to be rescued from it. God is now patiently waiting for you, anxious to show mercy, and inspiring you with good resolutions. Turn not away from His entreaties; be not deaf to His inspirations; this is the acceptable time; this is the day of salvation. You have no security of the future. Be not content with forming resolutions, but seek at once to put them in practice. Remember that no damned soul intended to be lost; it lived on in hope of a time which it was never destined to see, delaying from day to day its conversion until at last the measure of its iniquities was filled, and it was snatched away by a sudden and unlooked for death. If, then, you would not share the fate of the damned, be careful not to imitate their example. If you would receive the eternal reward which they have lost, pursue the life of virtue which they contemned.

THE DELAY OF REPENTANCE.

Then he began to upbraid the cities, wherein were done the most of his mighty works, because they had not done penance.

Wo to thee, Corozain, wo to thee, Bethsaida: for if in Tyre and Sidon the mighty works had been done that have been done in you, they would long ago have done penance in sack-cloth and ashes.

But I say unto you, it shall be more tolerable for Tyre and Sidon in the day of judgment, than for you.

And thou Capharnaum, shalt thou be exalted up to heaven? thou shalt go down even unto hell. For if the mighty works had been done in Sodom, that have been done in thee, perhaps it would have remained until this day.

But I say unto you, that it shall be more tolerable for the land of Sodom in the day of judgment, than for thee.—Matt. xi. 20-24.

And there were present at that very time, some that told him of the Galileans, whose blood Pilate had mingled with their sacrifices.

And he answering, said to them: Think you that these Galileans were sinners above all the men of Galilee, because they suffered such things?

I say to you, No: but unless you do penance, you shall all likewise perish.

Or those eighteen upon whom the tower fell in Siloe, and slew them: think you that they also were debtors above all the men that dwell in Jerusalem.

I tell you: No: but unless you do penance, you shall all likewise perish.—Luke xiii. 1-5.

THERE are but two ways by which a man can be saved; by innocence never lost, or by sincere repentance. This we all admit. Of this there can be no doubt. "Nothing defiled can enter heaven." If the soul has been stained by sin, it must be cleansed and made innocent again by true repentance. Heaven is open only to the innocent or the repentant.

Who is the man that expects heaven on the ground of never having lost his baptismal innocence; of never having committed grievous sin? You will have to search through thousands to find him, if he is to be found at all. We are all sinners. We deceive ourselves, if we believe we are without sin. We have all incurred the anger of God, and deserve His justice for the manifold sins of which we have been guilty. We may bid farewell to salvation on any other ground than that of deep and abiding repentance. This is our only hope. This is the only plank that remains to us after the fatal shipwreck we have long since made of the purity and innocence received in baptism. This divine instrument of salvation is necessary for every man; be he high or low, rich or poor, prince or subject, pontiff or priest.

Now, how few pursue this repentance by which alone they can be saved? Very few indeed are actually doing this necessary penance. We find no one who does not intend to do it. All delude themselves with the prospect of doing it at some future time. Of course, no one sins with the purpose of sinning always. No one wishes to die the death of a sinner. No one, be he ever so hardened in iniquity, but looks forward to the time when he imagines he will cease to do evil, and be restored to God's favor. In the midst of all his excesses, the sinner cannot quench the graces of sacraments once received; he cannot uproot from his soul the principles of virtue received in his early Christian education. Hence to extinguish the keen remorse which continually pursues him, if he be not altogether dead to the influences of grace, he tries to speak peace to his soul by promising himself to do penance hereafter; that in the future he will forsake his evil ways, he will cultivate virtue, and will wash away his sins by tears of repentance. Thus, he thinks, he will atone for the sins he is now committing, and save his soul. It is this fatal delay that is the greatest danger to the sinner, that sends multitudes daily to everlasting misery—it is the cause of the damnation of almost all who are lost.

The causes that induce this sad infatuation of deferring repentance, from the present time to some period in the future, are many. If we give our attention to the subject, we shall find them to be principally those which I am about to expose for your instruction.

A certain torpor or sloth gains possession of the soul, leading the sinner to defer his repentance from time to time. The soul is less sensibly affected by the truths of religion, than by the affairs of this life. Hence, he shows not the activity or energy in the care of his eternal salvation, that he does in the pursuit of some temporal end. It is not that he is ignorant of, or disbelieves the great truths of religion; his faith may be unshaken, but he does not keenly realize them; he does not think of them often enough, and seriously enough, to bring them home to his heart and mind. The faculties of his soul are benumbed with a sloth which hinders him from giving earnest thought to but what directly affects his senses; or, if at times, the subject of his salvation may occur to him, he at best defers it till some future period when he flatters himself he will be less disinclined to think of such matters. Of course, inspirations of God's grace come to him warning him of the dreadful peril in which he is placing his soul; but he speaks peace to himself by some excuse; sometimes one thing, sometimes another. Now it is that the confessor is too severe, or perhaps too just; now it is that he feels he is not as well prepared as he would wish to be before going to confession; now he fears the self-denial which he will have to practise after confession. It matters very little whether it be a good or a bad reason, anything that may quiet his conscience. Overcome by his sloth and by the apparent difficulty of doing penance, he falls into a sort of spiritual lethargy, defers his conversion from time to time, looking forward to a season when he imagines it will be easier and his repugnance not so great. The year passes around, the great festivals and fasts and penitential seasons of the Church come and go, always finding our sinner in the same state, never prepared and always deferring. It goes on for five or ten or twenty years, or perhaps throughout his whole life until the hand of God falls upon him in the shape of a sudden death, or until, prostrated upon his last sick-bed, he feels the icy hand of death, and that he has but a few days more to spend on earth.

Why, my brethren, it is the blindest of delusions to give way to this spiritual sloth and to defer your repentance from the present hour. Do you imagine that this sloth will diminish with time and habit? Do you imagine that indulgence in vice is the means of overcoming it? Would you overcome your passions by gratifying them? Would you cultivate chastity by impurity, temperance by drunkenness? Will you acquire energy by languor? Are not vices to be overcome by their opposites? He who wishes to be chaste, must he not cultivate the virtue by repeated acts of purity and by abstaining from everything impure? He who would be temperate, must he not practise abstinence? How then will you overcome your spiritual sloth? — by indulgence which feeds it, or by energetically rising from your torpor and shaking off the mortal lethargy that oppresses you?

Yes, my brethren, this is the hour to rise from sleep; this very hour, no future time. It is far easier now than it will be when habit and indulgence will have increased your insensibility a thousandfold. Make but the effort, and all your repugnances and the apparent difficulties that appall you will vanish. Make but the effort, and you will be surprised and confounded, as others have been, that such delusions and seeming obstacles could have withheld you so long from doing penance. Make but the effort, and the severity of the confessor which you now fear will become sweet; your apprehension of the lack of the due dispositions will be the best token of your contrition; the self-denial that you dread will be acts of virtue that you will cheerfully impose upon yourself; all your pretexts will disappear; your only regret will be that you allowed yourself to be imposed upon so long by such unfounded difficulties and frivolous excuses. Endanger not your eternal salvation by giving way to this torpor. Delaying your repentance from day to day will bring you to final impenitence. The time is short. This is the acceptable day, this the day of salvation. Delay not your conversion from day to day; for His wrath shall come of a sudden, and in the time of vengeance He will surprise you. Awake, arise, walk no longer on the brink of hell. Be about your salvation lest God's justice overtake you. This is the hour to rise from the sleep of sin in which you lie ready to fall into hell.

There is another class who defer their repentance, because they are so much engrossed with the world and its affairs that but little time remains to them to think of God and their soul. When we look out into the world and see the wonderful energy that men exhibit in the pursuit of the goods of this life, when we see them give their undivided attention to their pursuit, during forty or fifty years, or even during their whole life-time, when we reflect how little men think of their eternal destiny—the only end for which they have come into being—we are almost tempted to think that they believe not in a hereafter, that this is the only world for which they have been made. Look at men; what is their history from generation to generation, from age to age? Every one is engaged in the pursuit of some temporal end, and he pursues it with an energy and perseverance such as we should imagine an intelligent being would bestow only on what concerns his immortal destiny. One man is occupied in quest of riches; in them he places his whole happiness. He stops not when he has accumulated more than he will ever be able to spend. He must leave something to his children to quarrel about after his death. He would seem to have come into the world for no other end than to pile up a mountain of wealth. Of course, such a man thinking of nothing but of hoarding money, has no time for repentance. Another man spends his days in the acquisition of fame. He thinks to satisfy his soul's craving for happiness by this phantom—so unreal, so easily had and often with so little deserving. He seeks not the praise of God which would indeed be his true bliss, but prefers that of men; and to obtain it, he will not hesitate to trample on God's law, and, it may be, persecute His church. Another man spends his life in acquiring knowledge, in delving into the secrets of nature. Certainly, of all, he is the noblest. Yet what a fool is he, if, in the pursuit of human knowledge, he neglects God, the source of all true wisdom! How often is this human learning sought to show the unwisdom of God and to destroy religion! A man spends a few days in the study of science, and when he has learned a few of the secrets of nature, puffed up with intolerable pride, he imagines that he could have improved very much on the works of God, had he only been the creator. Or, with impudence unpardonable, he proclaims that religion must be thrown overboard, because, forsooth, its tenets are not compatible with the discoveries of his puny mind. Or, it may be that he spends the best part of his life in undermining belief in the Divinity of Christ, or in questioning the holiest truths of religion.

Thus it is the world goes on, thus it is that men pass their days in the pursuit of objects as trifling and contemptible as the toys with which children amuse themselves. No one thinks of God or of his soul. Men come into the world and go out of it, without once casting a serious thought on why they have come into it or whither they are going. Warnings are neglected, the truths of revelation are mocked at, he who talks devoutly, or gives evidence in his conduct of fearing God, is laughed at as a fool or derided as a hypocrite. Generation succeeds generation, son follows father, all are engaged in the same frivolities, all show as little fear of God. Thousands are daily plunging headlong into hell. So it is, so it has been, so it will be until God in His just indignation shall come and consume the world. It is unnecessary to say that all those who are engrossed in the fortunes of this life expose themselves to the danger of final impenitence.

Of course, if you ask the man intent on riches

or fame or learning, if he never intends to give thought to his soul, he will answer, Yes; but there is yet time enough; just now he has too much else to do; wait until he has provided for his old age and gained something for his children; wait till he has made a name; wait till he has learned something more of the truths of nature; he is yet young, he has his three score and ten; but in his old age his passions will not be so strong; and then his worldly ambitions being satisfied, he will give his exclusive attention to his soul. But, my brethren, this is the sheerest nonsense that a man could utter. Do not all these engrossing cares increase with time and indulgence? As I have said before, the passions increase and are intensified by gratification. Desires for wealth or fame or pleasure or learning increase by what they feed on. The more wealth a man gathers, the greater the desire for wealth becomes; the more he becomes famous, the more he desires to be yet further known and honored; the more learning he acquires, the better he understands how little he knows and how boundless the domain of knowledge is; and accordingly his thirst for learning becomes more and more insatiable. This is all in the very nature of things. But look around you and verify it by experience. See those who are now at that period of life to which you look forward as the time when all worldly cares shall cease and you will give yourself to God and your salvation; it is the period to which these people themselves looked forward as days of penitence, when they were as you are now. What is the fact? Are they engaged in the work of salvation? Have all earthly cares ceased for them? Do they give themselves more to God than they ever did? Have the concerns of life, the thirst of gain, the pursuit of fame, the acquisition of knowledge, less charms for them now, in their old age, than they had in their youth and manhood? Why, my brethren, we have but to look around us to see the reverse. The rich man pursues, in his old age, the passion for money which held him captive, in his manhood and youth. Even on his death-bed, his last thought is solicitude for his wealth, and the pain he feels at leaving it. The man who sought fame in his manhood, will seek it till the day of his death. The man who sought knowledge is as fresh in his pursuit at seventy or eighty, as he was at twenty. These passions exercise as despotic a sway over the soul in old age as in youth. They leave as little time and as little relish for God and salvation as in the time of youth. If, then, we neglect God and salvation in youth and manhood, we shall neglect them in old age. We gain nothing by delay, we endanger all. Far easier now to do penance, than it will be when these passions have increased and been strengthened by time and habit. It is clear, then, that those who put off their salvation are likely to die impenitent. What are we to do? This is the hour to rise from sleep; this hour, not to-morrow or the next day. This is the day of salvation. We have no guarantee of any but of the present moment. Let us not expose ourselves to imminent risk by remaining a single instant in hostility to God. Let us not die impenitent, by delaying our repentance. This is the hour to work; a time cometh when no one shall work.

There are others who endanger their eternal salvation, by delaying their conversion, because their love for sin is so great that they are unwilling to give it up. They find in it a pleasure which they are not prepared to sacrifice. They prefer the gratification of sin to the consolation of keeping God's holy law. They cannot think of doing violence to their sinful inclinations. God and His law find little place in their hearts. They find their only happiness in iniquity. Without it, life for them would have but little charm. It never enters their mind that their only business on earth is to declare and carry on an unceasing war against the flesh and its concupiscence; that for this only have they been born, for this only do they live. They give up sin! They cannot think of it. They restore their ill-gotten goods! What! strip themselves of what may be the greatest part of their fortune! They are not beside themselves. Restore the reputations they have destroyed by detraction or calumny! That is asking too much of human nature. Part with those persons, sever those affections, that lead them into sin! You might as well tell them to pluck out their eye, or cut off their right hand. You ask too much, they will tell you. We ask nothing but what the Gospel requires under pain of eternal damnation. Ask these people, if they propose to save their souls. They will fire with indignation, and answer, with the greatest confidence, that they do. If you remonstrate with them, and point out that they are not now in the way of salvation, they will admit, if they are not wholly blinded to their miserable state, that they know their souls are not now in the state in which they would have them when God will call them; but that they mean, before they die, to seriously take in hand the work of their salvation. By and by, when they have enjoyed the world a little more, when they have acquired a competency, when passions shall have grown weaker; then they will turn to God, obtain pardon and wash away sin by tears and works of sincere repentance. Here again comes the delusion which I have been trying to expose. Do you imagine that your passions will grow weak with gratification? Do you imagine that sin will be less seductive after twenty years' indulgence than it is now? No; all reasoning, all experience shows that the passions increase and grow strong with time and impunity. The more the soul gives way to them, the more they tyrannize over it.

If sin has for you now a fascination which you cannot think of denying yourselves, how will it be when time will have augmented it a thousandfold? If now you cannot think of restoring to those whom you have defrauded what is their due, how will you do it when your ill-gotten goods will have become mountain high, only to crush you down to hell? If now you cannot separate from those who are occasions of sin to you, how will you do it when these acquaintances will have multiplied, and when the bonds that enslave you to them will have become as adamant? If now you cannot stoop to the duty of restoring the good name you have destroyed, how will you do it when age will have rendered you keener to human respect, and less willing to perform a duty so humiliating? No, my brethren, flatter not yourselves with the hope that sin will exercise a less despotic sway over you hereafter, than it does at present. Its bonds will not relax with time. Easier far to overcome it now, than it will be at any future time. At all times it requires a sacrifice. And this sacrifice must be made. The slavery of sin must be broken. War to the death must be declared against the world, the flesh, and the devil. This task is done easily now when the chains of sin and passion are not yet firmly forged; when the flesh has not yet grown proud and stubborn by frequent victories; when the world's vanities have not yet made those deep impressions on the soul which with time will become ineffaceable; when as yet, you are not the trained soldiers, but the raw recruits of the evil one.

There is still another class of people who defer their repentance, because they realize not the supreme importance of saving their souls. The great truths of religion make little or no impression upon them. They listen to the priest announce, with all the vehemence of which he is capable, the most alarming truths; Salvation, Hell, Sin, Redemption, Death, Judgment; but they convey no terror to their hearts. They feel none of those compunctious feelings which other sinners, even the hardest, frequently experience.

They hear of some one's conversion; they imagine that he must be mad. They hear of some one making restitution; they account for it on the ground that it is all pretense, only another means of gaining more than he gives. They hear of some one putting away an occasion of sin; it is because he has been found out. They hear that such a one goes to church and receives the sacraments; it is all hypocrisy, they declare.

Now such a person cannot understand such workings of grace, because he is spiritually blind. And why? It is because his understanding is darkened, his will is made perverse, he has abused God's grace, he has trampled under foot his inspirations; and now God, as just retribution, takes from him the light that would enable him to see and to realize the truths of Religion. As physical light is necessary to the eye that it may see physical objects, so the light of grace is necessary to the soul that it may see and realize the importance of religious truth. It is unnecessary to remark that such a one is exposed to the most imminent risk of damnation. What must he do? Redouble his importunities: beseech God earnestly and unceasingly to remove the darkness that clouds his soul, to soften the obduracy of his heart, to rectify the perversity of his will, that he may see the truth and follow it with a docile mind and willing heart.

All — the slothful, those engrossed with the goods of this world, those too fond of sin to give it up, the impenitent and hard of heart, all, I say, flatter themselves with the prospect of doing penance at some future time. Some future time! Will it ever come? We cannot promise ourselves any but the present hour. God has promised grace to those that repent; but has He promised it to those who defer repentance? How many have been lost by deferring their conversion from day to day? How many have been on a sudden cut off with all their sins upon them, and, without a moment's repentance, hurried before the judgment-seat of God? They who have been thus lost, were once as confident of being saved as you are now. The sad prospect of reprobation was as far from their thoughts as it is now from yours. They looked forward as hopefully to the time when they would be restored to God's favor, and wash away their sins by penitential tears. But just as foolishly, they neglected the present moment. They delayed their conversion from day to day until, at length, the measure of their iniquities was filled, and God executed His vengeance upon them. "Delay not then to be converted to the Lord, and defer it not from day to day, for His wrath shall come on a sudden, and in the time of vengeance He will destroy thee." Taught by the dread example of those who have been lost, the tremendous danger of deferring repentance, nay, of remaining one single hour in mortal sin, we should put off our conversion no longer, but seek the Lord and His mercy while there is yet time.

Putting off repentance from day to day brings it to the death-bed. And woe to the man who rests his chance of salvation upon a death-bed repentance! Woe to the man who begins not his preparation for death until, prostrated by some mortal illness, he feels that his days are at an end and that death is upon him! Death-bed, did I say? Will he have a death-bed? May not the battle-field be his death-bed? May not the ocean be his death-bed? May not some of the numberless accidents that are taking place, continually, everywhere, be his death-bed? Death-bed, indeed! Why, there are ten thousand causes within us, and around us, that, in a moment, can put us out of life, without giving an instant to lie on a death-bed. Death is in the food that we consume, the water we drink, the air we breathe; a blow upon the head is enough to disorder the brain; a slight affection of the heart will cause death in a moment. Yet talk we of a death-bed!

But let us suppose that he who has delayed repentance all his life, lies upon a death-bed. What, if, at that hour, the brain be all on fire with some burning fever! What, if the poor intellect sink into utter unconsciousness! will repentance then be possible? Is it an unusual case? Ask any priest, how often he is called to attend someone, whom he finds unconscious. Frequently. He may anoint him; it will do no harm, if it can do but little good. He leaves strict orders to send for him again, if the sick person recovers his reason. How often is it that reason has taken its last farewell of the body? How often does the poor sinner pass from unconsciousness to death? But he retains his reason. He is furnished with whatever consolations his friends can afford. Think you that the difficulty, the sloth that has always been a hindrance to his confession, leaves him at that hour? On the contrary, does not this reluctance increase a thousandfold, now that he is tortured with pain, that the mind is delirious with agony, that the whole system is breaking up? In health, confession requires no small application of mind. Few would think of preparing for it, while suffering from a severe headache or toothache. How will the poor sinner apply his mind, now, when the shades of death are gathering, thick and fast, about him; when his will is weakened by the deadly anguish he suffers? How little capable of preparing for confession will he be, at that hour? Even then, he will be faithful to his habit of delay, and will suggest that it be put back until the next day, when the fever shall have abated and he will be more recollected.

The next day rises upon him a corpse. Or, it may be that the difficulty of confession will then seem so great that, with the aid of the devil suggesting that it is now too late, that he should have repented long ago, that such sins cannot be wiped out by a moment's repentance, he will give way to despair and die impenitent.

Thus it is that God abandons those who abuse His mercy, who spend their youth and strength and manhood in the service of the devil, reserving for Him the dregs of their old age, when they have no longer the power to offend him. "Because I called and you refused to hear; I stretched out my hands and there was none that regarded; you have despised all my counsels and neglected my reprehensions; I also will laugh in your destruction. When sudden calamity shall fall upon you, and destruction, as a tempest, shall be at hand; when tribulation and distress shall come upon you; then shall you call upon me and I will not hear."

Even if the sinner should not despair, his death-bed repentance will not be such as can be relied on. To rise from the death of sin to the life of grace, is a miracle far greater than to rise from physical death to physical life. As no one can come to life again, by his own power, so no man can, of his own strength, rise from sin to grace. We cannot make one effort towards our salvation, unless it be given us by the Holy Ghost. No ordinary grace will suffice to move the sinner's heart, at the hour of death. Proof against every feeling of compunction, dead to every good inspiration of grace, during life; great, indeed, must the grace be that can move it at the hour of death. Will he receive it? Can he expect it, who has drained the cup of iniquity to the dregs, and who turns to God, only because he has no longer the power to offend Him? What can he expect but to be abandoned in that hour?

There can be no sincere repentance, without a firm purpose of amendment, without repairing the evil effects of sin, without severing the bonds of sin, without giving up everything that is to us an occasion of sin. Think you, the sinner will be able to do this at the hour of death? that he will be able, in a moment, to separate his heart from affections which held him captive, even in health when he was fully master of himself? Such attachments are not easily sundered. Passions cherished from infancy, habits of sin which have become part of his nature, are not vanquished but by extraordinary grace and unceasing efforts. They are not overcome at the hour of death. Their purpose of amendment cannot be relied on. "Ease soon relaxes vows made in pain as nugatory and void." If they recover, they are apt to return to sin, just as if they had made no such purpose. "His bones will be filled with the disorders of his youth, and his sins will sleep with him in the grave."

What is it that the Holy Ghost, in the New Testament and the Old, most frequently gives warning of? What is it that Jesus Christ so often and emphatically declared during His mission on earth? What is it that the apostles, saints, and martyrs most earnestly and continually inculcated upon the faithful? What is it that the Church unceasingly puts before us in the Gospels and Epistles of the Sundays of the year? It is the suddenness of death, and the necessity of being always ready for it. "He will come as a thief in the night." "You know not the day, nor the hour, when the Son of man will come." "Watch ye and pray, for you know not at what hour the Lord will come." "For know you not that, if the master of the house knew at what hour the thief would come, he would watch and not allow him to enter?" "So be you always prepared; for you know not when the Son of man will come."

You know, then, from Jesus, from the Apostles, from the Scriptures, from the Saints, from the Church, from your own observation, that death will come when you least expect it. What are you to do? Be ready to meet it; put yourself in a state of grace. Do penance; for the kingdom of heaven is at hand. Do penance; or ye will all likewise perish. Do penance; for now the ax is laid to the root, and every tree that bringeth not forth good fruit, will be cut down and cast into the flame.

As I began, I conclude, by saying that there are but two means under heaven by which we can be saved: Baptism and Penance. Baptism is for us all a fountain closed. We have been washed in its waters; we have received its grace, and we have forfeited it. Penance alone remains. This is the salient, living spring of life eternal, which fertilizes the Church of God, and purifies the hearts of the faithful. Here we can be washed, without stint or measure, as often as we approach it with the necessary dispositions. It is always open. We have not to wait for any angel to touch its waters, nor for anyone to carry us to them, when they are moved, as at Bethsaida of old. We have but to draw near, and we shall at all times find Jesus in this Sacrament dispensing the priceless merits of His blood, applying to our souls, through the ministry of His priest, the fruits of His Passion, continuing the work of cleansing, not from the leprosy which afflicts the body, but from that worse and more fatal leprosy which destroys the soul and casts it into everlasting misery.

THE NEW YORK
PUBLIC LIBRARY,

ASTOR, LENOX AND
TILDEN FOUNDATIONS.

THE LAST JUDGMENT.

And I saw, when he had opened the sixth seal; and behold, there was a great earthquake, and the sun became black as sackcloth of hair, and the whole moon became as blood.

And the stars from heaven fell upon the earth, as the fig-tree casteth its green figs when it is shaken by a great wind:

And the heaven withdrew as a book rolled up together; and every mountain, and the islands were moved out of their places.

And the kings of the earth, and the princes, and the tribunes, and the rich men, and the strong men, and every bondman, and every freeman hid themselves in the dens, and in the rocks of the mountains:

And they say to the mountains and to the rocks: Fall upon us, and hide us from the face of him that sitteth upon the throne, and from the wrath of the Lamb:

For the great day of their wrath is come; and who shall be able to stand?—Apocalypse vi. 12–17.

And therefore we labour, whether absent or present, to please Him.

For we must all appear before the judgment-seat of Christ, that every one may receive the proper things of the body, according as he hath done, whether it be good or evil.

Knowing therefore the fear of the Lord we persuade men; but to God we are manifest. And I trust also that in your consciences we are manifest.

We commend not ourselves again to you, but give you occasion to glory in our behalf, that you may have somewhat to answer them who glory in face, and not in heart.—St. Paul, II. Cor. v. 9–12.

WHETHER we consider ourselves, our bodies so fearfully and wonderfully made, our souls gifted with divine attributes; or the universal order and harmony of the physical world; whatever we consider or wherever we turn our eyes, we see the most abundant evidences of the existence of a Supreme Being, and of one, too, of infinite power and boundless perfection.

But when we turn our eyes from the physical to the moral world; when we behold the cause of virtue, which is necessarily the cause of God, trampled in the dust; when we see the prosperous impunity which iniquity enjoys; when we see that it is not the God-fearing, but the God-defying, that, for the most part, possess the earth; when we see the virtuous poor piercing heaven with their cries against the wrongs they suffer from the tyrant rich; we find nothing, indeed, to invalidate the proof of the existence of God, which all things afford; but we find much to perplex the mind, much which we can, but with difficulty, reconcile with the existence of a God, all-wise and all-good.

Of course, this is because we take too contracted a view of things; all this is because we shut off from our minds the light of Revelation; all this is because we are not in a position to take in from end to end God's eternal designs.

But, if we expand our mental vision, if we let the light of Revelation fall upon our minds, if we trace the course of God's mysterious providence to its final consummation, in the day when He shall judge the world in justice,—when every man shall receive his deserts, when the wicked shall be covered with shame and confusion and the just shall receive glory before the assembled world,—

when the moral order, subverted during this life, shall be readjusted in the heavenly balance; then all perplexity ceases, and we find no difficulty in reconciling with God's gracious providence the permission of the grievous wrongs and black crimes which we see so frequently in the world. His ways are cleared up. His providence is justified before all men. The moral world, no less than the physical, bespeaks the wisdom and goodness of God.

Behold, in what we have said, the reason, why, in addition to the judgment which each one undergoes at the hour of death, a general judgment still awaits all men at the end of the world. On that great day, when an all-just God shall reward the just, and punish the wicked, we shall understand the mysterious dispensation which, in this life, so often permitted the good to suffer, and the wicked to prosper.

We may, perchance, think that divine providence is sufficiently made known, and justified, by the sentence pronounced on each one, at the hour of death. We must remember that this sentence is hidden from all, save him upon whom it is passed. It is not published to all men. At the general judgment, this sentence shall be re-affirmed before the whole world.

Besides; the purpose of the final judgment is not so much the trial of individual men, as the manifestation, before the whole human race, of the accomplishment of God's mysterious providence, in the midst, or, rather, in spite of human passions and human perversity. It will also serve to show, why divine goodness allowed the enormous evils which we see everywhere in human society.

When will this great investigation take place? "No one knows; not even the angels, not even the Son of God," says St. Luke. Of course, he is to be understood to mean, that the Son knows it not, in order to reveal it. For every thing that the Father hath, the Son hath. They are the same God. It is one of these things the knowledge of which God has reserved to Himself. We know that certain great signs will precede it. The Gospel must first be preached to all nations as a testimony, and then will come the consummation. The Antichrist must first come: "If, in that day, they say to you, lo! here is Christ, or there, believe it not, for the Antichrist must first come, the son of perdition; and then will come the end." Faith will have grown faint in the hearts of men: "Think you that the Son of Man, on his coming, will find faith upon the earth!"

Of one thing, however, we may rest assured. When it comes, it will come suddenly, and there will be no mistaking it: "The day of the Son of Man will come as a thief in the night." For what other purpose has God made it one of those things which no one knows, not even the angels, if it is not that it should come when we least expect it? "Be ye ready, for ye know not the day nor the hour, when the Son of Man will come." There will be no mistaking it: "For even as the light rises in the East, and sets in the West, so will the coming of the Son of Man be." It will be preceded by such signs, as will leave no doubt of its being at hand.

After all, it is a matter of no great practical importance, when it will come. It comes to every man at the hour of death. The day of our death is the day of our judgment. As we fall, so we shall remain. The sentence pronounced upon the soul, at the moment when it leaves the body, will never be reversed.

"Where will this great assize be held?" the curious may ask. This, too, is a matter of little moment. Yet, if we are to answer, we would say that it will be held, not in the different places where men may find themselves, but in some particular spot or locality. The very object of the general judgment,—the manifestation to all men of the glory of the just, and the shame of the reprobate,—would seem to imply the necessity of gathering together all men, in one place. It would appear, that the gifts of a glorified body do not include ubiquity, or the power of being present everywhere at once. Nor can a glorified body be cognizant of what is taking place elsewhere, than where it actually is. Yet, that the purpose of the general judgment may be fulfilled; that the wicked may be put to shame and exposed to the scorn of mankind, and that the just may be held up to the admiration of the world; it is necessary, either, that glorified bodies be endowed with ubiquity; or, that they be brought together in one place, to be made cognizant of all that will happen on that day. Even if a glorified body possessed ubiquity, we should still have to believe that men would be judged, not in the spot where they happen to be, but in some particular locality. For the bodies of the damned, for whose punishment the general judgment is especially destined, will not be glorified: "We shall all, indeed, rise again, but we shall not all be changed." Hence, we conclude that all men will be assembled together, according to the words of Scripture: "Then will men be gathered together from the four quarters of the world." Many are of the opinion, that the place destined for this great event, is the Valley of Josaphat.

But, let us hasten on to consider the words of our text: "We must all appear." Who will be judged? You and I and all of us; the young, the old, every rank and condition of life; those who die in the flower of youth, and in the vigor of manhood; those who go down to the grave laden with years. The king, the subject; the philosopher, and he who knew not his letters; the gifted, the giftless; the bondman, and the freeman; he who revelled in luxury, he who toiled in indigence, shall all be reduced to the same level, and stand before the same tribunal. All men; all races, tribes, peoples: Catholics and infidels and pagans; Jews and heretics; those who have never heard the name of Christ; those with whom it has been the first lisp and the dying sigh; the men who lived before the flood; those whose bones have lain within earth's bosom thousands of years; those who are born at the sound of the Archangel's trumpet; all who have ever trod the earth, or hereafter will appear upon it, till time shall be no more, must all, one day, stand before the judgment-seat of Christ.

A fearful multitude will this surely be; a multitude more numerous, by far, than the angels who fell from heaven; a multitude so vast, that the earth would seem insufficient to contain it. Yes; on that mighty day, decisive of the eternal destinies of our race, at the sound of the Archangel's trumpet, the graveyards of the earth will open, and yield forth the uncounted millions who lie beneath its surface; the earth itself will give back the untold multitudes, which it has, in all ages, in its horrible convulsions, swallowed up; the great ocean shall roll back, and disgorge from its horrid abyss, all those who have therein found an untimely grave.

While all this is going on; while men are hastening from their last resting place where death has laid them in the four quarters of the world, to the Valley of Judgment; while the vision of the prophet is, to the letter, fulfilled; and the bones of men are once more united together, and again clothed with the flesh, and reanimated with the spirit, the other words of Scripture are verified: "The sun is darkened, the moon is changed into blood;" the stars rush from their spheres, and fall from heaven; the powers of earth are shaken; the elements are in dissolution; the earth is convulsed to its very centre; continent is torn from continent; islands are submerged; the mighty ocean, partaking in the general disturbance, rising from its bed, mountains high, falls upon the earth, sweeping away the cities, and every other vestige of the pride and pomp and magnificence of man. The whole world is in the throes of dissolution. Already appear the lurid flames of the conflagration destined to consume the world and reduce it to eternal ashes. A dread, uniform silence, unbroken save by the sound of the Archangel's trumpet, and the noise of the warring elements, pervades all nature. Even irrational nature, the wild beasts of the forest, beside themselves with the terror inspired by the scene around them, start from their haunts, and seek the companionship of man. Then shall the tribes of the earth mourn; then shall the nations be distressed; then shall men wail and wither away with terror, at the sight of Divine Justice.

And yet this confusion, and these death-throes of an expiring world, are but a feeble image of the wild confusion, the bitter anguish and blank despair of every human breast. What idle regrets, what unavailing remorse will then fill the souls of men! I know not what, on that day, will be the feelings of the man, who has passed his days in acquiring, with infinite industry, his vast possessions,—in piling up mountains of gold, when he sees them all involved in the common ruin of all things. I know not what, on that day, will be the sentiments of the unbeliever who tortures his ingenuity to justify his unbelief; when he beholds, before his eyes, the very event which he has so often laughed to scorn. I know not what the satisfaction, on that day, the remembrance of the forbidden pleasures, enjoyed in this life, will give the sinner, when he realizes that they have caused the loss of the immortal pleasure of seeing God, and brought upon him unending woe. What then shall be thought of the bauble, which men pursue so eagerly, of human fame and glory; when every human soul shall undergo the rigid scrutiny of an all-seeing God who sees the secrets of hearts, and who will judge all things not according to the corrupt maxims of this life, but according to the eternal maxims of right and truth. How many of the judgments of this world shall then be reversed! What will be the bitter anguish of the man who feels that he has lost his soul! what profit will it then be, to have gained all things else, and to have failed in the one thing necessary! Loss it is, which eternity alone can declare, to have lost one's immortal soul. But who can measure the height, and depth, and breadth of the crime of having caused the loss of the souls of others. Then, will thousands arise, and demand vengeance upon the murderers of their souls. Nor will their demand pass unheeded by Him who has declared that it is better for a man never to have been born, or to be cast into the sea with a millstone around his neck, than that he should become a rock of scandal to souls purchased at the price of His all-holy blood.

He who can imagine the feelings of the human breast, at one of those awful moments which paralyze the hearts of a population, and which bring home to him, in accents which preacher never uttered, the vanity of all things human; when the earth reels and totters, in some terrible convulsion, and opens, in a yawning abyss, ready to swallow a whole people, can, perhaps, picture to himself the sentiments of the reprobate at the last day. They will call upon the hills to cover them, and the mountains to annihilate them, from the face of an angry God.

Do not think, for a moment, that I have exaggerated any statement, or that I have, in the least, overdrawn the picture. Bear in mind, that I have hardly departed from the words of Scripture. There may be those who, because they have sinned with impunity, all their lives long, and have experienced so little of Divine Justice, have become unmindful of it. There may be others, who delude themselves with the thought, that God is too merciful to visit His creatures with so searching a judgment. They may think, too, that He can not be so inexorably just, as to punish eternally. But the past history of our race supplies but little encouragement to this thought, so gratifying to human passion and sin. His attributes can not war with one another. His mercy can not exclude His justice. It is, indeed, above all His works; yet, He must ever remain, essentially, a God of justice.

Call to mind that day of judgment, when all, save those who were in the Ark, perished in the flood. Remember the one hundred and eighty-five thousand Assyrians put to the sword, in one night, by the Avenging Angel. Reflect upon the fate of Sodom and Gomorrah, and the other cities of the plain, which, together with their crimes, lie buried at the bottom of the Dead Sea. These are but a few of the signal instances of divine vengeance, which the holy Scriptures afford. Yet, from these, we may learn something of God's swift and fearful justice.

Then will appear the sign of the Son of Man in heaven: "And you will see the Son of Man coming in the clouds of heaven, with great power and majesty." He will come, seated upon a great white throne, surrounded with the powers and principalities of heaven. No human imagination can picture the unearthly grandeur, the awe-inspiring character of that tribunal; and the wild confusion of the sinner, at that presence, before which the angels tremble, and heaven and earth would fade away. How different from His first coming, will be that second glorious advent of the Son of Man! This difference is determined by the different character of the mission on which He will then come. On His first coming into the world, He came on a mission of love and mercy. When He comes again, He will come on a mission of justice and vengeance. He, then, came to ransom, at the price of His blood, a world of immortal spirits condemned to death. He came to teach them, that detachment from this life is the only hope and assurance of eternal happiness in the next; to teach this lesson, by His own high example; both, in the manner in which He came into the world, and the life which He led while in it, He exhibited the loftiest superiority to all human weakness; the most utter detachment from all human things; the sublimest contempt for the ways, and maxims, and wisdom of men.

But, on His second coming, it will be no longer on an errand of mercy. He will come, sent into the world by His Eternal Father, as the judge of the living and the dead. He will come not as the mediator, not extended upon the cross, as on a throne of mercy, offering Himself as victim, between the uplifted anger of God, and the sins of men; but as the avenger, charged with the interests of Divine Justice against those who, during life, have despised His mercy, made void His atonement, and put Him before men to an open shame.

The chaos and confusion of the physical world, will be but a feeble image of the bitter agony, the intense anguish of every sinful breast. The sinner shall look upon Him whom he has crucified; upon His thorn-crowned head; His nail-pierced hands; His opened side; and, filled with the consciousness of his base perfidy and black ingratitude, he will wish the rocks to fall upon him and annihilate him; he will curse the day in which he was born. He will not need any word of reproach from Jesus his Saviour. The repetition of the look which He cast upon Judas, will be enough to remind him of his treachery and baseness. Then, will come rushing upon his mind the remembrance of all that Jesus has done to save him; yet, in spite of all, he is lost; lost, in defiance of the priceless ransom of Christ's precious blood, shed so lavishly for his sake; lost, when a hundredth part of the time and care given to the world, and the gratification of passion, employed in the work of salvation, would have num-

THE LAST JUDGMENT. 117

bered him among the saints, who stand around the throne of God. The load of his sad misfortune shall crush him to the very earth.

Many things which now, we little understand, because we so little reflect upon them, and because they are so far removed from the sphere of our ordinary thoughts, in the light which will, on that day, fill the world and illume the souls of men, will present themselves to us, with an evidence and reality which we never before dreamed of. Then, shall we understand the mystery of Christ's redeeming love. Then, shall we realize, for the first time, the unfathomable depth of meaning contained in this, the most unsearchable of the mysteries of God. Then, in the light which this great mystery sheds upon all things, in heaven and on earth, we shall understand the nature of sin, the fall of Adam, the eternity of reward and punishment, God's wondrous providence, and all those other truths which, here below, we so poorly comprehend. Then, finally, will men learn and keenly feel, what before they would never learn and never felt, that, in all this wide world, with all its countless enterprises and manifold cares, with which men amuse themselves, and lose the time given them for a nobler purpose, there were four, and only four, facts of sovereign interest, of undying importance, and alone worthy the attention of immortal beings: God, the human soul, the Blood that was shed for it, and the soul's fidelity to God's holy law. Of all things else, except in so far as they will bear upon these supreme issues, no account will be made, on that day. They will form no part of the investigation of that final judgment.

And then will come the investigation of the hearts of men; the showing forth of the glory of the elect, and the shame of the reprobate. For we must all be manifested before the judgment-seat of Christ. Nor will this investigation be necessarily a lengthy one. For, as I have just said, the subject matter of this examination will be contracted to the very narrow limits of what the soul has done and suffered for salvation. Besides, our conscience, on that day, will be our worst accuser. It will bear its testimony; the thoughts of our hearts mutually accusing, or even defending one another.

Moreover, no man will need to learn his eternal doom. From the moment of his death, he knows that the general judgment will not reverse the sentence then passed upon him, but will be to him a re-affirming of that sentence, and the increase of his woe. For then, his body will be condemned to share the eternal sufferings of his soul.

Although not lengthy, this examination will be most searching. In the emphatic language of the Scripture, our hearts will be turned inside out. The light issuing from the throne of God, will penetrate into the inmost recesses of our hearts, and souls, and minds; and show, to the assembled world, our deeds of darkness, our works of shame; our fidelity as soldiers of Christ, fighting the battle of salvation against our sworn enemies, the flesh, the world and the devil, following our great captain along the narrow and rugged and bloodstained path that leads to life; or, our perfidy in abandoning the standard of salvation, and enrolling ourselves under the prince of this world, and treading that broad, and easy, and luxurious path, so easily found, and so generally pursued.

And then will come the separation. The whole human family will, in an instant, file off into two great divisions; the one standing to the right, and the other to the left of Jesus. And now, are fulfilled the words of Scripture: "Two women will be grinding at the mill; one will be taken, and the other will be left." You are a father and a mother: the mother is assiduous in the discharge of her religious duties, careful, by word and example, to imbue her children with a love of religion, and to form their minds, while yet young, to the practice of virtue; the father heedless of his duties to himself, his children, and his God; perhaps, even a member of some forbidden society, which has weaned his affections from the Church, and led to his entire neglect of the sacraments, leaving him a Catholic in nothing, but in name. "The one will be taken, the other will be left." You are two sisters: one modest, retiring, carefully shunning those frivolities, and vanities, and amusements which are sure, in the long run, to lead to sin; fearful, lest even the shadow of sin should cross her path; the other; bold, forward, devoted to fashion and pleasure, wantonly exposing herself to the occasion of sin. "The one will be taken, the other will be left." You are two men: both devoted to business; the one, however, keeping before him for his guidance the law of the Gospel, careful to avoid sin, frequent in the reception of the sacraments, and if he seeks the goods of this life, yet seeks them in reference to the one thing necessary,—the salvation of his soul, which he makes the object of his chief solicitude; the other; recognizing no law, but the law of gain, stopping at no crime that stands in the way of his interest or passion, never once bestowing a serious thought on his final destiny, living as if there were no future life, living as if his destiny were one with the beasts of the field, to sink into the earth to rise no more. "The one will be taken, the other will be left." Then will the pagan who has never heard the name of Christ come and take the place of the baptized Catholic; because, although not possessing the Faith, he was faithful to the natural law written in his heart, and corresponded with the grace sufficient for salvation, which is given to every man; while the Catholic having, as a birthright, a faith that would do credit to an angel, yet had charity so little, that of it a pagan would have been ashamed.

The separation made; what remains but that the eternal sentence be pronounced. Turning to the vast multitude at His right, Jesus will say: "Come, ye blessed of My Father, possess the Kingdom prepared for you, from the foundation of the world; for I was hungry, and you gave me to eat, thirsty, and you gave me to drink, naked, and you clothed me, in prison, and you visited me. Even as you did it unto one of these little ones, so did ye it likewise unto me. Enter into the joys of the Lord." Turning to the rest of mankind, He will utter the eternal curse: "Depart from me, ye wicked, into the everlasting fire prepared for the devil, and his angels. For I was hungry, and you gave me not to eat; thirsty, and you gave me not to drink, naked, and you clothed me not; in prison, and you visited me not. So long as ye did it not unto one of these little ones, ye did it not unto me."

Thus, will all things come to an end. Thus, will be the final consummation of the dread conflict between good and evil. Thus, will God's providence in this world be cleared up. Thus, will His ways be justified before all men. Thus, will be the end of time; the beginning of eternity.

I have placed before you the general judgment. It is appointed to each of us, one day, to undergo this judgment. What have we done, what are we doing, that we may receive the favorable sentence? what are we doing for our eternal salvation? Seventy years is the time allotted, in Scripture, to a virtuous and well-spent life. Few of us can hope to reach it; few of us actually do reach it. Yet, even if, in God's providence, we are destined to reach it, there are few who now hear me, who have not already passed one half, and, it may be, two thirds of it; while many of you are already in the decline of life. Take the few years that yet remain to any one of you, and reduce them to days, and you will find that but a few thousand days of life yet remain, even to the youngest among you. Yet what are you doing for your souls? Youth given to passion, finds but little time, and less inclination to think of salvation, and defers it to manhood. Manhood comes, and finds even less time and less inclination to attend to the one thing necessary, and postpones it to old age. Look around you, and you will see old age as eager in the pursuit of this world's goods, and with as little care of salvation, as in the bloom of youth. And thus, from youth to manhood, and from manhood to old age, and from old age to the grave, is the one thing needful neglected, in man's eager pursuit of the phantoms of this life. Not until the shadows of death are gathering, thick and fast, about our last sick-bed; not until we feel its mortal chill coursing through our veins and paralyzing all our faculties; not until we see the grave yawning to receive us; not until then, do we feel the emptiness of this life, the unprofitableness of all human pursuits, the all-importance of the one thing necessary. So has it been from the beginning; so it will be until the end. Age succeeds age, generation succeeds generation; and it has the same story of human blindness and wilfulness to narrate. Be assured, that the day of our judgment will be sudden and unlooked-for. As we fall, so shall we lie. It is high time to wake from the sleep of death; and to employ, in the work of salvation, the few days that yet remain to us. Be assured, that some of you shall have undergone judgment, before you shall again hear the minister of Christ announce it.

THE NEW YORK
PUBLIC LIBRARY

ASTOR, LENOX AND
TILDEN FOUNDATIONS

ON THE GREATNESS OF GOD.

Get thee up upon a high mountain, thou that bringest good tidings to Sion : lift up thy voice with strength, thou that bringest good tidings to Jerusalem : lift it up, fear not. Say to the cities of Juda : Behold your God :

Behold the Lord God shall come with strength, and his arm shall rule : Behold his reward is with him and his work is before him.

He shall feed his flock like a shepherd : he shall gather together the lambs with his arm, and shall take them up in his bosom, and he himself shall carry them that are with young.

Who hath measured the waters in the hollow of his hand, and weighed the heavens with his palm? who hath poised with three fingers the bulk of the earth, and weighed the mountains in scales, and the hills in a balance?

Who hath forwarded the spirit of the Lord? or who hath been his counsellor, and hath taught him?

With whom hath he consulted, and who hath instructed him, and taught him the path of justice, and taught him knowledge, and shewed him the way of understanding?

Behold the Gentiles are as a drop of a bucket, and are counted as the smallest grain of a balance: behold the islands are as a little dust.

And Libanus shall not be enough to burn, nor the beasts thereof sufficient for a burnt-offering.

All nations are before him as if they had no being at all, and are counted to him as nothing, and vanity.

To whom then have you likened God? or what image will you make for him?

Hath the workman cast a graven statue? or hath the goldsmith formed it with gold, or the silversmith with plates of silver?

He hath chosen strong wood, and that will not rot: the skilful workman seeketh how he may set up an idol that may not be moved.

Do you not know? hath it not been heard? hath it not been told you from the beginning? have you not understood the foundations of the earth?

It is he that sitteth upon the globe of the earth, and the inhabitants thereof are as locusts: he that stretcheth out the heavens as nothing, and spreadeth them out as a tent to dwell in.

He that bringeth the searchers of secrets to nothing, that hath made the judges of the earth as vanity.

And surely their stock was neither planted, nor sown, nor rooted in the earth: suddenly he hath blown upon them, and they are withered, and a whirlwind shall take them away as stubble.

And to whom have ye likened me, or made me equal, saith the holy One.

Lift up your eyes on high, and see who hath created these things: who bringeth out their host by number, and calleth them all by their names: by the greatness of his might, and strength, and power, not one of them was missing.

Why sayest thou, O Jacob, and speakest, O Israel: My way is hid from the Lord, and my judgment is passed over from my God?

Knowest thou not, or hast thou not heard? the Lord is the everlasting God, who hath created the ends of the earth: he shall not faint, nor labour, neither is there any searching out of his wisdom.

It is he that giveth strength to the weary, and increaseth force and might to them that are not.

Youths shall faint, and labour, and young men shall fall by infirmity.

But they that hope in the Lord shall renew their strength, they shall take wings as eagles, they shall run and not be weary, they shall walk and not faint.—Isaiah xi. 9–31.

THE human heart is instinctively Christian. When left to itself, it instinctively recognizes the existence of God, and of but one God. When polytheism prevailed throughout the greater part of the world, even then, the voice of rational nature, in times of peril, or when left to its spontaneous dictates, invoked not the Gods of the prevailing superstition, but, contemning the polytheism of the period, gave testimony to the truth written in its heart, by calling upon one supreme and infinite Being. The consciousness that proclaims the existence of God, proclaims at the same time His infinitude and perfection. It is to the greatness of God, His infinite nature and boundless attributes, that I would, this morning, invite your attention.

It is very easy to say that we know God is infinite. But to know something, is not to realize it and bring it home to the mind. We know our souls to be immortal. We profess to believe the great truths of religion; yet how few realize these truths, and bring them home to the heart and mind, so that they enter and become woven into the very character and texture of their lives? It is the same when we speak of numbers. We have no difficulty in repeating, and in seeming to understand, a million or a million million; but when we try to realize or picture to ourselves so great a number, then it is, that we feel the weakness of the mind, and its insufficiency to grasp so vast a conception. It is pretty much the same, when we speak of the infinitude of God. We find no difficulty in uttering the word; but when we try to realize what is meant by His infinitude, then it is, that the human mind having soared to the bosom of God, falls back to the earth, exhausted and undone. Yet, we should not be content with merely repeating that God is infinite, without seeking to give a meaning to the words we utter. It should be our pleasure, to weigh our words, to sound their meaning, to proclaim to ourselves the truths they contain. We shall never be able to conceive, even approximately, the attributes of God; but the very effort will impress them upon our mind. Besides, from the inability of reason to form even an inadequate notion of the divine nature, we shall draw the very important lesson, suggestive indeed of His greatness, that God must be wondrously great, when the human mind can form no idea of His nature.

When we apply the word infinite to God, it is well to remark that we use it, not in the sense in which it is generally employed, but in its strict philosophical meaning: so great that He cannot be greater; not merely that the mind cannot conceive a greater; but that outside of the human mind, and regardless of its efforts, there cannot be a greater.

First, then, call to mind that God is self-existent; that He exists from His own nature; that He draws existence from no external cause; otherwise, He were not God; nor even from Himself, as from a cause; otherwise, He were the cause of Himself, which is absurd. He exists from the very necessity of His essence, from the very exigence of His nature; essence and existence are identical in God. We cannot conceive

God, not existing. As we cannot think of a triangle without three sides, so, we cannot think of God, without conceiving Him in existence. The human mind is utterly powerless to understand, even in the most imperfect manner, how God can exist, and never have come into being. We cannot understand how anything can be without beginning. Our idea is this: everything has a beginning, and an end; it was, once, but in a possible state; a cause was required to lead it from its ideal state, and confer upon it the reality of existence. But God was never in an ideal or possible state. He always possessed the fulness of existence.

If God is so absolutely sufficient for Himself, that He is self-existent, He is necessarily an infinite Being; if God, in His own nature, includes existence, He necessarily includes all other perfections. Existence is the greatest of perfections; if He includes existence, He includes all perfections of inferior nature. Existence is the choicest gift, the noblest perfection. Even the smallest atom that God has made, by the mere fact that it exists, is a more perfect creature than the most beautiful world God's mind can conceive, if such a world is not in actual existence. Existence is, then, the greatest of all perfections. God, having existence, has all other perfections. It is only because God is infinite, that He is self-existent; self-existence is but the consequence of His infinite nature. If we establish that God is self-existent, we establish that God is infinite, as a consequence, and we also establish that He is infinitely perfect, with every manner of perfection, in His nature and attributes. He that is self-existent must, by the very impulse, the very tendency, the very force, of his being, (if we may so speak) be infinite in his nature and perfections.

Having shown you that God is self-existent; that he is independent of all things else; that He is not the cause of Himself; that He could not withdraw Himself from existence; and having shown you that God's self-existence is the proof and consequence of His infinite perfection, let us consider some of the effects that flow from this unspeakable prerogative of the Divine Nature.

First; if God is self-existent, He has always been in existence. There never was a time, when He was not. Go back in thought as far as you may; go back before man was created; before the foundations of the world were laid; before the heavenly spirits were summoned into being; reckon the uncounted ages of the past, as so many moments; travel back until your reason staggers and your imagination reels with your efforts to grasp the eternity of God; as far as you can go, you will find God in being; you will be as far from finding any beginning of Him, at the end of all your efforts, as at first. Surely, here is mystery greater than any that religion makes known to us; here is something that is enough to abash all human pride, and make it confess the all marvellousness of God, and the utter insignificance of all things else.

Again; travel forward to the time, when the world will cease to be; when the mountains will fade away, and the great seas dry up; when all nature will be reduced to its original nothing; when time will be no more; when eternities of eternities will have rolled around the throne of God, He, the Ancient of days, will be as young and as immortal, as in the first dawn of the aurora. This, surely, is a vast conception; infinitely greater than any our minds have yet conceived.

And now, I will make a remark in which, perhaps, our reason distressed by its efforts to grasp God's eternal duration, will find some relief. But, I fear, that if reason can find any comfort in it, it will be the comfort of despair; it will be because the thought is so absolutely beyond all human power of comprehension, that we cannot, at all, begin to comprehend it. It is this; that in God there is no such thing as past eternity, nor future eternity; no such thing as ages or thousands or millions of years. These are but the puny efforts of reason, to comprehend God's eternal being. God's eternity is but one indivisible moment. God foresees nothing. He sees all things. Eternity admits of no past or present or future. It is one uninterrupted day; no continuation, no succession, no change. It is the complete and simultaneous possession of all duration. Time is not a part of eternity. Time or succession is found only where there is change. There is no change in God. Time is confined to man. Time is but succession or mutation. In God there is no succession or mutation. Here is a thought, even greater than that which I suggested in carrying you back before the world was made to all eternity; and then carrying you forward to that period, when the world shall cease to be, and God shall continue to exist, even as before the first dawn of creation.

God is a being who is absolutely sufficient for Himself. We sometimes imagine that God's happiness depends, in some manner, upon us; that it was even some regard for His own felicity that induced the Lord to die for us. This is a great error. God is infinitely sufficient for Himself. He is independent of us; we are not necessary to His happiness or glory; our perdition would not, in the least, disturb His imperturbable tranquillity, His supreme bliss, His perpetual joy. Before the world was made, before time began, before He had balanced all things in the palm of His hand, " Before He had measured the waters in the hollow of His hand, and meted out heaven with a span, and comprehended the dust of the earth in a measure, and weighed the mountains in scales, and the hills in a balance,"—from everlasting, God existed by Himself. He was supremely happy with Himself. He found uninterrupted occupation, supreme felicity in the contemplation of Himself. He found in the contemplation of His Divine Essence, work enough for the tireless energy and inexhaustible activity of the Divine Intellect. We see then how little necessary we are for God; how little we are capable of marring, even for a moment, the course of bliss and glory which He has enjoyed from all eternity.

ON THE GREATNESS OF GOD.

God is immutable. This we cannot understand. Everything that is limited is changeable; therefore everything is changeable but God. St. Thomas says, "Life is motion;" and we may add, life is change. There is change within us, around us; change in all things that God has made. But in God there is no change, nor the shadow of change. What changes, loses that which it had, or acquires that which it formerly had not. If it loses what it had, it is no longer what it was; if it acquires what it had not, it shows its capacity of further increase; and in either case is finite. All that God has made, either, gets something it had not, or, loses something it had; hence everything is changeable. But God, alone, remains immutable amidst all-changing things. In Him there is not the slightest mutation. His counsels are from everlasting. The creation of the world was determined before all time. The incarnation and death of His Divine Son was ordained, before the foundation of the world. Nothing that God does is a mutation. It is but the fulfilment of what, from all eternity, He proposed at a certain period to do.

If, my friends, we pass from the consideration of God's nature in itself, to the works He has done; we find everything to fill us with wonder, to manifest to us, in the most vivid manner, His omnipotence and the infinite perfection of His divine nature.

God then at a given period created the world. Have you ever reflected on what it is to create? The word is so often used to designate that which is, properly, but formation or production, that we seldom give it its due meaning. To make, is to form or produce something out of that which already exists; to give something a form or shape which it had not already possessed. To create, is to produce not the form or shape, but the very material or substance; and that, too, out of nothing. To make is within the power of man. To create is the attribute of God alone. Between something conceived as possible, and that something in existence, there is an infinite distance; an immeasurable interval; an impassable gulf. None but infinite power can cross that distance, can measure that interval, can span that gulf. No human will can give us any idea of the creative power of God. We know what the human will is, and what it is capable of. We know the marvels it has accomplished among men, in science, in literature, on the field of battle and elsewhere. It is indeed man's divinest endowment, and that in which he most resembles his Creator. But the human will in its highest type, can give us no illustration of, nor explain the mysterious nature, and still more mysterious operation, and infinite fecundity of God's omnipotent Will; for this world, and all that God has made is the result of His Creative Power. Do our best, we can never, at all, understand the resistless energy, the all-mighty, all-effecting power of the Divine Will. The all-powerful Will of God has this prerogative: that it commands, and it is at once obeyed. He can say, let there be light, and, at once, there is light; let the seas be gathered together, and, in the same instant, the mighty oceans are formed. By this Will, inconceivable and irresistible, God has made all things. He has not been content to create this little earth on which we tread; He has made the universe, so vast, so stupendous, so illimitable!—the universe so boundless, that light travelling at the portentous rapidity of 186,000 miles in a second of time, sent on its mission ages ago, has not yet reached this planet of ours;—the universe made up of countless multitudes of worlds, and of systems of worlds, that roll in the distant realms of space.

It is when we consider some of the facts of astronomy, that we begin to catch some glimpse of the boundless power of God, and the all-marvellousness of His creations. When we reflect that the sun is one million times greater than the earth; that it would take a missile, sent with a velocity which the human mind cannot conceive, twenty-four years to reach the sun; 750,000 years to reach the nearest fixed star; 100,000,000 years to reach the farthest fixed star that we know of; we cannot but exclaim with the psalmist who fostered his piety with considerations such as I have been making use of: "When, O Lord, we consider the heavens which Thou hast made, and the sun and moon which Thou hast set; what is man, that Thou shouldst be mindful of him, or the son of man that thou shouldst visit him!" Well may we fall down before this God of power and majesty, and adore Him from the inmost recesses of our being, with every feeling of humility and every sentiment of reverence!

Well may we join in the unceasing adoration paid Him by the blessed spirits, and proclaim all praise, power and glory to this God who lives and reigns forever. He alone is great. All things else are nothing.

When we look upon some piece of mechanism devised with rare skill, say a watch or steam-engine, in which human genius is conspicuous, we marvel at its organization; how elaborately it is contrived; how harmonious in all its movements; how simple, yet how complicated; how multitudinous in its parts and joints; yet not one unnecessary. And we, deservedly, form a high idea of the wondrous intelligence required to conceive, and of the masterful ability to form, so exquisite a specimen of skill.

And yet, what is all this, compared to this mighty world that God has made! What is all this, to the divine workmanship exhibited in the heavens; to the mysteries of intelligence there revealed to our contemplation! What are all the works of man and all the contrivances of human ingenuity, to that work of God ever before our eyes;—worlds unnumbered in multitude, revolving in supreme order and harmony; by their mutual influences sustaining and controlling one another; some giving light to those dark of themselves; others nurturing and supporting life and fertility upon those distant millions of miles; their amazing size, perfect shape, dazzling splendor; resplendent mirror, in which are reflected the beauty, wisdom and power of God, their Maker.

My dear friends, we seldom reflect upon the

glory of God, as manifested in His works. We see them from childhood; we grow familiar with them, and heed them not. If the wonderful phenomena of nature did not take place every day; if they were but of rare occurrence, they would impress us with an awful idea of God's infinite power and greatness. The sun that rises in the east and sets in the west, and has done so for thousands of years; let this occur but once, and all men would fall down and adore the Being who created such a glorious body, and gifted it with such marvellous motion. Let the moon with her tranquil glory appear but once; and it would force from us the homage of our admiration. Let us be told that this earth of ours, which revolves upon its axis around the sun, will do this but once, or, for the first time, in a thousand years; we would realize so great and portentous a fact. If a man, full-grown should come into the world and see those wonders for the first time; the mild glory of the moon, or the glorious splendor of the sun, or the azure vault of heaven bespangled with the myriads of worlds, which the darkness discloses, he would be filled with the sentiments of awe, and reverence, and praise, and homage which they justly inspire; he would be impressed with a sublime idea of the nature and omnipotence and perfection of the Almighty Being, whom they bespeak.

It is not only in the distant realms of space, that we look for the manifestation of the greatness and power of God. On this earth of ours; in the smallest atom of matter, or in one of the countless insects disclosed by the microscope, we find fearful evidence, of the exactness and minuteness of God's omniscient, all-pervading intellect. The vilest insect which is swept from the floor of the noblest temple that man has ever built, is a far greater manifestation of power and wisdom, than the temple itself. That insect is a far greater creation than the loftiest conception or highest triumph of the human intellect. The smallest atom of matter contains secrets which the wit of man will never know; betokens a genius and wisdom before which pales all human genius and wisdom; discovers a divine workmanship and skill, which beggars the proudest efforts of human ingenuity.

These are considerations which should lift our hearts and minds in devout contemplation to Him, of whose omnipotence all these wonders are the result; whose glory they show forth. All the wisdom and power and glory and magnificence, that we see everywhere in nature; all the beauty and loveliness that has been so copiously poured upon it, are but the emanation and reflection of God's own uncreated goodness and perfection. There is no endowment in the creature that is not contained, in a higher and fuller sense, in the creator. All things good, all things beautiful, all things true descend from Him, the source of all beauty, light, and truth; the Author of every good and perfect gift.

The lessons to be drawn are these. Teaching us God's infinite majesty, it ought to teach us our own insignificance; and, at the same time, our own importance and rank, seeing that we have such a Being, for our first beginning and last end. If God is as great, as we say He is, we should be slow to offend this God of infinite majesty and boundless power. If He is so great: the consideration that His mercy is still greater, and above all His works, should inspire us with the most filial confidence and unshaken hope.

When we reflect, that even unaided reason discovers greater mysteries in God, than any revelation discloses; we can, with greater facility, believe the truths which the Catholic Church proposes to us. When we reflect upon His Divine perfection and absorbing beauty; we can easily elicit the love of God, which consists in preferring Him to all things, because He is infinitely good and perfect and loveable in Himself; and, therefore, necessarily deserving our love.

ALMSGIVING.

You shall tell my father of all my glory, and all things that you have seen in Egypt: make haste and bring him to me.

And falling upon the neck of his brother Benjamin, he embraced him and wept: and Benjamin in like manner wept also on his neck.

And Joseph kissed all his brethren, and wept upon every one of them: after which they were emboldened to speak to him.

And it was heard, and the fame was abroad in the king's court: The brethren of Joseph are come: and Pharao with all his family was glad.

And when they had brought them, he gave them food in exchange for their horses, and sheep, and oxen, and asses: and he maintained them that year for the exchange of their cattle.

And they came the second year, and said to him: We shall not hide from our lord, how that our money is spent, and our cattle also are gone: neither art thou ignorant that we have nothing now left but our bodies and our lands.

Why therefore shall we die before thy eyes? we shall be thine, both we and our lands: buy us to be the king's servants, and give us seed, lest for want of tillers the land be turned into a wilderness.

So Joseph bought all the land of Egypt, every man selling his possessions, because of the greatness of the famine. And he brought it into Pharao's hands.—Genesis xlvii., 13-20.

THE following sermon was preached in St. Patrick's Cathedral, in 1881, on occasion of a collection to relieve the people of Ireland then stricken with famine.

The appeal which is made this day suggests to me the fitness of speaking to you on the duty of almsgiving; the duty of relieving the poor.

There may be those who think that there is no strict obligation of giving alms; that it is good and praiseworthy and the evidence of a feeling heart; but, yet, a work of supererogation; that a man's goods are his own, and he is free to retain them, or dispense them, as he pleases. This is a great mistake. There is an obligation of giving alms, I do not say, to every one; but when the case is such as entitles it to our help. This may sometimes, not as a rule, however, become of strict obligation. That surely must be of grave obligation, upon which our Lord places the alternatives of salvation or damnation. He tells us that, on the last day, He will say to those who have fulfilled their duty in this respect to their fellow-men: "Come, ye blessed of my Father, possess the Kingdom prepared for you from the foundation of the world. For I was hungry, and ye gave Me to eat; I was thirsty, and you gave Me to drink; I was a stranger, and you took Me in; naked, and ye covered Me; sick, and ye visited Me; I was in prison, and ye came to Me. Then will the just answer Him, saying: Lord, when did we see Thee hungry, and did feed Thee; thirsty, and did give Thee drink? and when did we see Thee a stranger, and did take Thee in? or naked, and did cover Thee? or when did we see Thee sick, or in prison, and did come to Thee? And the King will answer and say to them: Truly, I say to you, as long as ye did it to one of the least of these my brethren, ye did it to Me. Then will he say to those also on His left hand: Depart from me, ye cursed, into the everlasting fire which was prepared for the devil and His angels. For I was hungry, and ye gave Me nothing to eat; I was thirsty, and ye gave Me not to drink; I was a stranger, and ye did not take Me in; naked, and ye did not cover Me; sick, and in prison, and ye did not visit Me. Then they also will answer Him, saying: Lord, when did we see Thee hungry, or thirsty, or a stranger, or naked, or sick, or in prison, and did not minister to Thee? Then He will answer them, saying: Truly, I say to you, as long as ye did it not to one of the least of these, neither did ye do it to Me. And these shall go into everlasting punishment: but the just into life everlasting." Indeed, our Lord seems to attach a peculiar emphasis, a surpassing importance to this duty of almsgiving, in seeming to make it the only matter on which the issues of the last day shall turn. Of our other obligations and of our accountability for them, He seems to make no account.

However, it is not my intention to entertain you with the explanations and distinctions of theologians, touching this duty of almsgiving to the poor. They are very useful in their place; but are not called for in a discourse such as the present. If I can succeed in infusing into you a charitable spirit; if I can impress upon you the duty, in general, of being charitable to the poor; if your hearts feel aright on the subject, you will not fail to share charity, when a suitable occasion arises and a deserving object presents itself.

Men say that they have a right to their property. I admit it. It is inviolable. But I contend that with that right, they have received a duty; that the duty, in a manner, limits the right; that often the duty becomes more sacred than the right; that, in extreme cases, the right of men to what will save them from starvation, is greater than the right the rich man has to his property. In the beginning, the earth and all things were given to men in common. But, as society progressed, its existence and welfare required that the right of the first possessors of the land should be held inviolable. You have then a right, an indefeasible right to your property; whether you have received it by inheritance, or it be the fruit of your industry. Your right in this matter resembles nothing more, as has been advanced by a great writer, than one of the great growths of nature. It is planted by God. It cannot be defeated by any human law or convention. It does not depend upon any human reasoning. It is not the result of any human compact.

The welfare, nay, even the existence of society requires that there be grades in the condition of men. This is necessary to extinguish sloth, to stimulate energy, to foster and sustain human enterprise, to call into requisition men's abilities, and to develop the resources of nature. They are as necessary to society, as the varied levels of the earth are to the fertility and productiveness of nature. But we have only to look around, and we shall often find that the disparity in the condition of men is greater, by far, than that which is required for the well-being of society. We shall find some revelling in luxury, with every gratification which caprice can suggest or wealth procure. While others are reduced to utter destitution; often crying for the food whereby to support life. Can God ever have intended such a state of things as this? Is He not the Father of all, but especially of the poor? Does He not make His sun to shine and His rain to fall upon all, just and unjust? Can He who tempers His wind to the shorn lamb, without whose high permission, not even a sparrow falls; who has counted the hairs of our head; who clothes the lilies of the field, which to-day are, and to-morrow are not, with a raiment more glorious than that of Solomon; who feeds even irrational beings, with so plenteous a profusion ;—can He have ever meant that man, the noblest work of His hands, should perish from want of food to support the life which He has given him?

How, then, are we to justify His providence, to vindicate His goodness, seeing the appalling destitution of some, and the limitless resources of others? Has He supplied no means for the relief of the poor? Yes, my Brethren, He has. He has supplied such means in the superfluity of the rich. The superfluity of the rich, is the sustenance of the poor. The rich are His almoners to the poor. The rich are the divinely appointed custodians and guardians of the poor; the channels through which He wishes to communicate His abundance.

And thus, in the inscrutable wisdom of God, the inequality which we see here below in the condition of men, subserves His final providence in the affairs of this life; subserves the glory of the elect. It becomes a source of merit to the rich man, in affording him an opportunity to practise that charity to the poor which is the first of virtues. It becomes a source of merit to the poor, by giving them an opportunity to bear with patience and resignation that state of life, in which it has pleased God to cast their lot. And, as it is the highest duty of the poor, to bear with patience their lot; so, it becomes the highest duty of the rich, to see to it, that God's providence be not cursed, nor His goodness called in question by the impatient poor.

This duty of almsgiving to our fellow-man, is taught us by the very best feelings of our nature. God Himself has made the human soul; and made it in His own image and likeness. He has communicated to it something of His own divine goodness. It is God Himself who speaks in the heart through the emotions and voice of pity. Who does not sympathize with the suffering? Who will not relieve the needy? Who that is true to the best instincts of his nature, does not fire with indignation at the wrongs inflicted upon the innocent, the fatherless, the destitute? The human heart left to itself, instinctively expands and goes out in feelings of Christian sympathy and active benevolence.

With what honest pride and just complacency, do we look upon the acts of generosity of our ancestors in the Faith or in the state; when, some great calamity, hunger or pestilence falling upon society, the great heart of our common humanity was stirred to its lowest depths, and there welled forth a generous supply of the holiest sympathy and abundant charity! It is at such times, one learns of what great things human nature is capable; how much nobleness is united in it with so much meanness; how, with all its downward tendencies, it can still lift itself heavenward, and is capable of such divine instincts.

This same duty is taught by our conscience. We find in our hearts an intimate persuasion of the duty of assisting our fellow-men. It is not the result of any reasoning. It seems to be one of the original intuitions of our being. We find it in the applauding voice of conscience, when we have done an act of well-doing. We find it in its condemning reproaches, when we have been wanting to the just needs of our neighbor.

The somewhat slower conclusions of reason confirm the same duty. Reason in proclaiming the common origin, the common nature, and the common destiny of all men, proclaims the common duties of mutual love and help which should exist between them. It were the height of selfishness, the basest cruelty, the rankest crime, to hoard our substance; and see our fellow-man, our equal in all respects save the accidental one of riches, perish from want.

Yet, my brethren, this duty of charity to our fellow-men made known to us by the feelings of our nature, the dictates of conscience, and the voice of reason, is not Christian charity. It is but pure natural goodness; the noblest product of the human heart, it is true; but yet only a natural virtue; natural in its origin, natural in its motives, and, like all things merely natural, limited in its scope and influence. Besides, it is mixed up and its beauty, in a measure, marred with the human frailty and imperfection with which it is commonly found. But, take this human goodness in its highest and purest form; take the pure gold of human goodness, separated from the alloy of imperfection and selfishness, in which it generally lives buried in the human heart; raise it to the rank of a supernatural virtue, by making its animating principle, the love of God—the love of man in God, and for God; let it be compassionate, bringing balm to every wound and solace to every grief; let it be active and efficacious, dwelling not merely in the heart, but going forth in deeds of active benevolence and inexhaustible generosity; let it be constant, abiding while there is human suffering to be relieved, or human want to be supplied; let it be universal, bringing aid to every form of want, spiritual and corporal, and knowing no limits to the sharers of its bounty, but the limits of our common humanity; let it be disinterested, and if it seek a reward, let it be the reward of one day gaining God; in a word, let it be an unfailing fount of divine charity springing up in active benevolence; do all this with human goodness, and you have Christian charity, the most sublime of virtues; first brought on earth from heaven by Jesus Christ. Christian charity!

the sacramental bond in which He has united all men together and to God; the mysterious union which binds all men, as the common creatures of the same Creator, and sharers of a common destiny; the sacred duty which prompts man to see in his fellow the image of God, washed all pure in the blood of Christ; and, as such, worthy of our love and assistance. Jesus was the author of this divine virtue. It could have none other. He alone of all men has made the one supreme, complete act of love of God and man, which this world has ever seen. It was sealed in His blood. It was ratified by His own great sacrifice for its sake.

Of this charity the pagan world never dreamed. They who worshipped not a common God, could have no bond to unite them in a common brotherhood. It was reserved for Jesus Christ, as introducing men to a knowledge of the true God, to make known to them the bond which could hold them together. It was the new commandment which he brought into the world. "Heretofore it hath been said: thou shalt love thy friend and hate thine enemy; but I say to you, love your enemy, pray for them that persecute and calumniate you." In the New Testament, the rich glutton is condemned to hell, because of his insensibility to the wants of Lazarus, the type and representation of the poor and needy. The good Samaritan is not far from the kingdom of God, because of his charity to the sick and needy. "Give and it shall be given to you." "Religion before God and man is to visit the widow, the fatherless, and the orphans in their distress." But why give passages? The New Testament is one continued lesson of charity and beneficence to the poor. It is written in every passage; it breathes in every sentiment. It is the new mandate given to all Christians. It is the characteristic feature of the Gospel. It is the mark by which all men were to recognize His disciples.

Human goodness and Christian charity are often so blended together that it is hard to discriminate between them; even as reason with faith in religion. It is wonderful what mere human goodness has done and is doing for the world. The deeds of generosity, disinterestedness, and self-sacrifice prompted by human goodness, throw a lustre upon the history of our race. Wherever, then, we find it, let us congratulate ourselves that our nature still possesses so much of its original and inherent goodness. Wherever we find it; in whatever race or nation, religion or sect, community or person, let us pay to it the tribute of admiration and praise, which is its due; and thus render homage to God, the author of the human heart.

Yet, in giving philanthropy its due, let us not forget the claims of truth, by calling goodness, Charity; and Charity, mere goodness. One is all human; the other is all divine. As Christ has exalted the passion of love, anointed it with His grace and made it the foundation of the sacrament of marriage; as He has founded Penance upon the natural inclination of the heart to disclose its sinfulness; so has he raised human goodness to a supernatural virtue, by infusing into it the love of God, as its animating principle.

Real human goodness involves self-denial and self-sacrifice. Far from seeking self, it destroys self. Human benevolence which gives only from abundance, and brings with it no act of self-denial, is scarcely worthy of the name. No great mercy is seen in him who gives of that only which is not required, either for his well-being or comfort. It argues no great virtue to give that which, otherwise, must perish. He who gives that which may be conducive to his luxury, does a little; he who gives that which is useful for his well-being, does more; he who gives that which he cannot part with, except with injury to himself, rises higher in the rank of goodness; he who, for the sake of his fellow-man, parts with what is necessary to his life, or who even is prepared to sacrifice life itself, would possess goodness in a supereminent degree, and such as is never found among those in whom Christian Charity does not flourish. There is very little sacrifice to be seen in goodness as it is practised among men. Who gives but of his abundance? who gives that which is useful for even his luxury? who thinks of self-denial in order to practise generosity? who denies himself the smallest pleasure, in order to relieve the needs of others? who would deprive himself of one meal out of three, that his suffering fellow-man may have the one? And in giving even out of his abundance, who is willing to overcome the repugnance created by the defects, and shortcomings, and ingratitude of the objects of his bounty? How many excuses do we find for discontinuing our beneficence, in the personal character of those we assist? How seldom does human goodness expose itself, by hanging over the poisonous breath and pouring into the ear of the dying, words of comfort and consolation?

All this, because human goodness springs only from human motives. It is destitute of a principle, which can sustain it in the sacrifices and compensate it for the losses, which it necessarily involves. Not so with Christian charity; it is based upon a principle which supports it under all circumstances; which it feels is more than compensation for the sacrifice of worldly goods, of our ease and convenience, nay, even of life itself. The assurance of possessing God eternally, is enough to stimulate to loss of comfort and pleasure; to all acts of self-denial and self-sacrifice; to unbounded generosity to the poor; to even personally assuming their hardships and sufferings; it even makes it a profitable exchange, to lay down life itself for our neighbor. This is what lifts charity above all human motives, and makes of it a heavenly virtue. This is what enables it to overcome all defects in its objects, even ingratitude; ministering to every want, and bringing balm to every suffering. This is what urges the Christian hero to strip himself of all worldly goods for the poor; to expose himself to contagion and death for the relief of his fellow-man. It was this, that nerved the martyr's heart to meet death in its most appalling forms. It is this, that gives the missionary courage to leave home and kindred, and go forth to preach the Gospel to the heathen and barbarian. It is this, that gives constancy to the virgin, in her life-long martyrdom of the flesh with its lusts, that keeps alive and fresh in her heart the vestal fire of angelic purity. It was this, that made St. Paul wish to be an anathema from Christ, for his brethren; that made St. Francis Xavier content to risk salvation, so as to remain longer on earth for souls; that made the monk Telemachus rush into the amphitheatre, to separate the gladiators, and to be crushed to death by the showers of stones hurled at him; thus purchasing with his blood, the law that forever abolished those cruel sports. It was this, that made St. Vincent de Paul sell himself into bondage, as a ransom for a captive. This it was, that inspired all the marvellous acts of self-denial and heroism which history records. It is this principle that discriminates charity from every other virtue, making it immeasurably superior.

The Church has inherited the spirit of her Divine Master for the poor and destitute. He has breathed it into her, in its fulness. She renews His life among the poor, continually. Daily is she going among them; preaching the gospel to them, sympathizing with them in their sufferings, and relieving their wants. Her history teems with benevolence in their regard. From the beginning; from the day when all things were in common at Jerusalem, when the faithful of Corinth beggared themselves to relieve the poor, her whole history has been one long apostleship of God-like charity towards those whom she is to have always with her. It was only His spirit dwelling in her that could have inspired such charity. Innumerable have been the Apostles of Charity, whom this mystical spouse has brought forth to Christ. They were not content with spending their lives in the service of their fellow-men; but sought to perpetuate their usefulness, by the orders and institutes which they established. Through them, they have continued their mission of charity, and transmitted their spirit to generations untold, and will so transmit it till time is no more. This, true of all founders of religious societies, is conspicuously true of him whom the Church esteems as the Apostle of Charity in these latter times, St. Vincent de Paul. His spirit is still preserved in the community, which he founded and which bears his name. Though dead, he lives; lives, by his example; lives, because his spirit is still among his children. They carry on the great work of their Father. They are to be found on the battle-field, in the slums and hospitals of our great cities, by the side of the plague-stricken bed; wherever affliction needs a solace, wherever destitution needs relief, wherever the soul seeks to see and to hear something of the charity of Christ, there they are to be found. No plague is too pestilent, no misery too abject, no sinner too loathsome, to deter them, to intimidate them.

Now, if ever, you have an opportunity of showing charity to your fellow-men. To-day, the people of Ireland appeal to you, by our common humanity, our common Christianity, and for sake of the blood of Jesus Christ shed for us all, to rescue them from the jaws of famine. Such an appeal has been seldom made. But very few of you have ever heard such an appeal before. God grant, that need for such an appeal may never again arise.

It is, my brethren, no ordinary appeal. It is not the appeal of one, or of a few particular cases. It is the cry of millions; it is a nation that stretches out its hands for bread! Sad; sad, indeed, it is to think that, in the teeming abundance with which God has blessed the earth, even one creature should perish from want. But, how oppressive to the heart and to every feeling of nature, to think of millions reduced to utter starvation; threatened with a death, the most awful the human mind can conceive.

It is no ordinary appeal; for it is the cry of hunger. And of all the calamities and miseries which beset the life of man, there is none that appeals more powerfully to the human heart, than the cry of man for bread with which to support life. And if there be one thing more than another, which can pierce the heavens, and call down God's vengeance upon the human avarice that permits it; it is the cry of the starving victim sent up to heaven, in the midst of the pangs of hunger—of that creature for whom Christ did not hesitate to shed His blood. This is not so much a cry for charity, as it is a cry for justice. For every human being—every being into whom God has breathed the breath of life—has a right, an absolute, an indefeasible right to what will save him from death.

Besides; in the case of Ireland, there are special claims upon us; claims of race, claims of blood and kinship, claims of religion, claims which I forbear to dwell upon, because I know they are present to the heart of every one of you, this morning. Nor shall I stop to tell you, what you so well know, of the history of Ireland: her steadfastness in her religion, her long-continued suffering for the preservation of her faith. Her faith is, indeed, spoken of in the whole earth. She has, indeed, filled the world with the sacrifices which she has made, and the persecutions which she has undergone for its sake.

It is for you, to-day, by your generous offerings, to lighten, and, in a great measure, to avert the curse which now hangs over her, blasting her fair fields, and hastening to a premature death her gifted children. Let not the scenes of 1847 be renewed; let not the red graves of those countless multitudes be reopened; let not the details of that famine, so loathsome, so degrading, so revolting, that their mere recital makes the blood run cold, and forces shame of our human nature that could permit it, be re-enacted! Let not the victims who have already fallen, or who will hereafter fall, ascend to the throne of God and accuse us before His tribunal, of having hoarded our substance when we saw His creatures perish! Let all hasten to the assistance of Jesus Christ, in the person of the starving people of Ireland; and, at the last day, we shall hear these words, " Come, ye blessed of My Father, possess the kingdom prepared for you from the foundation of the world ; for I was hungry, and you gave me to eat ; thirsty, and you gave me to drink ; naked, and you clothed me. Amen, I say to you, so long as you did it to one of these starving people in Ireland, you did it unto me ; enter thou into the joy of the Lord."

THE NEW YORK
PUBLIC LIBRARY

ASTOR, LENOX AND
TILDEN FO   S.

THE IMMORTALITY OF THE SOUL.

But some man will say: How do the dead rise again? or with what manner of body shall they come?

Senseless man, that which thou sowest is not quickened, except it die first.

And that which thou sowest, thou sowest not the body that shall be; but bare grain, as of wheat, or of some of the rest.

But God giveth it a body as he will: and to every seed its proper body.

All flesh is not the same flesh: but one is the flesh of men, another of beasts, another of birds, another of fishes.

And there are bodies celestial, and bodies terrestrial: but one is the glory of the celestial, and another of the terrestrial.

One is the glory of the sun, another the glory of the moon, and another the glory of the stars. For star differeth from star in glory.

So also is the resurrection of the dead. It is sown in corruption, it shall rise in incorruption.

It is sown in dishonor, it shall rise in glory. It is sown in weakness, it shall rise in power.

It is sown a natural body, it shall rise a spiritual body. If there be a natural body, there is also a spiritual body, as it is written:

The first man Adam was made into a living soul; the last Adam into a quickening spirit.

Yet that was not first which is spiritual, but that which is natural; afterwards that which is spiritual.

The first man was of the earth, earthly: the second man, from heaven, heavenly.

Such as is the earthly, such also are the earthly: and such as is the heavenly, such also are they that are heavenly.

THE IMMORTALITY OF THE SOUL.

Therefore as we have borne the image of the earthly, let us bear also the image of the heavenly.

Now this I say, brethren, that flesh and blood cannot possess the kingdom of God: neither shall corruption possess incorruption.

Behold, I tell you a mystery. We shall all indeed rise again: but we shall not all be changed.

In a moment, in the twinkling of an eye, at the last trumpet: for the trumpet shall sound, and the dead shall rise again incorruptible: and we shall be changed.

For this corruptible must put on incorruption; and this mortal must put on immortality.

And when this mortal hath put on immortality, then shall come to pass the saying that is written: Death is swallowed up in victory.

O death, where is thy victory? O death, where is thy sting?

Now the sting of death is sin: and the strength of sin is the law.

But thanks be to God, who hath given us the victory through our Lord Jesus Christ.

Therefore, my beloved brethren, be ye steadfast and unmovable; always abounding in the work of the Lord, knowing that your labor is not in vain in the Lord.—1 Cor. xv., 35-55.

WE all understand very well what is meant by the immortality of the soul; not mortal, not liable to death, not tending, like all other things, to dissolution; endowed with such vitality that it will live forever.

Before we go further, we may observe that as there are but two ways by which anything can come into existence, so there are but two ways by which anything can go out of existence. Something is made from some pre-existing material, by a certain disposition and ordering of its parts; this is properly called making or formation. This is within the power of man; and is all that man with all his wondrous inventions has ever accomplished. Such a thing will go out of existence, by a disintegration and separation of the parts of which it is composed; and is properly called destruction. Again; a creature may come into existence, formed from no pre-existing material, the result of no combination of parts, but springing into being by the Almighty fiat of its Creator; such an act is creation and belongs to God alone. Such a being will depart from existence, not by a corruption of parts, which it has not; but by the same Almighty fiat which, first, summoned it into existence. For it requires the same effort of divine omnipotence to destroy such a creature, as was first required for its creation. Such is the human soul; which is created by the almighty power of God, and which cannot but by annihilation die. Such annihilation, we claim, God will never inflict upon it. When He created it, He destined it to last forever.

Man received this gift at his creation. Nor did he forfeit it at his fall. God had conferred it absolutely; irrespective of man's future infidelity. It is true the prospect of immortal happiness closed upon him; but there was reserved for him the sad assurance of immortal misery and woe. Before the fall, the knowledge of his immortality was revealed to him. And this knowledge never perished from the minds of men. They ever felt a consciousness of it. It was written in the human heart by the very finger of God. Its promptings were felt in the aspiration of the soul after the infinite and eternal. It may have been mixed with, or obscured, or partly effaced by the superstition and idolatry with which it came in contact; but it was never wholly obliterated from the minds of men. All the religions of the world bear vestiges of this original revelation. During their sojourn in bondage, the Jews found belief in the immortality of the soul, the belief of their pagan masters. In the East, the doctrine of the transmigration of souls must, in its origin, have been intimately connected with this belief. In our own country, on its discovery, were found traces of this same belief among its primeval inhabitants.

The Jews, of course, entertained the liveliest faith in the immortality of the soul. It is true that the Sadducees, not knowing the Scriptures nor the power of God, denied the resurrection of the body; and by an easy consequence, called in question the immortality of the soul itself. But they were held as heretics for departing from the faith of their fathers, and the universally received belief of Judaism.

The pagan philosophers of antiquity were divided in the belief of the soul's immortality; as they were on every question that concerned man, or his destiny. Cicero with a beauty of language befitting the subject, represents the sentiments which prevailed among them, touching belief in the imperishable nature of the soul; which, he tells us, was almost the unanimous belief of them all. And, after discoursing on the subject in a strain worthy of a father of the Church, he says that even should he be mistaken in the belief that the souls of men are immortal, yet would he cling to his pleasing error; nor does he wish the belief by which, during life, he was filled with consolation, to be taken from him. Then he exclaims: "O blessed day! when I shall set out for that divine assembly and society of souls; when I shall depart from this misery and confusion." Plato reasoned so well on the immortality of the soul, that in reading him, we seem to read some discourse of St. Augustine, on the same subject. There is one error that stains the writings of some of the ancients on this matter. From the reasoning which to their minds demonstrated the soul's immortality, they inferred also the sou 's past eternity. And it is no wonder that they fell into this error on so mysterious a subject, as the origin of the soul; an error which even some of the fathers of the Church did not escape. Even to-day, after all the development of Christian Doctrine; after the enlightened studies of the greatest theologians; it remains one of the darkest and most mysterious subjects of Christian theology.

I have thus dwelt at some length, in pointing out that the immortality of the soul was believed before the Christian Revelation was made; because it is for the good of religion to show that this truth is made evident by mere human reason, unaided by the light of Revelation.

If we come to consider the arguments which reason by its own natural light supplies for believing in the soul's immortality; we shall find the first in the very nature and tendency of the soul itself.

Our soul is unlike anything else in nature. All things are made up of parts; are endowed with extension. So true is this, that some have claimed that extension is the very essence of matter. But the human soul is a simple, spiritual, angelic substance; infinitely superior in its nature to anything composite. The nature of any creature should proclaim its destiny. As we rightfully conclude that everything natural has its final end in the world, we ought, by analogy, to conclude that the human soul has an end proportioned to the excellence of its nature. As God has expended more of His divine power upon it, and made it more excellent than anything else in nature, we must believe that He has decreed to it a destiny higher, than that of all other creatures. All things else tend to dissolution and decay. Made up of parts, by the very law of their nature they tend to corruption from the first moment of their existence. But the human soul knows no decay; is subject to no dissolution. It constantly renews its youth; and is possessed of an immortal vigor, which permits no diminution or abatement. As the soul, then, is so superior in the tendency of its nature to all things else, we ought to infer that its destiny is infinitely higher than that of corruptible matter, which to-day is and to-morrow is not.

Then consider the gifts with which man has been ennobled, and which mark his superiority and pre-eminence to all things else; and in consequence, bespeak his destiny. His appearance; his stature; his mien; his human face divine, looking up to heaven; the freedom of his will,— that God-like gift which leaves him free in all his actions, and puts it in his power, as far as concerns himself, to accomplish or frustrate the design of God in his creation; the power of his intellect, which penetrates the secrets of nature and unfolds the wonders of knowledge; which, abstracting from particulars, forms universal ideas that embrace all things; which lifts him even to the bosom of God, and forms no unworthy idea of the divine nature and perfections; and all the other faculties which he possesses, and which stamp him at once as the noblest work of God, as the masterpiece of His hands.

We may speak of man's insignificance. We may say that he is but a worm of the earth; and it is true. But yet, he is God's creature endowed with wondrous gifts, which make him but little less than the angels. We may say that he is but the dust of the earth; and it is true. Yet in that casement of dust there dwells a spirit which exalts and sanctifies it, and makes of it a tabernacle in which God Himself did not refuse to dwell. Man is, indeed, the very combination of littleness and of greatness; of what is low and of what is noble; a very animal, by his downward tendencies, an angel, by his heavenly aspirations. He is the very point where heaven and earth do meet; the union of divinity with humanity.

Behold man's dominion over all things. The earth and all therein have been made for his use and benefit; and they have fulfilled their mission. He has always been their absolute master. From the day, when all animals passed in review before our great parent, acknowledging his dominion, and receiving from him their names, to the present, man has shown that he is, what God destined him to be; the Lord and Master of all things. Not to speak of those creatures, the most familiar to us, and which we all know are subject to man, and do his pleasure:—even those works of God over which man seems to have but little power, yet acknowledge his dominion and subserve his purposes. What he rules not by strength of body, he rules by the light of his genius and the power of his mind. He may not ascend to the heavens, and travel among the stars; but he calculates their distances, and describes their motions, with such wonderful precision, that it would almost seem in obedience to his calculations, that they exist where they are, and describe their courses. Again, if he ascends not to heaven, he calls down its lightnings, and makes them subserve the conveniences of life. He contracts, by the speed with which he traverses it, the broad expanse of the mighty ocean, and rides in security upon its breast. He delves into the earth; and from its teeming womb draws forth everything required for his comfort and support. He is, verily, the Lord and Master of all things.

Is he, then, for whom all creatures have been made, who is the Lord and Master of the earth and what it contains, destined for no higher purpose than those very creatures; is he, like them, to sink into the same common earth; to be reduced to the same nothingness? Could God have ordained man—by his gifts, the flower of creation, the masterpiece of His hands—for no other end than that common to brute and inanimate creatures? the very instruments and servants meant for his use and pleasure.

Why, if this were so, we ask, has God made the world? If all things are to find their final destiny here below; if man and beast and all nature, animate and inanimate, are all to sink into the grave of corruption; to rise no more, and to be dissolved in the same common nothingness; why, I ask, has God made the world? Was it not for the manifestation of His power and glory? But; if there be no future life, if all end here; how can this purpose be accomplished? If we are to imagine the world to end here, and man to have no higher destiny than the brute; we must confess that God's design, in the making of the world, has been frustrated; and that the Divine purpose is by no means advanced, by a world constructed on such principles.

Indeed, we must own that, if man has no other end than that like the brute—to sink into the earth to rise no more—the brute is far happier, and far more highly privileged than man; the servant more fortunate than the master crowned with glory and honor. In proportion as he is exalted above all creatures, by his transcendent gifts, does he sink below them all; and does his misery increase; because, capable of greater felicity, and entitled to a nobler destiny than they, he is absolutely less happy, and sinks to a worse fate. For the instincts and wants of irrational creatures are simple and natural, easily supplied and at once satisfied. They cannot think; hence they do not know and cannot desire but what affects their senses; their desires are limited to what they feel. They cannot, therefore, aspire to a condition other or better than that which they at present enjoy. Not having an intellectual memory, they are not afflicted by remembrance of their past sufferings and pains; nor are they troubled with solicitude for the future, nor molested with the ever-present certainty of their death. Much less are they tortured by the incessant struggle which every man experiences of virtuous with vicious inclinations.

If man be not immortal, why this longing after immortality? Why this terror at the prospect of annihilation? Why this desire for perfect happiness? For, the desire of immortality is one with the desire for perfect happiness; no happiness can be perfect, unless it be immortal. "Who is the man," asks the Psalmist, "who desires not good days; who is the man that seeks not to be happy?" And if I were to ask you, do you desire not happiness; your hearts and every instinct of your being would cry out, that you live and breathe for nothing but happiness. It is the motive of all we do. It is the motive of every man's endeavor to get on in life; to better his condition. It is the spring of this feverish thirst for prosperity, this discontent with the reality, this looking forward to the future. It dominates the heart of every man. No one is exempt from its sway. It is the one tendency of our nature that is irresistible. Think not, that it can be satisfied with the pleasures of life. Ask the rich, the great, the powerful; consult all human experience, and you will find, that the spiritual cravings of man's soul cannot be satisfied with the corrupt pleasures of sense.

Nor can it be said, that this desire is like other passions of the human heart; honor, love of power, avarice. Those, absolutely speaking, can be overcome; but this cannot. It is the original instinct of our being; the sovereign inclination of our nature. It is the principal and supreme tendency of man's rational nature, implanted in him by an all-wise Providence, to direct him to his final destiny and supreme beatitude.

This desire for a happiness, which includes every good, excludes every evil, and lasts forever; this surfeit and disgust of the heart with all human pleasures; this aspiration of the soul to the infinite and eternal; is but the manifestation of our nature seeking the God from whom it came, and to whom it must return to attain perfect repose and bliss. Thou alone, O God, hast made us, and in Thee alone can we find rest. God could never have infused this desire into man, if He meant that it should never be satisfied.

What is it that consoles us in the miseries, and trials, and disappointments of life? What is it that, in the dark hour of adversity, bids us hope and fills us with the promise of better things? What is it that, when relations and friends are taken from us, lightens our sufferings and assuages our grief? What is it that animates the expiring soul, and gives fortitude to the martyr, in the midst of his torments? What, but the hope of receiving, in a better life, that which we lay down in this; the hope of gaining more than we lose; the hope of reaching, in the next life, the happiness we sought, in vain, in this; the hope, of one day, joining those relations and friends, whom we now see grieving around our own death-beds. These feelings of our soul are the expressions of its nature, the manifestations of its eternal destiny. "It is the divinity that stirs within us, and points out an hereafter."

Look out upon the world, and behold the scene that presents itself. See, if you find nothing that bespeaks that future life, which we claim for our souls. See the intense, wide-spread prevalence of sin, impiety, irreligion; see the disregard of truth, the contempt of obligations, the black treacheries, the base perfidies, the deadly hates, the direful wrongs, the rank pride, the foul lusts, with which the world is filled; making of human society a seething mass of corruption. See how piety and godliness are laughed from the face of the earth; how iniquity is exalted; how the poor are trampled on; how the wicked possess the earth; how the just are, for the most part, in poverty. It is not the God-loving; but the God-contemning that, for the greater part, flourish. Consider all this and tell me, if you think there is no future life; no state of rewards and punishments; but, rather, that God's providence ends here. If there is a God, He is essential goodness in His nature. He must be an approver and rewarder of virtue; a punisher and avenger of vice. If there is a God, the cause of virtue must be His cause, and the votaries of virtue must be His chosen ones. If there is a God, the cause of iniquity must be the cause of the prince of this world, and the votaries of iniquity must be his followers. If there is a God, He cannot be indifferent to the fearful, deadly conflict going on, in this life, between virtue and vice. He cannot but reward the struggles, and patience, and long-sufferings of just men. He cannot but punish the iniquity, and injustices, and crimes of the wicked. I would rather believe that there is no God, than to believe that there is one, and yet that He is indifferent to the sufferings and hopes of the just; while He permits the wicked to glory in their wickedness, and to enjoy the goods of this life.

If, then, the soul be not immortal; if there be no future life, how can the order of things in this life be readjusted? How can the heavenly balance be reset? How can the wicked be punished? the good rewarded? How can divine justice be avenged? How can God's ways be cleared up and justified?

Is the just man who, from early youth, has walked faithfully in the ways of God; who, carefully, throughout the years of a long life, till the moment of death, avoided all grievous sins, to obtain no reward? is he to sink into the same nothingness, as the one who never thought of God; who lived as if there were no God; who offended Him whenever caprice, humor, or interest suggested? Is the virgin, who, in early youth, plighted her virginity to God, and all the years of life, struggled to keep burning that sacred fire, to receive no other reward than that of the profligate, who did nothing but gratify passion, and draw to destruction the souls of men? Is the martyr, who paid to the truth the highest testimony, which human nature is capable of; who sealed, with his blood, his belief of God's truth; to sink into the same grave as the tyrant and persecutor who shed his blood, and caused him to meet death, in its most awful forms?

Perish, then, these false teachings which would degrade man,—by his nature and endowments the noblest work, the masterpiece of God,—to the condition of the brute. Perish the philosophy, which would confound the end of man,—the Master and Lord of creation,—with the end of the brute and inanimate creatures; his servants and his instruments. Perish from the earth the doctrine, that God has infused into the human heart the desire, and impressed upon the human soul the consciousness of immortality, never to be realized. Perish from the minds and hearts of men a philosophy, which represents God as indifferent to the struggle going on, in this life, between Himself and the prince of this world; as indifferent to the trials of the just; as loading favors upon the wicked;—a philosophy which destroys virtue; by denying to it that future retribution, which alone can compensate for the difficulties, and trials, and dangers which beset its path;—which would open the way to every outrage and every crime, by destroying that future life, which is the only barrier against the deluge of immorality which would, otherwise, overwhelm human society.

Yes, my brethren, there is a future life; and we are made immortal to enjoy it. The blessed Gospel of Jesus Christ puts an end to all our speculative reasonings; and places the seal of divine unerringness upon our conclusions. "You err, not knowing the Scriptures or the power of God," said He to the Sadducees, who denied the resurrection of the body. "For, in the resurrection there shall be neither marriage, nor giving in marriage ; but ye shall be as angels of God in heaven. He is the God of Abraham, and the God Isaac, and the God Jacob. He is not the God of the dead, but of the living."

Yes; existence begins in this life, but ends not here. This life is but the bud, the spring, the source of our eternal being. It is not for this life that we have been made. Our true life begins, when this ceases. We shall die ; our bodies will sink into the grave and will be reduced to their original dust; but our souls will defy the dominion of death, and will pass from hence to enjoy God for evermore. Even our bodies will rise, at the end of time, to be re-united to our souls, and to partake of the glory and bliss of seeing God. It is necessary that they should first perish; that this corruption should put on incorruption, that this mortality should put on immortality; but from the grave of death and corruption, all hideous though it be, they shall come forth, endowed with gifts which will render them fit companions for evermore of the immortal soul.

This world will pass away; the great seas will dry up, and the mountains disappear; all that we see will be as if it had never been. Perhaps, new worlds and new universes will take its place, and a new order of things begin on high. The human soul will, alone, survive the dissolution and destruction of all things else; will, alone, escape unscathed from the war of jarring worlds, and the chaos and confusion of a universe hastening to its doom. Ages will roll away; eternities of eternities will revolve around the throne of God; yet it shall abide, young with its immortal vigor, and happy in the embrace of its God. This is your destiny. This is your hope. This is the immortality for which you have been made and to which you unceasingly aspire.

It is sad to think that the soul, which of all things is most precious; which alone, on that day when God will come to judge the world, shall be deemed worthy of thought; is now accounted the cheapest of all things, and receives the least share of men's attention, and which they are ready to barter for every vile advantage. Is it not wisdom, —is it not the highest wisdom,—is it not the only wisdom,—to live for the salvation of this immortal soul?

THE EXAMPLE OF THE SAINTS.

AFTER this I saw a great multitude, which no man could number, of all nations, and tribes, and peoples, and tongues, standing before the throne, and in sight of the Lamb, clothed with white robes, and palms in their hands:

And they cried with a loud voice, saying: Salvation to our God, who sitteth upon the throne, and to the Lamb.

And all the Angels stood round about the throne, and the ancients, and the four living creatures; and they fell down before the throne upon their faces, and adored God,

Saying: Amen. Benediction, and glory, and wisdom, and thanksgiving, honour, and power, and strength to our God for ever and ever. Amen.

And one of the ancients answered, and said to me: These that are clothed in white robes, who are they? and whence came they?

And I said to him: My Lord, thou knowest. And he said to me: These are they who are come out of great tribulation, and have washed their robes, and have made them white in the blood of the Lamb.

Therefore they are before the throne of God, and they serve him day and night in his temple: and he, that sitteth on the throne shall dwell over them.

They shall have no more hunger nor thirst, neither shall the sun fall on them, nor any heat.

For the Lamb, which is in the midst of the throne, shall rule them, and shall lead them to the fountains of the waters of life, and God shall wipe away all tears from their eyes.—*Apocalypse*, VII., 9–17.

THE Church has been often charged with giving to the saints and angels an undue honor: if not placing them on a level with God, by transferring to them the honor which belongs to Him alone; at least, dividing this honor with Him, and extending a part of the worship to them, which should be simply and entirely rendered to the Supreme Being, the Lord and Maker of all things.

If this were true, it would expose the Church to the charge of idolatry. But she well distinguishes between the supreme and absolute worship due to God, and to Him alone, and the inferior or relative honor paid the saints. They are to be honored, as God's special friends and servants; not for their own sake, but for the sake of God, to whom they owe all their excellence and glory. God is to be honored for His own sake; because of His intrinsic and absolute perfection. As we revere a relic or a picture, not because of its own innate merit, but because of the saint to whom it belonged, or whom it represents; so we honor the saints because they are images or reflections, however feeble, of God's own perfection and holiness; His own handiwork, formed and fashioned out of our poor nature; the noblest offerings we can make to Him out of this sin-smitten world.

Even the inferior honor which the Church permits us, nay, calls upon us to give the saints, springs from the love she bears to Christ. The glory we give the saints redounds to Him. We but praise the Lord in His saints. The Man-God is the exemplar the saints have followed. He is the model, as well as the embodiment of all sanctity. The saints have loved Him, and from loving, they have sought to imitate Him. They shadow forth, they are the closest resemblances we have of Christ's uncreated holiness. They are the medium through which we are permitted to catch a glimpse of the splendor of God's sanctity. Through them its dazzling brightness comes to us, subdued and softened; as the glorious rays of the sun are mellowed and tinted, when they come pouring through the stained-glass windows of some old cathedral. Thus we are enabled to look upon the splendor of His glory, and yet live. As we can only bear to look upon the sun, when the eye is protected by some medium; so it is only when God's sanctity is reflected in the saints, that we can look upon its dazzling splendor.

Thus, we see that in honoring the saints, we take away nothing from the honor due to God. On the contrary; His honor is our motive in their worship. We acknowledge not only that He is holy, but that He is capable of communicating His holiness to His creatures. We but honor those whom God Himself has honored; whom He has raised to His highest friendship; on whose souls He has poured His choicest gifts, and shed the brightest influences of His grace; whom He has conformed to the image of His Son, because He has predestined them to be partakers of His glory.

It is not my purpose to defend the worship which the Church renders to the saints. Neither is it my purpose to pronounce the panegyric of the saints. I wish only to remind you that we are called upon not only to ask their intercession, to honor their memory, to celebrate their virtues; but also, to imitate their example. This is one of the objects the Church has in view, in presenting them to our attention and devotion.

We are apt to imagine that the saints belonged to a nature superior to our own; that their superiority is something arising not only from grace and fidelity thereto, but from a disposition naturally prone to virtue ; in them we scarcely believe that those passions found root, which we find so deeply rooted in ourselves. This, of course, is an error. The saints were men like ourselves; hewn out of the same rock, born in the same sin, subject to the same passions, and, before their conversion, probably guilty of the same sins. It was God's grace that made them what they became; and, were it not for its sovereign power and their fidelity to it, they would forever have remained what they were. It was God's own potent hand that elaborated and fashioned them out of the general wreck of our fallen nature. They are the masterpieces of His grace. They are not, then, so far above us, that we cannot hope to imitate them. We are called upon to be perfect. There is not one of us who cannot, by the same fidelity to grace and perseverance in good, attain unto something, at least, of their perfection. We may be forever strangers to the depth and intensity of their charity, to the firmness and brightness of their hope, to the steadiness and loftiness of their faith, to their spirit of self-sacrifice, to their utter contempt for the world ; but we can, at least, fol-

THE EXAMPLE OF THE SAINTS. 177

low them from afar off, and acquire something of their great virtues. We are not called upon to attain these virtues, in their most exalted degree; but we are called upon to possess them in their germ or principle. The saints, then, are our models.

In contemplating the lives of these servants of God, we are struck by the sublimity of the motives and views which guided all their actions. The saints lived on a plane far above that of the rest of men. Their motives and views were incomparably superior to the motives and views of those who live but for this world. They sanctified the least of their actions, by directing them to the honor of God. No sordid or unworthy feeling found place in their hearts. Hence it was, that they were generally misunderstood, and even misrepresented, by the world. Men are slow to acknowledge that anyone can be prompted by motives, other or better, than those which, for the most part, actuate themselves. Men are loath to acknowledge that others possess qualities, or gifts, or attainments, or graces, which they have not themselves. They are disposed to judge of others, by themselves; denying to them what they have not; granting them, at most, what they themselves have.

The principles of the Saints were immeasurably above the rules of mere worldly wisdom. Hence, the world, gauging them by its own standard, fell into error; and since it could not understand them ended by calumniating them. Compare the sublime principles and motives of the saints, with those that actuate the world's votaries. What the world calls the best and noblest of the sons of men were prompted in all their actions, by motives which the saints contemned. Men are thought noble-minded, if they live to hoard treasures, to pursue knowledge, to acquire fame that may, perhaps, live after them and transmit their names to posterity. What sublimity in motives which lead to that which is, at best, but vain, transitory and perishable? Of what avail is it to hoard treasures, which must, one day, be abandoned? How absurd to consume ourselves in the pursuit of mere earthly knowledge, and neglect the knowledge that would lead to God: the source and fountain of all true knowledge? How ridiculous to be so solicitous for the immortality of our name, and to be so indifferent to the immortality of our souls? How criminal to wade through seas of blood, to destroy the lives of innumerable beings, in order to gratify ambition? to damn countless souls for the sake of human glory? a passing breath, the veriest of delusions. What sublimity is there in principles like these?

The saints sought not such ends; they despised them; they were dead to the world and to all its allurements. They cared not for its riches, its praises, its distinctions, its glory. They placed not their happiness in such toys. They opened their minds to know, they expanded their hearts to embrace, the infinite and eternal good. They felt the craving of their souls for a perfect, a boundless happiness. They felt that, as God alone had made them, in "Him alone could they find rest." They knew that the vanities of this world could never fill the void, nor satisfy the insatiable craving of their God-destined souls. They looked beyond the horizon of this world, and placed their happiness, and their hopes, and their ambitions, where only they can be found: in the bosom of God, in the contemplation of His infinite and adorable perfections. Here, and here alone, can be found true riches, true pleasure, true wisdom, true glory, true felicity. "I know that my Redeemer liveth, and that in the last day, I shall rise out of the earth; and I shall be clothed again with my skin, and in my flesh I shall see my God, Whom I myself shall see, and my eyes behold and not another. This my hope is laid up in my bosom." This was the motive, the mainspring of the lives of the saints.

In this consideration, we are to seek their wonderful independence,—not that independence which is born of pride and nourished by vanity,—but that virtue which springs from detachment from the world, which contemns all human respect, which regards not what others may do or say, and which finds a law for its actions in its conscience and its duty to God. The saints were the most independent of men, because they were the most independent of the world's esteem.

No wonder that the saints, animated by such lofty principles in their daily actions, afford us also the most remarkable examples of self-denial and self-sacrifice. We admire the lofty courage that prompts the soldier to deeds of heroism: the fortitude, that, in a worthy cause, hesitates not to lay down even life itself, extorts the homage of the noblest feelings of our nature. But after all that can be said of the courage that stimulates to acts of self-denial; what is it to the courage of abandoning the world, of denying ourselves its pleasures, of separating ourselves from its vanities, of passing life in the mortification of the passions, of living simply and utterly for the purpose for which God has made us? Men who are capable of the loftiest heroism, in the world's sense, would be absolutely incapable of practicing the apparently humbler, but really transcendently superior courage of dying to the world to live to God. How many are there ready to sacrifice life itself, for the sake of courage? How few are they who have the courage to mortify one sinful passion, to practice one single act of virtue for God? "Greater far is he that ruleth his spirit, than he that taketh a city." Consider, what it is to abandon the world: to forsake fortune, position, influence, bright prospects, the enjoyment of all the world's goods; to exchange, as many of the saints did, the luxuries of a palace, for the privations of a cell; couches of down, for the bare earth; the choicest viands, for the simplest fare; the society of the world, for the solitariness of the desert and the companionship of wild beasts. Consider, how few men are willing to make such a sacrifice; and from their fewness, learn the marvellous fortitude it calls for.

The noblest acts of heroism which history records, were acts whose performance lasted but for a very short time; and then the courage that animated them was relieved. But the fortitude of the saint must be continual and inexhaustible, to sustain him in his unceasing warfare against himself, his passions, the world, the concupiscence of the flesh, and the pride of life. No sudden, momentary, transitory courage suffices for this. Many are equal to impulsive bravery, but few are equal to sustain it any length of time. The saints had to pass years, nay, their whole lives in self-denial and in deeds of self-sacrifice. No isolated acts, nor sudden triumphs, were sufficient to give them the victory over their passions, to enable them to overcome the allurements of the world. They had always to nourish, to keep alive, to intensify the holy flame that burned in their hearts, when first they forsook the world; continually wasted in the conflict, it had to be continually replenished. The world never slackened in its assaults; they had to perpetuate their resistance; until, finally, having fought the good fight and finished their course, they received the crown which was laid up for them in heaven. Their sufferings may well be compared with the sufferings of the martyrs. And the man who, for the love of God, voluntarily relinquishes the world and spends his years in privation and suffering, may well lay claim to the martyr's crown; for his life is a continual martyrdom. He has to crucify the flesh with its concupiscence, to sacrifice those feelings and desires which are the strongest and most ineradicable of his nature. He knows that the kingdom of heaven suffereth violence, and the violent only bear it away.

Even the love of power, of glory or reputation, and of those other objects which even good men think they may pursue without blame, can have no place in the affections of the saint. He must learn to contemn these things and to seek his happiness in the possession of God. For Him, alone, must he live; in Him, alone, must he centre all his affections. Few can realize the disinterestedness and the heroism required for such a sacrifice.

Far from seeking the good opinion of men, and the glory of the world, the servant of God must incur their odium, and bear with patience their scorn. How lofty, how unworldly, how indifferent to human respect, must be the courage which not only endures, but even despises hate and contempt? Self-love is so strong in the human heart, that it is with difficulty we can bear reproach, or brook insult. Hearts invulnerable to all things else, are keenly sensitive to even the least look of contempt. Men brave to rush upon certain death in its most awful forms, are cowed, and sometimes unmanned, by the slightest scorn. In fact, fear of contempt is often the motive that urges men to the most daring deeds. Men fear the world's opinion, and prefer to die rather than risk its odium. The saints were far above all such weakness; they minded not the judgment of the world; as they sought not its praises, so they feared not its censures. The principles which guided them, were the dictates of their conscience; not the judgments of men. It is to be remembered that, in despising the world's opinion, they were not prompted by pride; they did not compensate themselves for the world's contempt, by the pleasure they found in despising the world. There were pagan philosophers, who affected to contemn the world, but their contempt was the result of pride. They made amends to themselves, for the loss of the world's esteem, by the secret pleasure they found in contemning its opinion. But with the saints, contempt of the world sprang from their humility; they pitied the world, and lamented that men should be the victims of its delusions. They rejoiced that they were accounted worthy to suffer reproach for the name of Jesus. They were made a spectacle to the world, to the angels, and to men. They were esteemed the refuse of this world. There are none truly brave, but the truly humble. It is pride that makes cowards; it is only by trampling it under foot, by annihilating it, that we can aspire to the noble fortitude, which enabled the saints to endure the scorn and censures of men.

But all the virtues of the saints would be as nothing, if they did not have goodness; it is the essential mark of all holiness. Goodness, prompted by no interest, awaiting no command of duty, looking to no reward, seeking not its own, is the grandest prerogative of the saints; as it is of God Himself. No one is truly great, who is not truly good. Men have been great, only in so far, as they have been possessed of goodness. God is the source of all goodness; it is the greatest of His attributes. It was His goodness that moved Him to create the world, to redeem man: the most perfect, disinterested goodness. The saints are the images of God. The more goodness they possess, the more clearly do they reflect their great Exemplar. In contemplating the marvellous goodness of God in Himself and in dying for men, the souls of the saints were fired with goodness. Next to their love of God, there was in them nothing greater than their goodness, or, love for men. In all their actions, we see a goodness which was but an emanation of the goodness of Christ; their model and master.

We reverence the memory of those who are the benefactors of our race; who pass their lives in the alleviation of its sufferings; who travel the world, not to behold the evidences of its grandeur, nor the relics of its past greatness, nor to gather wisdom in its schools, nor to be entertained by the novelty and beauty of its languages and customs; but in search of the fallen whom they may raise, the destitute whom they may assist, the suffering whom they may relieve, the wicked whom they may reclaim. And we should; for these philanthropists are the best and noblest specimens of our race. Their works of goodness and disinterestedness are the lights that illumine, the deeds that ennoble this dark, and dreary, and selfish world of ours. Were not such acts of devotion recorded up and down the page of history, it would present but one vast record of suffering, unrelieved by the generous impulses of our nature.

But this goodness, after all, springs but from a natural motive, and can exert but the limited influence of a natural virtue. What is it to the goodness, the supernatural goodness of the saints, proceeding from a love of God, unlimited in its influence, and extending to all men? The saints lived for no other purpose than to do good; their lives were but records of beneficence. It was their continual study how to succor humanity, how to improve the condition of all. For this, they resorted to all the means which a heavenly wisdom could suggest; for this, they exhausted all the energies of body and soul. No obstacle was insurmountable, no toil too wearisome, no prospect too hopeless, no opposition could deter them, no fear could intimidate them. If seas were to be crossed, if countries were to be penetrated where life and health were exposed to the most imminent danger, if the gospel was to be preached among nations where its announcement was sure to be sealed with their blood, the saints hesitated not; no danger was too appalling, no fatigue was too insupportable, no death was too cruel, if there was hope of gaining souls to Christ. Their lives are but the record of what they have done and suffered for their fellow-beings. Not only did they spend their lives, not only did they undergo sufferings untold, but even their liberty and their blood were freely offered on the altar of their charity.

We read of saints who delivered themselves into captivity to redeem some prisoner; of others who offered even to die for the ransom of slaves;

of others who would even risk their eternal salvation, by preferring to live longer on earth for the salvation of men, than to go to heaven at once. From St. Paul, who wished himself to be an anathema from Christ for his brethren, to St. Vincent de Paul, who sold himself into slavery to redeem a captive, the history of the Church is but one series and brilliant record of enterprises undertaken and carried out for the redress of human grievances and the alleviation of human suffering. The Church in her saints has been but re-enacting the mission of her Divine Founder. Into the saints has He infused His spirit. By them has He perpetuated His example.

We are called the children of the saints; we have the same mother Church. Are we really their children, or is it but an empty name? We are called upon to honor and imitate, or rather, to honor by imitating the saints. Do we so honor them? or does our honoring consist in saying a few prayers and litanies in which their names are mentioned? How stand we in this matter? Let us look to ourselves. We may not be called upon to practice their eminent virtues. But do we follow them, even from afar off? have we their virtues even in germ or root? are we even desiring to tread in their footsteps? Are we pursuing that narrow way, beset with trial and danger; blood-stained on every side, telling of the hard struggles and fierce conflicts of those who have gone before?—that royal road of the Cross, which all the predestined must travel; that narrow way, that so few find and which alone leads to glory. Or are we pursuing that broad and beaten path, which shows no vestiges of conflict, which tells no tale of blood-shedding or of suffering for salvation, which suggests no lesson of self-denial: that broad and easy and sinful way which almost all pursue?

You will say, that you are doing as well as your neighbor. Then you are on the wrong path. If you do no better than the majority you will be lost. Most men are not in pursuit of salvation. The saints were not like the rest of men. I wish not to discuss the question of the fewness of the elect. Yet, when I consider the solemn words of Scripture, I see no justification for those who would improve upon the Gospel; who broaden the way, that Christ has declared narrow; who ease the path, that He has declared difficult; and who enlarge the number, of those whom He has declared few. Rest assured, that, if you are no better than the rest of men, as they are found in the present state of society, you are not of that " Little flock " which Christ calls His faithful followers.

You will say that you keep the commandments and avoid grievous sin; that you are not called upon to be saints. True; you are not called upon to be saints in the highest sense of the word; true, strictly speaking, you are only obliged to avoid mortal sin. But think you, that you will succeed in so doing, while you scruple not venial sins? He who would avoid mortal sin, must begin by avoiding venial. He who would hit the mark, must aim a little higher than seems necessary to his purpose. He who rushes along a precipice, must be careful not to run too close to the edge, lest he stumble and be dashed to pieces upon the rocks below. He who would keep the law in its integrity, must not begin by shaving it. You must make allowances for the wear and tear of the conflict; and give yourselves some vantage ground on which to hold your own against the fatal assaults of mortal sin.

Think not that you will be without reward. What is the recompense of the saints? I answer; what is the object of creation? What is the end of all things, but the glory of the elect? For this alone did God create the world. All things else are subordinated to this one great purpose. God's primary providence in the affairs of the world, is the preservation and diffusion of His Church: that, through her, may be brought forth the saints who alone of all men subserve the final design of God in the creation of the world. But for the saints, and their works, the history of the world, on the last day, would be but a universal blank. God made the world for man, to manifest to him His glory. Man fell: the work was spoiled. Jesus came: all things were restored. The saints, alone, co-operate with Him in the work of restoration; alone, make themselves partakers of the benefits conferred by Him. Only they, of all men, seek to further the purpose God had in making the world; hence, at the last day, the history of the world, and even of individuals, will be narrowed down to what concerns the design of God in creating the world and man.

THE EXAMPLE OF THE SAINTS.

Let us imitate the saints, for we are their children. We belong to the same Mother Church, who brought them forth to Christ. We may never reach the loftiness of their motives, the sovereign degree of their self-denial; we may forever remain strangers to their unapproachable goodness. Yet, we are called upon to possess these virtues, at least, in their element or principle. If we are to share their glory in the life to come, their virtues we must have, if not, in fulness, at least in a measure proportioned to our mediocrity. Let us, then, study our models, imbibe their spirit, and make their virtues our own.

The world may laugh, may think our life without purpose, and our end without honor; yet it will, at the last day, honor us, as it now honors them. Iniquity will be forced to pay its tribute to virtue: " These are they whom we had sometime in derision, and for a parable of reproach. We foolish ones esteemed their life madness, and their end without honor. Behold, how they are numbered among the children of God, and their lot is among the saints. We have therefore erred from the way of truth; and the light of justice hath not shined upon us; and the sun of understanding hath not risen upon us."

Not only can we expect the reward prepared for the just; but even in this life we shall not be without recompense. Where are, now, those that persecuted the saints? Where, now, is the world of their day? Yet, the saints are remembered and honored by all men. They have inherited the glory which in life they contemned. And those who lived but for glory and this world, are sunk in oblivion. Like Jesus Christ, contemned, and persecuted, and put to death, the saints have emerged from their obscurity, and the contempt of men, from their sufferings, and hidden holiness, and heroic deeds of charity, all glorious;—to be honored, throughout all time, together with their Master and Model. Their names are enthroned in the hearts of the faithful, they are enshrined in the prayers of the Church; their intercession is invoked, wherever, from the rising to the setting sun, the clean oblation of Christ's body is offered up. They are as immortal as the Church itself.

Thus it is, that virtue is rewarded; that the Church triumphs; that the ways of God are justified; and that He overcomes the world.

ON PRAYER.

And when ye pray, ye shall not be as the hypocrites, who love to stand and pray in the synagogue and at the corners of the streets, that they may be seen by men. Truly, I say to you, they have got their reward. But thou when thou prayest, enter into thy chamber, and when thou hast shut the door, pray to thy Father in secret: and thy Father who seeth in secret, will repay thee. And when ye pray, gabble not as the heathen do: for they think that for their many words they may be heard. Be not ye, therefore, like to them; for your Father knoweth what is needful for you, before ye ask Him. Thus, therefore, shall ye pray: Our Father who art in heaven, hallowed be Thy name. Thy kingdom come. Thy will be done on earth as it is in heaven. Give us this day our daily bread. And forgive us our debts, as we also forgive our debtors. And lead us not into temptation: but deliver us from evil. Amen. For if ye forgive men their offences, your heavenly Father will forgive you also your offences. But if ye will not forgive men, neither will your Father forgive you your offences. And when ye fast, be not of a sad countenance, as the hypocrites. For they disfigure their faces, that to men they may appear to fast. Truly I say to you, they have got their reward. But thou, when thou fastest, anoint thy head, and wash thy face: that thou appear not to men to fast, but to thy Father, who is in secret: and thy Father, who seeth in secret, will repay thee. Lay not up for yourselves treasures on earth, where rust and moth consume, and where thieves break through and steal. But lay up for yourselves treasures in heaven, where neither rust nor moth doth consume, and where thieves do not break through, nor steal.—St. Matthew vi., 5–20.

PRAYER is defined to be the raising of the mind to God, whereby we praise Him, give Him thanks for His benefits, ask for good things, and to be freed from evil.

Prayer is the raising of the mind to God: by this, it is clear that words are not necessary to prayer; that thought and meditation are its essential ingredients. We praise God because of His intrinsic excellence and boundless perfection. For this He is entitled to our love and worship. By asking for good things and giving thanks for His benefits, is implied the duty which rests upon us of giving thanks to Almighty God for all the blessings, temporal and eternal, that He confers upon us. We are also taught to pray to God for all things necessary to the salvation of our souls; always keeping in mind the admonition of Christ: " Seek ye first the kingdom of God and His justice, and all things shall be added unto you." We are to ask submissively, and upon the condition that what we ask, it be pleasing to God to grant. We are not to expect absolute immunity from evil; but that we may not be tempted beyond our strength, that we may be led, uninjured, through temptation. This is a short explanation of the definition of prayer.

When it is said to be a raising of the mind to God, we have the substance and essence of what prayer should be. It answers those who say, that they pray not because they know not how to pray. Who is he, that knows not how to raise his heart to God, to ask Him to lighten the burdens under which he suffers, to give him light enough to know the truth, and grace to follow it? As we can raise our hearts to God, we can pray. Prayer consists not in any skilful arrangement of thoughts or sentiments, nor is it any effort of the mind, nor any elaborate argument; nor does it require any profound erudition or recondite research, nor any deep knowledge of God's mysteries, nor extensive acquaintance with His law. It is not any lofty speculation or logical discourse. Prayer is the cry of the soul conscious of its miseries and trials; it is the outpouring of our hearts conscious of their weakness, and surrounded on every side by temptation. It is the confession of our disrelish and disgust with all things human, and of our own insufficiency; and the acknowledgment that all our hope and reliance is in the goodness of God alone. Prayer is not something in the heavens, that we need to have brought down to us; nor something across the seas, that we should say, who shall bring it to us. It is in the power, as it is the duty, of everyone. It is the law of our spiritual life, it is the essential condition of our salvation. The high, the low, the ignorant, can pray, no less than the highly stationed or the highly gifted. The essential duty of every man does not depend upon any external circumstances. All can pray, because everyone can understand his misery, and can look to God for strength and assistance. The rustic who can scarcely name the Trinity, may be more of an adept at prayer than the great theologian who, while he talks learnedly of the Trinity, may fail to do the will of the Trinity. He who is filled with salutary fear of God's judgments, and with hope in His boundless goodness and mercy, and who falls down in worshipping the greatness of

His majesty and His adorable attributes, is better prepared for the duty of prayer than if he possessed all human erudition expressed in language the most embellished. The more keenly one feels his misery, the more he realizes his own nothingness and his absolute dependence upon Almighty God, the more unreservedly he commits himself to Divine providence and looks to it for strength: the more perfectly he is able to pray.

Theologians tell us that there are various kinds of prayer: the best is that, in which the soul ascending from virtue to virtue, from holiness to holiness, mounts even to the bosom of God: and finds in the contemplation of His divine nature and perfections, unspeakable joy and bliss supreme. If it were necessary to aspire to this kind of prayer; if it were necessary to be, like Saint Paul, transported out of one's self to heaven, and to hear those secrets which it is not permitted him to utter, we might, indeed, claim dispensation from the duty of prayer. But we must content ourselves with the lower order of prayer; that in which, feeling our weakness and our dread proclivity to sin, and surrounded by temptation on every side, we beg God to grant us grace not to yield to our enemies; or, having yielded, we implore Him to come to our rescue, to raise us from our misery. We can beg Him Who watches over us, Who has counted the hairs of our head, and Who makes His sun rise and His rain fall upon the just and unjust, that He will supply our wants and grant us all we need for our temporal and spiritual welfare. As the hungry know how to ask for bread, and the thirsty to ask for drink, and the naked for covering, so he who feels the needs of his soul, can ask God in His goodness to supply them. See the entreaties, long and persistent, with which men seek some temporal object: no less should be our earnestness in beseeching God to grant us the virtues and graces necessary for our eternal salvation: even greater zeal and assiduity should mark our prayers, because of the greater urgency and necessity of our eternal salvation. No man can excuse himself from the duty of prayer, because he knows not how to pray. Let him but feel the end for which he has been made, and he cannot fail to have an instinctive knowledge of the divine art of prayer.

The advantages of prayer are many. By it we render to God the worship, which is His due; and we acknowledge His supreme dominion over us, and all things. We recognize Him, as our sovereign benefactor, from Whom we have received all, and from Whom we are to expect all. Everything has been made for His honor and glory. Inanimate nature cannot subserve this end, but imperfectly, except through man. Man, then, by prayer gives the glory to God, which He expects from all creatures. Man's adoration and love, free and spontaneous in its nature, is alone worthy of the Creator.

Prayer opens heaven. Prayer ascends, mercy descends. God hears the prayer of men; it is the ordinary channel through which we receive all blessings. He wishes to be asked for His gifts. If we do not receive them, it is because we do not ask; it is the established means of receiving divine grace; even the sacraments depend upon it; for, by prayer we must obtain the dispositions which they require for their fruitful reception. If it is the appointed channel of obtaining grace, all other means are excluded. As God has ordained prayer as the condition of granting us His grace, it is through prayer that we must seek it.

Prayer improves all our virtues: increases our faith, animates our hope, inflames our charity, nourishes confidence in God, augments diffidence in ourselves. Taught to have recourse to Him in all our needs, and to look to Him for light and assistance in darkness and temptation; and always obtaining what we ask, or something better in lieu thereof, we come to mistrust ourselves and all human resources, and to place all our trust in His goodness and mercy.

Frequent interviews are necessary to excite love for anyone. The more intercourse we have with God in prayer, the warmer becomes our love; because the clearer our knowledge of Him is made. All things else lose, by too close a scrutiny; but God gains upon us, the greater our intimacy. Human society and individuals appear happy and great: but examined closely, there is nothing but misery and discontent, sin and anguish. But God closely examined by holy meditation, and sought in prayer, is full of beauty, and of holiness, and of every perfection that can charm or satiate the soul. He fills the soul united to Him by prayer, with all the content, and joy, and exultation, that are the outcome of these divine perfections. We shall never rise to a perfect knowledge of Him in this life; but, in whatever measure we apprehend Him, the same shall be the degree of our love. In communion with God, we come to learn the beauty of virtue, the hatefulness of sin, and the emptiness of all things earthly: enamored of the divine beauty and goodness, we come to love holiness, and aspire to the Eternal Good.

Prayer is a vital necessity of the soul. This arises from the necessity of grace. By myself, I am nothing; by the grace of God, I can do all things. To purchase for us this grace, Christ became man. St. Thomas says that, without prayer, we cannot be saved. Some hold that, without prayer, there is no grace; wherefore, without prayer, there is no salvation. Some things are necessary for salvation, as a means; some, as a matter of precept. Prayer is necessary, both as a means and as a precept. "We ought always to pray, and not to faint." "Amen, amen, I say to you, if you ask the Father anything in My Name, He will give it you. Hitherto you have not asked anything in My Name: ask, and you shall receive, that your joy may be full." Christ, by His example, taught us to pray. After the fatigues of the day, preaching, curing the sick, ministering to every want, working miracles, He spent the night in prayer. He was in constant communion with His heavenly Father. In His agony, in Gethsemane, the day before He died, He prayed. He prayed on the cross for the penitent thief; he prayed for the Jews, for they knew not what they did. This He did for our edification. He did not need to pray for Himself; for in Him there was neither sin nor the shadow thereof.

The temptations that surround us, teach us the necessity of prayer. Born from a corrupt source, bearing within us an earthly, and a heavenly element, which war continually; feeling the law of our members alluring us to sin; with nothing in the world but the lust of the flesh, the lust of the eyes, and the pride of life; exalted and made proud by prosperity, cast down by adversity and disappointment; what resource have we only prayer? to whom shall we have recourse in our misery? whither shall we repair from our enemies, except to God, by prayer, fervent and sustained? Christ gave us a form of prayer, which contains all that is necessary to our eternal salvation, and to our temporal well-being.

Prayer is one of those duties, from which nothing can dispense us. Other obligations there are, and these, urgent; yet, there are causes that dispense us from their fulfilment, or extenuate the guilt of neglect. As grace is necessary to the fruitful reception of the sacraments, and as there is no grace without prayer; so whatever is the necessity of the sacraments, the same is the necessity of prayer. Without prayer as a preliminary to obtain the grace which they require, the reception of the sacraments may be fruitless, or even sacrilegious. Few question the necessity of prayer; but few are faithful to the duty which the necessity implies.

We frequently hear people say, that they pray, and yet receive not; that they ask, and it is not given to them; that they seek, and they do not find; they knock, and it is not opened to them. What, then, is the use of prayer? Yet nothing is better established in religion than the unfailing efficacy of prayer. We have the assurance of Jesus Christ that, if we ask, it shall be given to us. Prayer, then, reaches the very heart of God. How shall we explain this? on the one hand, there is the word of God assuring us of the infallibility of prayer; and on the other, the unmistakable fact that we sometimes pray and do not receive. St. James explains the difficulty and reconciles the two: "Ye ask and ye receive not, because ye ask amiss." You ask not what you should, or you ask what you should not, or asking what you should, you ask it not with the proper disposition. What then should we pray for? What should be the subject matter of our prayer? Reflect on the object for which we are come into being. What is our final destiny? Is it riches, or fame, or passion, during life; then to sink into the grave and be no more? But if we have come into the world for a destiny which ends not here below; if we have an immortal soul, and its eternal welfare depends upon our fidelity to God's holy law; then, it is plain, that the object of our prayers should be far above any of the interests or objects of this life. Our petitions should beseech God to have mercy upon our weakness, to grant us grace to overcome temptation, to slacken the fire of lust; in a word, they should concern our eternal destiny and what may be necessary thereto. Our requests should be in harmony with the providence of God, and with the design that He has had in making man and revealing to him his supernatural destiny. The incarnation and death of Christ are luminous facts to manifest God's providence with regard to man. To save the soul, and to use all things that God has given, in so far as they may conduce to this salvation, and to refrain from them, in so far as they may hinder it, is the highest Christian philosophy. It was not that we might enjoy any temporal advantage that Christ died. The salvation of humanity was the only object worthy of that mysterious sacrifice: that man might have supernatural life and abundant grace to attain it, was the only fruit and reward worthy of that incalculable price. Put out of mind all thoughts and all the concerns of this world; banish from it all things of a transitory nature, or contemplate them as they will appear to you in the day, when Jesus Christ will come to judge the world: what are the objects which, in that day, will seem important in our eyes and to have been alone worthy of our attention during life? They will be our soul and its eternal destiny: God and His eternal kingdom. These, then, are the objects for which, now, we should pray.

Why should we pray for anything outside of these eternal realities? Why should we ask God for favors that have no relation to our immortal destiny? If it is true, that this body is hastening to the grave; that, in a few short years, it will be, as if it never had been in this world, why should we pray to escape sickness? If, in a little while, your reputation shall be followed by the silence of the grave, why give so great part of your thoughts to its attainment? If pleasure lasts but so short a time, if no human gratification can entirely satisfy the cravings of the soul, why pray for human enjoyment? why pray for temporal advantages? Why not, rather, pray for the light of the Holy Ghost; that it may dwell with us, and keep our eyes open to the vanity and emptiness of all things human? Our soul and its salvation should be always in our thoughts. It is no wonder that our prayers are not heard, because we pray, truly, amiss.

Every prayer that the Church offers is in the name and through the merits of Jesus Christ. Every supplication is through His blood and sacrifice. The prayers of the Church are to be the models of our own. Think you to ask anything save what concerns salvation, in the name of Him, Who has died for no other object than to purchase it for us? With His unspeakable sacrifice for our sins and our redemption before our eyes, can we dare to profane it by asking worldly gratification, or any temporal benefit? Can we ask anything except what He came to obtain for us, and for which His blood was shed? We should confine our prayers to the model which He has taught us; and in it there is no mention of temporal benefits, except the daily bread wherewith soul and body may be kept together.

We have an advocate before the Father: Jesus

Christ Who makes continual intercession for us. He is our great High-priest, Who is entered into the heavens, not one who cannot have compassion for our infirmities; but one tried in all things in like manner without sin. Can we imagine that He asks the Father for anything except what regards our eternal salvation? It is clear, then, that we pray amiss; that we do not obtain what we ask for, because we forget the rightful object of prayer.

See the man who is united to God by continual prayer: how calm; how great the serenity of his soul; nothing can disturb the heart where the Holy Ghost dwells. Upon how high a plain does he live and move. How pure and lofty an atmosphere does he breathe. Nothing disconcerts him. Calamities do not cast him down; calumny, disgrace, misery, death, may come: they find him tranquil and resigned. People who know not the grace that strengthens and irradiates his soul, wonder at him. Such a man has solid religious convictions; realizes that life is short, that death is sure, that the world is nothing but deceit, that there is but one thing necessary. It is the consciousness of living for the one thing necessary, which fills his soul with a peace that worldlings fail to understand. They who place their happiness in the objects of this life, sink into despondency when worldly misfortune befalls them. They must needs: because they lose the only happiness for which they have appreciation. Religious convictions are not deep in their souls.

How must we pray? Left to ourselves and to the promptings of our hearts, we all are instructed in the art of prayer. We may pray for the rightful objects of prayer, and yet we may not always obtain what we ask, because we pray not as we ought. When you pray, prepare your hearts and be not as those tempting God. Our prayers should be animated with the spirit of humility. God resists the proud and gives grace to the humble. The proud Pharisee went down from the temple unpardoned, because of his self-conceit and self-sufficiency. The poor publican with sins uncounted and black in their dye was justified, because of his humility. With what lowly entreaty do we seek a favor from some temporal potentate; nor do we think our pains lost, if we obtain what we ask. The Canaan woman obtained what she sought, because of her humble earnestness. Confidence that we shall obtain what we ask, is another quality which should mark our prayers. It has the virtue of working miracles. "Thy faith hath made thee whole." "He could not perform any miracles because of their unbelief." Nothing is more essential to prayer than perseverance. It belongs to God to say how long we shall beseech Him; and on what conditions He will grant our requests. From the nature of prayer, as a communion or colloquy with God, it is obvious, that this duty is to be performed with due preparation of soul, free from all wilful distractions, with all fervor and attention of mind, with all earnestness and affection of heart.

For what shall we pray? For what does the

thirsty, the sick, the starving pray? If we understood our misery, we would not ask the question. We have so much to pray for, that we scarcely know where to begin. Are we in sin, pray to be delivered from it. Are we in grace, pray for perseverance. Pray for strength to overcome temptation. Have you ever committed sin? Pray for its forgiveness. Be not without solicitude for sins supposed to be forgiven. Thank God for your conversion; for enlightening and leading you from iniquity. Pray for yourselves, for your relations, for your friends, for your enemies. Pray for the young, in whom passion is strongest; for the old, in whom time has not diminished sinfulness; for those who are in sin, that they may rise from it. Pray for infidels; for heretics; for the sheep not of the true fold, that all may be brought to see the truth. Pray for those whose faith is a dead one, who lie in sin in the bosom of the Church. Pray for the Head of the Church; for the Church's triumph over its enemies, and its diffusion throughout the world; for the accession to the priesthood of priests filled with the spirit of their vocation, men after God's own heart. If you are in the world, pray that you be not contaminated; if you are in solitude, pray; for a man's enemies are those of his own household, his passions follow him wheresoever he goes. Pray at all times, especially during temptation, that you may not fall; and if you fall, pray after temptation that you may rise again. Peter was safe while he prayed; he fell when he ceased. The sinner should never despair, until he despises prayer. "There is nothing left me," says Holy Job, "but the teeth above my lips." "Much is left to thee," says St. Hilary, "because there is left to thee, the power of raising your lips in prayer."

MOTIVES TO HUMILITY.

Two men went up into the temple to pray: the one a Pharisee, and the other a publican.

The Pharisee standing, prayed thus with himself: O God, I give thee thanks that I am not as the rest of men, extortioners, unjust, adulterers, as also is this publican.

I fast twice in a week: I give tithes of all that I possess.

And the publican, standing afar off, would not so much as lift up his eyes towards heaven; but struck his breast, saying: O God, be merciful to me a sinner.

I say to you, this man went down into his house justified rather than the other: because every one that exalteth himself shall be humbled: and he that humbleth himself shall be exalted.—St. Luke xviii., 10-14.

OFTEN does the Church place before us, in the Gospels read to us, the lesson of Christian humility. In doing this, she but imitates our Blessed Lord, who by word, and deed, and example, never ceased to inculcate upon His followers the necessity of this virtue.

Not to speak of His incarnation, which is, perhaps, after all, a manifestation of His power and wisdom rather than of His humility: throughout the varied circumstances of His life, He affords a wondrous example of lowliness. Born of a poor virgin, having not whereon to lay His head, passing through life in poverty and obscurity, enduring privation and suffering, bearing without resentiment, and even with meekness, the blackest of outrages and most grievous wrongs; and, finally, for our sake, dying the death of a malefactor, He presents to us an example of humility of which God alone was capable. When, during His short-lived earthly triumph, they would make Him king, He fled; when He performed miracles, He charged His disciples that they should tell no man till He had risen from the dead; when He was transfigured on Thabor and the light of the Divinity shone about Him, He commanded that it should not be made known till after His resurrection. He even washed the disciples' feet, to afford an impressive example of the spirit of humility which should characterize them. "Learn of me, for I am meek and humble of heart."

And to carry on the work which He had begun, He made not use of the means which human pride and prudence would suggest; but He consecrated holy humility and sent it to convert the world. "The foolish things of this world did He choose to confound the wise, and the weak to confound the strong, and the things that are contemptible and those that are not to bring to naught the things that are." "Father, I give Thee thanks that Thou hast hid these things from the wise and prudent, and hast revealed them to little ones." "You know that the princes of the Gentiles lord it over them, and they who are great exercise authority on them. It shall not be so among you; but whoever will be the greatest among you, let him be your waiter. And whoever would be first among you, shall be your servant." "Unless you become as little children, you shall not enter into the Kingdom of heaven. Whosoever shall humble himself as this little child, the same is greatest in the Kingdom of heaven." The poor publican with sins grievous and beyond number was forgiven, because of his deep sense of unworthiness. Ths self-sufficient Pharisee with his rank conceit and festering pride, went down from the temple as he had gone up; probably, even with his heart still further hardened to the influence of grace.

Humility is the foundation of Christian virtue. As pride may be traced in every sin, humility is found in every virtue. As every sin is, in some sense, an act of pride, so every act of virtue is the result of humility. No virtue can exist without it. From it all the virtues spring, and have their nourishment and life. He is humble who realizes that he is but a creature, that he has nothing of his own, that of himself, he is but sin and misery, that all his sufficiency is from God; and who infuses this belief into his will, giving him an abiding sense of his nothingness. The more fully we apprehend and realize, and the more fully we impart to the will, this sense of our insufficiency and nothingness, the more truly humble we become. Humility does not consist in lowering ourselves below that which God has made us. Humility is founded upon truth. They cannot be opposed. Pride as the opposite of humility, consists in esteeming one's self beyond that which God knows him to be. Humility accordingly is found in knowing what one really is. If a person has received gifts from Almighty God, true humility will show itself, not by attempting to believe that he has not, but by improving, and making them subserve the glory of God; and acknowledging that they are His alone. As true humility teaches us to know ourselves, it leads us to understand and confess our relations to God. The more profound our knowledge of these relations, the truer and deeper our humility. Thus, the saints by the light and grace of the Holy Ghost, had a most vivid perception, a most intense realization of their nothingness as creatures; and of the all-sufficiency and greatness of the Creator. It was because of this, that they sometimes expressed themselves in words, which in us would simply seem affectation: that they felt themselves to be the greatest of sinners and the most miserable of men.

Many are humble in their words and modest in their exterior deportment, yet entire strangers to the virtue of humility. Modesty usually accompanies true humility; and, sometimes, even passes for the virtue; a counterfeit, which is not always and at once detected. Yet the two are quite distinct. The pride of Lucifer may be concealed under the garb of modesty. Of all the virtues, humility is the least easily discerned, and may long remain hidden. Humility never obtrudes itself, never seeks to be known as such. It were but exquisite pride, to seek to be thought humble.

The man whose soul is filled with true Christian humility will place the law of God before all things: rather than contemn it, he will suffer the loss of all he holds dearest, even of life itself. Convinced that outside of God there is no real pleasure, no real riches, no real honor, nothing worth living for; he will not seek these objects, except in reference to his one great paramount duty of loving God and saving his soul. He may be compelled to pass his life in obscurity and poverty; he will not demur. He will see, without envy, the elevation of those to whom he may be superior; but who are carried forward by the spurrings of a higher ambition, or by more favorable caprices of fortune. The soul of such a man will be filled with a blessed peace; noble sight to the anxieties and pains that harass the heart of the proud; an imperturbable tranquillity will possess him. He destroys, from its roots, and by a blow, the network of sensitiveness, the soul's torment, whose fibres reach the heart and make life miserable for so many. No matter what may befall him, whether he be scorned, or neglected, or calumniated, or his inferiors preferred, or he pass his life in misery, his heart is in God: nothing can disturb him. What bliss like this! A foretaste of heaven! It is not my purpose to give you a lecture on humility. I wish rather to invite you to consider some of those things that are apt to produce sentiments of this virtue. "It is better to feel compunction than define it, better to do the will of the Trinity, than to talk learnedly of the Trinity."

To become thoroughly humble; we have but to consider, what we are, how absolutely we are nothing of ourselves, and how utterly dependent we are upon Almighty God. We are creatures: no word expresses a dependence more absolute, a self-insufficiency more complete. To create implies to bring forth from nothing: a thing created has nothing of its own. Whatever it is, and whatever it has, it must receive from its Creator. Whatever, then, man is, or has, all comes from God. Our bodies, our souls, our faculties; all are the gifts of God entrusted to our keeping, for our own use, and yet to subserve His honor and glory. Of the gifts, whether of nature or of grace, which we have received, we shall one day be required to give a rigid account: and as of those to whom much has been given, much will be required, so, those who have received more than others, will have to give a more rigid account.

As we have been created, there was a time when we were not. But a few years since, we were nothing; and, had it been the will of Almighty God, such we should have remained forever. It was His omnipotent power and goodness that called us forth from nothingness and endowed us with existence; that gave us our bodies, and created our immortal souls, gifted with wondrous faculties, and capable of achieving an eternity of bliss, or an eternity of woe. And, once in existence, we had been insufficient for ourselves: were it not for the Almighty Power which called us into being and continued to sustain us, we should have fallen back into our original nothing.

This continual dependence upon God, is a subject suitable to excite the deepest humility. It is obvious, too; but, in proportion as it is obvious, it is neglected. Why, even the elements which surround us and are necessary for our support and life, may become fatal to us. There is death in the air we breathe, in the water we drink, in the food we consume. Take air: how soothing, who could exist without it? Yet, let that air become the hurricane; what can withstand its destructive fury? Take heat: what more necessary for life? Yet, let the spark fall upon an inflammable substance; and soon it is a conflagration which will reduce to nothing the most enduring structures of human workmanship or the noblest efforts of human art; burying in its ruins, it may be, thousands of human beings. Take water: how useful, how obedient in its littleness! But, let the boundaries which Providence has put between land and sea be removed; and how soon will it carry havoc and destruction through a country. No; man is not the master of nature, though he seems to be: he is the creature and victim of the elements. It is only God's conserving hand that preserves him from ruin. This earth would crumble and be dissolved but for God. You have heard of earthquakes. The word carries terror to the bravest heart. Yet this earth of ours is continually quaking; imperceptibly to us, it is true; but ascertainable by the instruments and observations of scientific men. In three thousand five hundred years, there have been eight thousand earthquakes; an average of about two a year. I need not refer to history for instances of these dreadful visitations, which reveal how utterly we are dependent upon the hand of God; how, if that hand were for one moment withdrawn, destruction and nothingness would at once ensue. How profoundly humble should we not be! how gladly, and with what deep thankfulness should we not confess that, of ourselves, we are, indeed, nothing; that what we have, is all from God, Who alone is good and exceedingly to be feared and adored!

Created and sustained by Almighty God, how miserable is man! Born of a woman, he lives but a short time, and has many miseries entailed upon him; and, notwithstanding the wonderful faculties with which he has been endowed,—his form and gifts of body, his power of intellect, the freedom of his will, the universality of his ideas, his capabilities of acquiring knowledge and of practising virtue, his dominion over all things, all of which but too clearly mark his exaltation over all other created things,—how prone to sin, how subject to passion, how full of misery! With all his great endowments, how contemptible he is! He has heaven-born aspirations, the proof of his destiny; but hell-born passions, the result of his fallen nature; he aspires to the true and the good; but is deluded with error and pursues evil. How much of nobleness, how much of meanness; how much of generosity, how much of selfishness; how much praise for virtue, how downward a proclivity to vice; how emphatic an approval of the law of the mind, how abject a slavery to the law of the members.

See a man in his health and vigor: broad shoulders, powerful chest, well-knit sinews, elastic step, no trace of sickness, a picture of health; he walks the earth a very king in his strength, glorying in it, and feeling himself equal to any effort or endurance. How much is required to unman him? Why, a three days' pneumonia will bring that strong man to his death-bed. A slight blow on the head will send him into howling madness. It is well to feel the humbling hand of sickness, or the icy touch of death. Then it is, that we look at things in their right light; for then a light as from another world shows us how contemptible man is. It is then, that we understand that God is great, that man is nothing.

Well does the Psalmist say "What is man or the son of man, that Thou shouldst visit him?" What is a man to all men? what are all men to the world? what is the world to the universe of worlds? what is all that God has made to God Himself? Think you that, if you were dropped out of existence, you would be missed among men? No more than the bud is missed in the forest. Think you that, if all the men now on the earth were to perish, they would be missed before God? No more than the leaves which strew the earth in autumn time are missed in the fruitfulness of nature at the return of spring. Nay, more; think you that, if this atom of nature which we call earth, the solid earth, should thaw and melt into the elements that compose it, and the great seas should dry up, and the laws that hold all things together should fail, and the sun and stars and moon disappear forever;—think you that all these would be missed from God's works? No more than the ocean shrinks because of the continual evaporation; no more than the earth crumbles because of the removal of an atom; no more than the glory and splendor of the sun is lessened by the loss of a ray. Other suns and stars and moons would shine, other earths would revolve; and, perhaps, God would be worshipped by other and more faithful adorers. His name would still be glorified. In such considerations, then, we may learn how insignificant we are,—not as much to God as the lowest creature is to us.

The termination of our earthly career, the prospect of the grave, to which we are insensibly yet continually hastening, is equally calculated to excite in us sentiments of the most unfeigned humility. The advantages of wealth, of mind, and of body, which we at present enjoy and which are apt to make us proud, will not be ours forever. We have them but in keeping for a time. Every day brings us nearer to the period when we shall have to give them up, with a rigid account of the use we have made of them. Soon the bodies which you now pamper and treat with every indulgence, will be the food of worms; your beauty of form and feature will be lost in dissolution. Your riches will be followed by the poverty of the grave. Your distinctions will give way to its obscurity. Your reputation will be inherited by another. Your very names will perish from the minds of those by whom, you now think, you will never be forgotten.

More eloquent, by far, than any sermon that

preacher ever preached, is the lesson taught us by the grave. There, we see how insignificant, how truly contemptible man is. There we learn our real value. It is there, by contemplating what we shall be, that we can best understand what we are. It is there that every feeling of pride goes out, that we learn how cheap are human treasures, how short are human pleasures, how vain are human distinctions, how empty the pride and pomp and magnificence of this world: the shortness of life, the nothingness of all things human. Carry all human pride and avarice and pleasures and honors and power,—all that men live for, and, sometimes, even die for,—to the mouth of the grave; contemplate it all in the light which issues even from that darkness, and what is it all worth? Not even the dust to which it shall one day be reduced. There we learn that God alone is great, and that man is but misery and sin.

The uncertainty of our eternal salvation and the continual risk of falling from God's grace and being lost, is another motive to preserve in the soul an abiding sense of our weakness, and of our continual dependence upon God's help and mercy. With fear and trembling are we to work out our salvation. Whatever may be our present dispositions, we have no security of continuing in them till the end. After persevering for years, we may fall, to rise no more, to be lost forever. The just man of to-day, may be the obstinate sinner of a time to come. We are no better than others who, at some period of their lives, were much holier and gave even greater promise of being saved than we, and who afterwards fell. We should enter into the sentiments of the great Apostle who, although he had converted nations, was so inflamed with charity that he wished even to be anathema for his brethren; and yet feared that after he had preached to others, he might become a reprobate himself. They who stand should take heed lest they fall. How far removed should every thought of pride be from souls, so continually and imminently exposed to the danger of falling into sin and perishing eternally.

If ever there was a time and country in which this virtue was needed, it is now and in this, our own land. Here, where every novelty finds its partisans: where so many arrogate to themselves the right to interpret the Scriptures in spite of the admonition of the Apostle: where men who find it as much as they can do, in the time at their disposal, to master some knowledge of their professions, and who spend the week in worldly affairs, undertake to decide the most important truths of religion, in odd half hours: where men have that little learning which is always a dangerous thing, and lack that deep philosophy which will always lead to the Church: where it is accounted a degradation of reason to believe; while it is, in fact, an exercise of the noblest reason to prostrate our minds before the truth and authority of God: here, I say, there is need of that humility of the intellect which enables one to give a prompt and unfaltering submission to the truths of faith which God has vouchsafed to reveal.

Moreover, there is need, too, of humility of the heart. We may not be bound to acquire the deep self-abasement of the saints: but every man is bound to have that degree of this virtue, which will enable him to bring his passions into a prompt and abiding conformity with the law of God.

Neglect no opportunity of practising this twofold humility. Remember you can only become humble, by practising humility. St. Bernard says: " If we do not exercise humiliation, we cannot attain unto humility ; for humiliation is the road to humility and produces it, as meekness in suffering tribulation and injuries, produces patience."

Frequently pray to the Holy Ghost to grant you this two-fold humility: that of the mind, by which we may ever know the truth and abide therein; that of the heart, by which we may ever keep God's holy law.

THE LOVE OF GOD OUR TRUE INTEREST.

And one of them, a doctor of the law, asked him, tempting Him:

Master, which is the great commandment in the law?

Jesus said to him: Thou shalt love the Lord thy God with thy whole heart, and with thy whole soul, and with thy whole mind.

This is the greatest and first commandment.

And the second is like to this: Thou shalt love thy neighbor as thyself.

On these two commandments dependeth the whole law and the prophets.—Matt. xxii. 35-40.

JESUS had closed the mouths of the Sadducees respecting the resurrection of the dead. One would think that from their discomfiture, the Pharisees would have learned wisdom and held their peace. But they, hearing that He had silenced the Sadducees, determined to tempt, that is, to try whether he was, indeed, possessed of the extraordinary wisdom which the people gave Him credit for; or it may have been for the purpose of having the opinion of Jesus concerning a question agitated among themselves as to which was the greatest commandment. Then the doctor of the law asked Him, "Teacher, which is the great commandment in the law?" Jesus replied: " Thou shalt love the Lord thy God with thy whole heart, with thy whole soul, and with thy whole mind. This is the greatest and first commandment. And the second is like to it: Thou shalt love thy neighbor as thyself. On these two commandments hangeth the whole law and the prophets."

These two commandments are, indeed, the substance of the whole law; the fulfilment of all justice; the discharge of all the duties which we owe to God, our neighbor, and ourselves. Love is the keeping of the law. "Little children, love one another," says St. John, "for love is the fulfilling of the law." Of course, the love spoken of in our text is that supernatural love which is founded on faith and animated by hope; and therefore necessarily includes in itself the three Theological virtues, which are required and which suffice for salvation. There is no duty which is not taught, there is no sin which is not forbidden, by this Divine command of love.

The command of loving God and that of loving our neighbor are so intimately connected together, the one so necessarily springs from the other, that one cannot exist without the other. We cannot love God unless we love our neighbor. "If you love not your neighbor whom you see, how can you love God whom you see not." We cannot love our neighbor unless we love God. There would be wanting a sufficient motive to animate us to the love of our neighbor. Hence, these two commandments may be reduced to one. If we love God, we love our neighbor; if we love our neighbor, we love God. Thou shalt love the Lord thy God with thy whole heart, with thy whole soul, and with thy whole mind; and thy neighbor as thyself for God's sake.

We are called upon to love. We are not called upon to fear. God would be served as a loving Lord. He would have us regard Him with the filial confidence, the tender love with which the child regards his parent. God is love. Love is the keeping of His law. He would unite us to Himself by the closest bonds of love. The fear of the Lord may be the beginning of wisdom; but it is only the beginning; it is not the perfection of wisdom. No one should be content with a love of God so imperfect; he should seek to advance to that perfect love which casts out fear. This is why the Council of Trent admonishes confessors to do what they can to excite in penitents sentiments of contrition springing from the love of God, and from the consideration of His Divine Goodness.

What then is it to love God? To love God is to prefer God to all things, to be willing to lose all things rather than offend Him. When we speak of preference, we are not to be understood of any mere speculative or theoretical preference, nor logical deduction that God is greater than all things else; but of the preference of the heart and mind; and the working of this preference into our lives, making it to control and give shape to our thoughts, and words, and actions; in fine, to our whole life. Thus it becomes a practical preference.

This love need not contain any degree of sensibility or feeling or fervor. Intensity of love is not required. Such love may be had for sensible objects, and is not always in our power. Our love should be the highest we are capable of, not intensively but appreciatively, as theologians say. We should prize or value or appreciate God above all other things: even life itself we should lose rather than offend Him. The man who has not this love, who is not in such disposition of soul as to be willing to die rather than offend God mortally, is not in the grace of God.

We should love God with our whole heart and soul and mind. At first, it might seem that each of these words did not have a direct and proper meaning, but that they are instances of the repetitions which abound in Scripture for the sake of emphasis, or to make the truth plainer to the reader. But the Fathers of the Church attach a distinct meaning to each. The heart is the seat of sensible love, the dwelling-place of the emotions. There is nothing more intimate to us than our hearts: hence, the heart is the synonym for everything sincere. Although we are not called upon to love God with a sensible love, yet there is a way in which it is possible for the heart to have its place in loving Him: by allowing nothing to take precedence of Him in our heart, by restraining its affections and denying the desires of the flesh so far as it may be required by His holy law. In this way, we shall love God with our whole heart. By our souls we think, reflect, reason, will. When we are convinced that God is the greatest good in Himself and the greatest good to us, and when we are determined to lose all rather than lose Him; then we love God with our whole soul. If the office of the mind in loving God is to be distinguished from that of the soul, it will be found in meditating upon Him, in abiding continually in His thought and remembrance. In this continual reflection on God we shall gain the highest wisdom. We shall not need the aid of books. We shall find it the very source and fountain of all knowledge.

We wish to present some motive to urge you to the love of God. Men generally are influenced by considerations drawn from duty, gratitude, interest, or pleasure.

Whatever influence duty may have among men in the affairs of life, it certainly has but little in the affairs of religion. Men are not induced to love God by the conviction that it is their duty. It is futile to attempt to urge men to the love of God by motives drawn from this consideration. It is beating the air, to demonstrate that it is our duty to love God. For it is before all reasoning and is made known to us by the very instinct of our nature. There is no one who is not fully persuaded of his duty of loving God. Yet, how few fulfil this obligation, obey this instinct!

Gratitude may be a higher and more potent motive. But gratitude, as a motive to the love of God, can only find place in one who has already advanced considerably in His love, and in appreciation of what Divine Goodness has done for him, and in a just feeling of what he in return owes Him. It argues a sensitiveness and delicacy of conscience which dreads to offend the Being from Whom we have derived so much, and for Whom, in return, we ought to make any sacrifice.

We find that, as in worldly affairs, so in religion, men, for the most part, are influenced by their interest or pleasure. Men may be induced to love God when they see that in it they will find their advantage or their happiness. Hence, we proceed to show how even your own interest and pleasure call upon you to love God: how that, without the love of God, you will never obtain that which everyone desires and labors daily to obtain.

Think not that a love of God springing from self-interest or pleasure may not be a true and perfect love of God. If we exclude self-interest from the love of God, we render love of God impossible. Man is created for, and is only happy in the enjoyment of perfect happiness. He seeks it in all he does. He places it in this, rather than in that object, because he hopes there to find it. What determines him to place it in God, unless the belief that he will there surely find it? Therefore, it is self-interest that prompts man to elect God as the object of his happiness. Besides, it is a proposition condemned by Innocent XII., that perfect love of God excludes all thought of self-interest. When St. Augustine speaks of charity consisting in the love of God for His own sake, he would exclude loving God for any temporal advantages, or for any good outside of Him; but he never thought of excluding the motive which urges us to elect God as our final end, as our supreme good, as the only source of our eternal beatitude.

It is our interest and our pleasure to love God with our whole heart and soul and mind.

Let me ask you, what it is you are all in search of? What is your first thought when you awake in the morning, and the last when you go to bed at night? What is the aim of the constant effort of every man to better his condition? What is the meaning of the unceasing change going on in the life of persons and of nations? why this discontent with what they have, and this greed for what they have not and yet believe within their grasp? It is that man seeks happiness: there is nothing nearer to his heart. In all things he seeks the purpose of his being. We are so constituted that we shall never be truly content except in the possession of perfect happiness. This desire has been planted in our breasts by an All-wise God, to direct us to our last end and final destiny. Our intellect apprehends a happiness which contains every good, and excludes every evil, and which lasts forever. Our hearts follow the guidance of the intellect and aspire after this infinite bliss. It is the vain endeavor to satisfy this desire with the limited and perishable goods of earth, that causes those struggles of man of which I have spoken.

And who has ever obtained this happiness? Has there ever been one, the cravings of whose soul were satisfied by the objects of this life? Ask the rich man who possesses everything that most men seek; who revels in luxury and gratifies every caprice that wealth can suggest: he will tell you that he is as little free from wants as the poor man; that his wealth gives birth to desires of which the poor man never dreams. Ask the man who seeks pleasure in passion: and he will tell you that it is vain to seek happiness in that by which strength is destroyed, health impaired, diseases engendered, death brought on; that his pleasure is nothing, compared to the keen and soul-consuming remorse with which it is followed. Ask the man who lives for distinction and who places his happiness in honors: and he will tell you that he enjoys far less peace of mind than the most obscure and despised of men; that he has not even the poor satisfaction of contemning the world, by whom, even if honored, he will soon be forgotten. No, my friends, the spiritual cravings of man's immortal soul cannot be satisfied by the corrupt pleasures of sense. It is a substance all spiritual; it can only rest in a happiness all spiritual. The cry of Solomon, "Vanity of vanities and all is vanity," is the experience of every son of Adam. The divine saying of St. Augustine, "Thou alone, O God, hast made the human heart, and in Thee alone can it find rest," is the voice of our common humanity. When Adam fell, happiness became an exile from earth never to return. From that day to the present, man has sought it on earth in vain; and will in vain forever seek it, till he possess it once more in the bosom of Almighty God.

You may ask, why cannot the human heart be satisfied with such happiness as this life affords? It matters little about the reason, when the fact is evident; yet, the reason is at hand. The human heart cannot be satisfied with this world because it was not made for it. Its destiny is higher, nobler, diviner. Everything is made for an end and can only be satisfied in its attainment. As the eye is made to see, and is only happy in the exercise of its function; as the intellect is made for knowledge, and is only at rest in the possession of wisdom; as the will is made for love, and is only content when loving and loved; so man with all his faculties is made for an infinite and eternal felicity, and can be satisfied with nothing less.

What, then, is our interest, what is wisdom for us? Should we not profit by the experience of all men? Can we imagine that the universal disappointment of humanity will be reversed in our case? Do we doubt our death, because we have not yet died? What would you think of him who could believe that he would never die? Now, you might as well doubt your death, as doubt that you shall never come by felicity in the things of this life. Why not, then, lay the lesson to heart at once? Since universal experience teaches the impossibility of finding real happiness here below, why not detach yourselves from the goods of life, and seek your happiness where experience and reason and religion teach that it can alone be found? Is it not wise to profit by the experience of others? Must we endure calamity before we take measures to avoid it? Do we wait for death to teach us that we all must die? Why wait for disappointment and misery to teach us, that, here below, there is nothing but disappointment and misery?

But go, plunge into the pleasures of life, enjoy them to the full: amass riches, acquire honors and rise high in the world ; seek to gratify your heart's desires with all that life affords: yet a time will come, if no other, at least that solemn hour in which you close your eyes forever upon this world to open them to eternity, when you will keenly realize, in all the bitterness and agony of an unavailing regret, the divine truth I would to-day teach ; when you will feel, in your heart of hearts, that " All is vanity and vexation of spirit;" when the sad experience of a disappointed life will wring from your soul, " Thou alone, O God, hast made the human heart, and in Thee alone can it find rest."

Learn wisdom while there is yet time. Be assured of this all-important lesson which you have not yet learned. Detach your hearts from this world before it is too late. Seek happiness where alone it is to be found. Delude not yourselves with the broken and empty cisterns of human felicity. Defile not your heaven-destined souls by contact with the dross of this world. Let not your hearts rest upon its objects, for its glory soon passes away. Seek not its pleasures, its riches, its honors, for they bring not peace but rather affliction to the soul.

What is the history of every man ? What is the history of the world? What is it but the record of human hope and human disappointment? of human misery and human despair ? All those objects in which we find pleasure or place our happiness,—youth with all its promise, manhood with all its vigor, old age with all the love and respect which it inspires, talent and genius with all the interest which they create, beauty of face and form, grace of accomplishments, the projects of human ambition, the enterprises of human industry, the distinction and honors which adorn or emulate men,—all quickly pass away and leave the soul devoid of any real or lasting contentment.

Is it not, I ask, your interest to love God, and thus attain to that happiness which, with every pulsation of the heart and every effort of your soul, you are seeking in vain in this life? Be wise. What you are in quest of is not to be had here below; in God alone is it to be found. Raise your hearts to the Beatific Vision, if you would attain happiness, pure and unalloyed. It will be in the possession of God, in the contemplation of His boundless beauty, His absorbing loveliness that our souls will be at perfect rest. He will fill them with such torrents of delight that they shall neither know nor desire any other felicity.

Here below, encased in this body of flesh and surrounded with a world of sense, we have but little understanding and less taste for spiritual pleasure. But when our souls shall have been separated from their bodies, they will seek only the bliss proper to a spiritual substance. Even the desires of sensible felicity which we feel are but the outcome and expressions of the one great, sovereign desire which possesses the soul of man. God will so satisfy this desire that it can seek nothing more. He will be knowledge to the mind, love to the will, unfailing bliss to the memory. What more can man desire? What else is necessary to satisfy his aspirations, to consummate his happiness?

And now, when I come to this part of my subject, the infinite perfection, the unutterable glory, the illimitable goodness of the God-head, and the bliss and the delight and the love and the transport thence resulting as the eternal destiny of the souls of the elect, I must confess that its description is beyond all powers of comprehension and all reach of the imagination. It would require words which it is not given to man to utter. This it is that it has never entered the heart of man to conceive.

I might reason upon the subject, and tell you that marvellously beautiful as this world is, God could have created a world infinitely more perfect. I might argue from the infinitude of the Divine Nature, and show you that God must be a Being of boundless goodness and sovereign perfection. I might remind you that, although the angels have been in contemplation of God from their creation, they have not yet begun to comprehend His infinite glory and unspeakable attributes; that the Blessed Virgin, permitted as she doubtless is to see more of God than all the blessed spirits together, has as yet but caught the merest glimpse of His Divine Nature. Yet all this would be but to reason; we should have still to infer what God's beauty and glory really is; and to infer a thing, is not to have that vivid perception of it which description, when it is possible, alone can give. It would require some Saint of God to speak worthily of the divine beauty: some St. Theresa, who was so beside herself with the love of God, inspired by vivid realization of His divine goodness and perfection, that she went about continually calling upon trees, flowers, rocks and all nature to love Him: some St. Philip Neri, whose love of God was so sensible that it caused an enlargement of his side.

However, Holy Scripture supplies us with some facts from which we can form a faint idea of what divine beauty must be, and of the love which it engenders in the human soul. We are told by Scripture that "Moses saw God," and as if astonished that he could survive the vision of glory and majesty which must have filled his soul, it exclaims, "and he yet lived." St. Peter and two other of the apostles were permitted a glimpse of the glory of God: when Jesus was transfigured on Thabor the splendor of the Divinity shone about Him. They were so overcome with delight that they fell down in ecstatic homage and wished no longer to return to the world; they lost all relish for this life; longed there for ever more to abide, and to build three tabernacles: one to Jesus, one to Moses, and another to Elias. St. Paul was transported to the third Heavens and saw things which it is not given to man to utter. He was so overwhelmed by the glory which he beheld, that he knew not whether it was in the body or out of the body; that is, he knew not whether it was the soul separated from the body, or the body and soul together, that was raised to the throne of

God. And ever after was he anxious, did he vehemently long to finish his course, to receive his crown and be united to his God. "Lest the greatness of the disclosures made to him should puff him up, there was given to him a sting of the flesh, an angel of Satan to buffet him." To St. John, in Patmos, the island of his exile, the heavens were opened. He tells us what he saw in his Apocalyptic vision: the glory of the Son, the angels casting their crowns before Him, the presence of all the heavenly hosts. So transcendent was the glory of the God-head revealed to him that he exclaims: "Eye hath not seen, nor ear heard, nor hath it entered the heart of man to conceive what God has prepared for those who love and serve Him."

We read of saints, who, being permitted a mere gleam of the glory of God, were so ravished out of themselves that they were lifted from the earth and remained suspended in mid-air; of others, who, similarly divinely favored, became insensible to all around them, unmindful of their human condition, and whom, neither raging heat, nor fiercest cold, nor the most cruel torments could recall from their fond ecstacy. How else can we conceive the sufferings of the martyrs; how can we believe that they were ever able to meet death in such awful forms; how endure the frightful cruelties which for the most part attended their martyrdom, except that their torments were lightened, and their pain and agony assuaged, by the glory of God filling their hearts and rendering them in part, at least, insensible thereto. Is it too much to believe that that was granted to the martyrs which we knew was vouchsafed to St. Stephen the First of Martyrs? He, when he was stoned to death by the Jews, saw the heavens open and the Son of God standing at the right hand of the Father.

In view of all that I have said, I ask, is it not our interest, our highest, our only interest to love God? Can any acquisition compensate for the loss attending the want of the love of God? Can any happiness be compared to the happiness of loving God? What matters, then, how it fares with us in this world? What matters it to lose this world, if we gain the next? What profit will it be to gain this, if we lose the next? Should we not be willing to take up our cross and deny ourselves, and follow Jesus along the narrow path ensanguined with the blood and tears of martyrs and penitents that leads to heaven, in view of the eternal reward there awaiting us? or should we rather choose the broad and beaten and luxurious path so easily found and trod by the multitude of men which leads to eternal misery? What matters it how the short years of life be spent, if the unending years of eternity shall be passed in the glory of heaven? what matters it if we pass time in obscurity and in the contempt of men, if we shall be known and rewarded by God forevermore? The misery and poverty of this life cannot be weighed against unfailing riches in the life to come: the pleasures of this life cannot be an equivalent for the immortal pleasure of possessing God hereafter.

If, then, you would enjoy this undying happiness which comes from the presence and the possession of God, begin your eternal union with Him here below; bind yourselves to Him in the bonds of love so closely, that nothing can separate you from Him: be able to exclaim from your heart with St. Paul, "Who then shall separate us from the charity of Christ? tribulation? or distress? or famine? or nakedness? or danger? or persecution? or the sword? For I am sure that neither death, nor life, nor angels, nor principalities, nor powers, nor things present, nor things to come, nor might, nor height, nor depth, nor any other creature, shall be able to separate us from the love of God, which is in Christ Jesus, our Lord."

THE NEW YORK
PUBLIC LIBRARY,

ASTOR, LENOX AND
TILDEN FOUNDATIONS.

THE INCARNATION.

In the beginning was the Word, and the Word was with God, and the Word was God.

The same was in the beginning with God.

All things were made by Him: and without Him was made nothing that was made.

In Him was life, and the life was the light of men.

And the light shineth in darkness, and the darkness did not comprehend it.

There was a man sent from God, whose name was John.

This man came for a witness, to give testimony of the light, that all men might believe through him.

He was not the light, but was to give testimony of the light.

That was the true light, which enlighteneth every man that cometh into this world.

He was in the world, and the world was made by Him, and the world knew Him not.

He came unto His own, and His own received Him not.

But as many as received Him, He gave them power to be made the sons of God, to them that believe in His name.

Who are born, not of blood, nor of the will of the flesh, nor of the will of man, but of God.

And the Word was made flesh, and dwelt among us, (and we saw His glory, the glory as it were of the only-begotten of the Father) full of grace and truth.—St. John i., 1-14.

THERE are truths supreme in their character and of the mightiest import which become the tritest. We learn them in infancy, we grow up in their knowledge; we hear of them continually and on every side, until we become so familiar with them that, by reason of our very familiarity, we never reflect upon them; we are content to think and to talk of them by rote and custom without weighing the meaning of the words which we employ. Many of these truths are of so surpassing a nature, so unfathomable in their depth, that reflection, serious and long-sustained, would be necessary to obtain even the most imperfect and superficial knowledge of them.

Of these truths that of the mystery of the Incarnation of the Second Person of the Blessed Trinity stands pre-eminent. To say that the Incarnation is the most stupendous fact that has ever taken place on this globe of ours, is to say nothing: to say that it is greater than the creation of the world or than all that God has made, greater than even the creation of ten thousand worlds, would be but to declare the truth without at all giving any just idea of the greatness of the Incarnation: to say that it is the utmost limit to which God could exert His omnipotence, is only to repeat what St. Augustine has already declared. Yes; in the Incarnation, Divine power no less than Divine love is exhausted.

The Incarnation is the foundation of all religion: the fulfilment of God's promises; the accomplishment of the prophecies; the reversal of the doom of our race; the only source of our hope. It is the keystone in the arch of heavenly truths, which, if displaced, would involve all the other mysteries of religion in hopeless confusion and inexplicable disorder. It gives meaning and harmony and consistency to the truths of revealed religion, clearing up what is dark, and harmonizing what otherwise would seem discordant. It is the focus where converge all the rays of light which illuminate the moral world. As well might you extinguish the sun and see the physical world, as to understand the moral world, shutting off from view the mystery of the Incarnation.

Fix, then, the great fact of the Incarnation in your mind. Try to realize what we mean, when we declare that God has become man. Mind that these words are to be taken to the letter. When we say that God became man, we are not to be understood to speak figuratively or symbolically, as if we meant that the man Jesus was overshadowed by the spirit of God ; nor as if He was called the Son of God, as were many holy men in the Old Law. Nor must we think of the Incarnation in that dreamy, misty way, which so many do outside of the Church, and excuse themselves from expressing any definite opinion on the subject, as too high or mysterious. We must assent to and believe in the simple truth that the Eternal God became very man, and prostrate ourselves before Jesus Christ as He walked on earth and adore Him as the Eternal God. Dwell upon this thought, and let it sink into your hearts.

Think, then, of God, in whatever view gives you the most exalted idea of Him and His greatness. Contemplate Him as a Being, self-existent, drawing existence from nothing external to Himself, nor from Himself as from a cause: as a Being Who has existed from everlasting: Who when the world and all things will have passed away and been forgotten, yet will remain as immortal and as young as in the first dawn of the aurora: as the infinite Creator in Whose mind was formed the type of all things, and Whose infinite power called them into existence: as the ever-watchful Conserver, without Whose all-sustaining arm everything would at once relapse into its original nothingness: Whose far-reaching and efficient providence directs all things to an end worthy of His divine intelligence:—contemplate God in whatever light you can form your most exalted idea of Him, and then consider that it was this same, self-existent, eternal, all-knowing, all-powerful God Who came down upon earth and became man. Yes, it was the Eternal God Incarnate Who was conceived in Mary's womb, Who was fondled in Mary's arms and nourished at Mary's breast; Who reduced Himself to the condition of a helpless babe; Who grew as other children grew, Who suffered as others suffer, Who was subject to pain and want as others are; Who worked at a lowly trade, receiving no defilement therefrom; Who disputed with the doctors in the temple, Who went down to Nazareth and was subject to human parents; Who walked pensive along the blue lakes and banks of Judea, Who lived in poverty and suffering, and died in agony and torments. This is the stupendous, amazing fact which we must seek to realize. Fix it well in mind, and keeping in remembrance all that I have told you, overpowered by the thought that it is the Eternal God Who is born into the world, draw close to His lowly crib; and in prayerful recollection and devout contemplation, receive into your hearts some of the lessons and the lights which are to be drawn from the earnest contemplation of God becoming man to save mankind.

Why did Jesus come into the world? Alas, the story is an old one and a familiar one. It was to save us from the effects of Adam's sin, and from the effects of our own. Adam had sinned, and had entailed irreparable consequences upon all his descendants. He was the moral head of the race: in him we stood: as his obedience would have brought us eternal happiness, so his disobedience involved us in eternal misery. In strict justice, God could have allowed us all to perish; even as the angels who fell and are suffering unending woe. But He determined to show mercy to man. The angels understood better than man the malice of sin. Man was circumvented and surprised by the devil. No angel fell but through the act of his own will. The sons of Adam could have had no personal participation in his sin. There were circumstances then which mitigated the sin of man, and softened the anger of the Almighty.

Was the Incarnation absolutely necessary for man's redemption? Could he have been redeemed by no other way known to Divine wisdom? If a condign satisfaction was to be made, of course, nothing short of the Incarnation would have sufficed. But God could have been content with something less than a condign satisfaction. He could have accepted even an inadequate expiation. For, even the sacrifice of Christ, full and exhaustive even to overflowing as it was in every respect, yet needed to be accepted;—and, therefore, supposed some indulgence on the part of God the Father. A less ransom, then, than that which was actually offered, could have been accepted by Him. It was only because from eternity an adequate atonement had been decreed, that it became necessary for Christ to become man. But, since man could have been saved by something less, why had it been determined that a full and perfect satisfaction should be required? Why did God foreordain a sacrifice of so great price, when one of inferior value would have served the purpose of redemption? It was to manifest His infinite love, and to manifest it in the infinite manner which His infinite nature required. The Incarnation may have been, and was, the fittest, the most congruous manner for the redemption of mankind. Yet, it must ever remain true that the desire on the part of God to manifest His infinite love was its principal cause. You may meditate upon the subject until the mind grows weary, until the imagination is bewildered; you may consult the inspired writings, you may seek relief in the productions of the illuminated minds of the saints and doctors of the Church; and, so far as it is permitted to mortal to penetrate into this great mystery, you will never find any adequate cause for the Redemption other than that which St. Thomas, following St. John Damascene, gives: the infinite love of God, manifesting itself in the infinite manner proper to the infinitude of His nature.

God becomes man to manifest His infinite love!

This would seem, surely, enough to stagger human credibility. It would seem almost trifling with human reason; a far-fetched effort of fancy. Our minds are so limited, our little hearts are so filled with themselves; we are such utter strangers to disinterestedness, so self-seeking in our every feeling and every action; we so measure all things in heaven and on earth by the narrow rules of our philosophy, that it seems little short of preposterous to talk of a man dying for another; much less, that the Eternal God should stoop to our low condition, become man, and suffer and die out of love for us!

How few are there who give even of what is superfluous of their temporal goods, to relieve the needs of their fellow-men? How fewer still give of what is necessary, to them? How seldom will a man give that highest test of love, the laying down of his life for his friend? Here we see that God's ways are not as our ways, nor His thoughts as our thoughts. There is no proportion between the goodness of an infinite Being, and the little ray of that same goodness which is shed abroad in our poor hearts.

No human illustration can convey to us any idea of the depth and intensity of Divine love: of the vehement, mighty longing of God for every human soul. Not the pelican, striking open her breast and nourishing her young with her heart's warm life-blood, which is so often used to symbolize the love of the Saviour of our souls; not the love of the Roman matron who fed her famishing father with the milk from her own breasts; not the maddest love of the most frenzied lover; not the burning love of the bounding heart of the fondest mother at the return of her long-lost son, can give us even the faintest conception of the height, and depth, and breadth, and infinite tenderness of the love of God for the souls of men, redeemed and purchased at the price of His blood. Holy Scripture tries to declare this love to us under images, the most expressive of passionate, burning human love: "Can a mother forget her infant, so as to be unmindful of the fruit of her womb?" "Jerusalem, Jerusalem, how often would I have gathered thy children together, even as the hen gathers her chickens under her wing; but thou wouldst not." "Even as the bridegroom waiteth for his bride, so will God wait for thee."

Consider the nature of God. What is it but simple, ineffable, infinite goodness? Goodness is His very essence; it is not merely the most glorious attribute of all, but it is the very source of all. It is hard to describe those truths which we have by intuition, rather than by reasoning,—truths with which God Himself has lighted up our souls. It is hard to lift our minds to the contemplation of things so far above us, and so far removed from the ordinary sphere of our thoughts. But, lift your hearts, contemplate God as He is in Himself. What is He but goodness? What has His life been from the beginning? upon what has He spent the activity which is inherent in His nature, or, rather, which is at once His nature and His life? upon what, but in the contemplation of His infinite goodness? Behold the mysterious relations of the Three Adorable Persons! the Everlasting God-head! the Eternal Generation of the Son! the Eternal Spiration and Procession of the Holy Ghost! and you have the life of God from all eternity. The goodness of God is His very nature, when from it is generated the Second Person, coeternal, coessential, consubstantial with the Father; when the Second Person is the Infinite and Personal Expression of the Eternal Goodness of the Father. How infinite is this goodness and how infinite the loveliness of its nature, when from the mutual love which it engenders in the Father and in the Son, proceeds the Third Person, coeternal, coessential, consubstantial with the Father and the Son; when the Third Person is the Infinite and Personal Expression of the Eternal Love of the Father and of the Son. Let me explain. God from all eternity contemplating His essence, forms to Himself a perfect image of His goodness; "the very Figure of His substance and Splendor of His glory." This is the Eternal Generation of the Son. This image or knowledge of Himself is so pleasing to Him that He loves It and It loves Him with an infinite love. This Infinite Love is the Holy Ghost. Behold, then, how God is goodness in and by His very nature: how His goodness is infinite, in that it engenders the Infinite Person of the Divine Word: how it is infinite in its loveliness, in that proceeds from it the Infinite Person of Divine Love.

Goodness is in its nature diffusive. It cannot remain absorbed or centred in itself. It must go forth and communicate itself to some being or object outside of itself; otherwise it would cease to be goodness. The river must flow on from its source. The sun must necessarily diffuse light and heat. As water cannot but flow, as we cannot think of fire not giving forth light and heat, so we cannot conceive of goodness except as manifesting itself to others.

Goodness, too, must communicate itself in a manner and degree proportioned to the nature and capacity of him possessing it. The rush and flow of the water bear proportion to the volume and strength of the stream; light and heat are in the degree of the intensity of the fire. He who has much, should give much. We talk of princely generosity, kingly munificence, regal profusion; because from the reputed wealth and superabundant resources of kings and princes, we expect a manifestation in proportion.

When we think of Divine goodness, we expect it to correspond to the Divine nature. As God is infinite goodness, we expect it to be manifested in an infinite manner. God works not after the manner of men. He does nothing by measure; everything in an infinite, God-like manner. It is as natural for God to act in an infinite manner, as for man to work by limit. When God would declare His power, He made the marvellous and illimitable world which we see around us. When it pleased Him to disclose His justice, He opened the great pit with its endless duration. When He came to reveal His goodness He did it in the same infinite way. When He made the world,

THE INCARNATION. 247

He made it to show forth His goodness; still it was but a limited exhibition, and by no means exhaustive of His resources. When He made man, He did it, too, from goodness; yet, after all, it was only a finite revelation of His love. But in the Incarnation, He shows forth His goodness in the infinite manner in which we should expect an infinite being to act, and His divine goodness carries Him as far as His divine wisdom can devise.

Divine wisdom could go no farther. God's goodness in a manner exhausted itself when He became man. The Incarnation was the utmost limit, the final consummation, the infinite exhibition and expression of Divine goodness. Behold the reason of the Incarnation: God's infinite goodness manifesting itself in the infinite manner which the infinitude of the Divine Nature required.

Why! so true is it that the Divine Incarnation was the influence of Divine goodness that it is an opinion entertained by the greatest theologians, that God would have become man, even if man had never fallen. St. Thomas admits it as, at least, probable; and theologians like Suarez, second only to St. Thomas, advocate it strongly. It is this thought that Cardinal Newman has before him when he says: "I had had it in mind to come on earth among innocent creatures, more fair and lovely than them all, with a face more radiant than the Seraphim, and a form as royal as that of Archangels, to be their equal yet their God, to fill them with my grace, to receive their worship, to enjoy their company, to prepare them for the heaven to which I destined them; but, before I carried my purpose into effect, they sinned, and lost their inheritance, and so I come indeed, but come, not in that brightness in which I went forth to create the morning stars and to fill the sons of God with melody, but in deformity and in shame, in sighs and tears, with blood upon My cheek and My limbs laid bare and rent."

We have meditated upon the Incarnation as the Infinite Expression of Divine Love. I have tried to explain, in words how feeble, I am fully conscious, the stupendous mystery of Christ's amazing love. Let not the effort have been in vain; let not your meditation be without fruit. Let the remembrance of Divine love excite in your heart reciprocal sentiments of love. And, as he who wishes to gain the love of another does it by narrating to him his acts of goodness, so let the recital of Divine goodness excite in you sentiments of love. Let the claim of God for your love be recognized. His love will save us, or His love will damn us;—save those who hearken to it, and give love for love;—damn those who despise the riches of His goodness, and patience, and long-suffering; not knowing that the benignity of God leadeth to repentance.

May the union which Jesus Christ, in this mystery, takes up with our humanity be for each of us an eternal one: may it be the symbol and pledge of our eternal union with Him hereafter. May all men come to believe and to adore this great mystery of the Incarnation, that it may be no longer to the Jews a stumbling-block, and to the Gentiles folly; but to all, the wisdom of God and the power of God. May those who already believe it, come to practise the lessons and imitate the examples set by their Redeemer. May all come to know the truth, and in their lives be faithful to it. May all come to share in the blessings and happiness which Jesus has purchased for them by His incarnation.

THE BIRTH OF CHRIST.

And it came to pass, that in those days there went out a decree from Cesar Augustus, that the whole world should be enrolled.

This enrolling was first made by Cyrinus, the governor of Syria.

And all went to be enrolled, every one into his own city.

And Joseph also went up from Galilee, out of the city of Nazareth into Judea, to the city of David, which is called Bethlehem: because he was of the house and family of David.

To be enrolled with Mary his espoused wife, who was with child.

And it came to pass, that when they were there, her days were accomplished, that she should be delivered.

And she brought forth her first-born Son, and wrapped Him up in swaddling clothes, and laid Him in a manger; because there was no room for them in the inn.

And there were in the same country shepherds watching, and keeping the night-watches over their flock.

And behold an angel of the Lord stood by them, and the brightness of God shone round about them; and they feared with a great fear.

And the Angel said to them: Fear not; for, behold, I bring you good tidings of great joy, that shall be to all the people:

For, this day, is born to you a Saviour, Who is Christ the Lord, in the city of David.

And this shall be a sign unto you. You shall find the infant wrapped in swaddling-clothes, and laid in a manger.

And suddenly there was with the angel a multitude of the heavenly army, praising God, and saying:

Glory to God in the highest, and on earth peace to men of good-will.

THE BIRTH OF CHRIST.

And it came to pass, after the angels departed from them into heaven, the shepherds said one to another : Let us go over to Bethlehem, and let us see this word that has come to pass, which the Lord hath shewed to us.

And they came with haste ; and they found Mary and Joseph, and the infant lying in the manger.

And seeing, they understood of the word that had been spoken to them concerning this child.

And all that heard, wondered ; and at those things that were told them by the shepherds.

But Mary kept all these words, pondering them in her heart.

And the shepherds returned, glorifying and praising God, for all the things they had heard and seen, as it was told unto them. —St. Luke ii., 1-20.

WHEN we contemplate the birth of Christ on a winter night, in a miserable stable, destitute of all the comforts of life, with the meanest animals for companions, with a humble virgin for a mother, and a poor carpenter for a foster father, we naturally ask ourselves, why Christ came into the world in such a state? Why did the Eternal, when He condescended to come among men, come in such squalid poverty, such utter self-abasement? Why was He not created by God without human parents, or at least, why was He not born of some great queen? Why was not some mighty king His foster father? Why was He not born in a palace instead of a stable? Why was not His crib, of gold set with precious stones, instead of a manger? Why did not all the choirs of heavenly spirits sing that song of glory, instead of a few? Why were not all men ready to follow the star, and coming fall down and adore Him, instead of the three wise men from the East?

Why did He not appear in such a manner as to arrest the attention of all men? Why was He not surrounded with a magnificence that would reflect, however feebly, the splendors of His heavenly court? Why was He not attended with that pomp and ritual of ceremony by which even earthly kings hedge in and seek to maintain their dignity? Why was He not surrounded by the noblest of the sons of men to do His every pleasure? In a word, why should God be born in a condition from which even the meanest of men would shrink?

We answer that He was born in such utter humiliation because He was God. Had He been born as we would have Him, He would not have manifested, so clearly, His divinity, as He does, when He comes into the world in profound contempt of all that we prize, when He shows Himself superior to the vain thoughts of our soft and sensual nature. Why should He, the Lord of all things, surround Himself with the inventions of our pride and sensuality? Why should He have sought the luxury and pomp which only reveal the weakness of our nature? Why should He have obscured His glory, by clothing Himself with our meanness? Man seeks to exalt himself by such means; God would have bemeaned Himself by having recourse to them. If Christ had come into the world after the manner that human wisdom would dictate, His birth would be too human, to be divine. It would be too redolent of human weakness and human pride. In it would be seen the thoughts of man; of the earth, earthy. In it we should in vain seek the infinite difference there must be between our manner of conceiving the birth of a God, and what the birth of a God should really be. In it we should fail to see those lofty thoughts which are alone worthy of the Divinity: that immeasurable superiority which must exist between the wisdom of God and the folly of man.

Human weakness may seek to exalt itself by glorious raiment, may surround itself with a ritual of ceremony, may fence itself round with exclusive bounds, within which no man may enter. But the Eternal God, the source of all true greatness, stands in no such need. He only manifests His greatness, He only shows that He is God, by His sublime contempt for such human contrivances.

If Jesus had shown a partiality for the arts and inventions of human effeminacy, could we ever have believed Him divine? Where would be the simplicity and austerity which we instinctively attribute to an all-perfect being, to a God-made man to reform mankind by His example? Who, in reading the life of Mahomet, can believe that he was what he pretended to be, because of his proneness to human weakness and gratification? He who would reform mankind, must show that he is not himself a slave to the vices and passions which he condemns. He who preaches a doctrine higher than that which he practices, cannot be divine.

But, in the way in which Jesus comes into the world: bereft of His glory, destitute of every comfort, reduced to the condition of the most abject creature; showing Himself superior to all human weakness, so completely detached from all things human; exhibiting such lofty contempt for the ways and maxims and wisdom of this world, we see all divine: the elevation above all human notions, the simplicity, fortitude, sublimity, which we necessarily attach to our idea of God.

Men marvel at the self-humiliation to which our Lord brought Himself in this mystery of His birth. Will they bear in mind the depth of the abasement to which He reduced Himself, by at all becoming man, by ever leaving His seat at the right hand of His father? Unspeakable was the condescension that He should at all think of our redemption. Birth in a stable, is a fitting birth for a God who vouchsafed to be conceived of a woman; of a God who relinquished His glory and even His divinity, so far as it was possible, to become man. Birth in a crib, is a fit prelude to a life of suffering, to a passion of unutterable woe, to death upon a cross.

Men wonder at His lowly birth. Let them look around them in this world. Do they see His visible presence anywhere? True, all things proclaim His existence; but, where is God to be seen so visibly manifested, that even the infidel cannot indulge his doubts? Is He not a hidden God in the midst of the most splendid manifestations of His being and perfections? He is, indeed, a God of mystery: existing everywhere, yet visible nowhere. If, then, He hides Himself in His birth, He only does that which he has done in the world; He only acts in consistency with the other mysteries by which He has disclosed Himself to us. In it, His humiliation is infinite because His love is limitless. His love is to be calculated by what He has done to show it. The depth of His humiliation, is the measure of His love. He could not have stooped lower: His love could not be greater.

Christ came into the world not only to redeem it, but to unteach men the errors into which they had fallen, and to teach them the lessons of true life and divine wisdom.

Since the first estrangement of man from his Creator, since this first breaking up of the harmony in which his faculties of soul and body were held by the supernatural grace in which he was created, there have prevailed in this world three mighty evils, the source of all others. To these may be reduced all human passion, human avarice, human ignorance, human error, and all that is comprehended in the "Lust of the flesh, the lust of the eyes and the pride of life." Track any evil to its source, and you will find it to spring from inordinate self-love or blind attachment to sense or that wisdom so emphatically called the wisdom of this world. But Jesus comes to reclaim man from his errors, to undo the work of the fall, to point out to him the way of freedom from the tyranny which self-love, sense, and worldly wisdom have established in his heart. In the external circumstances of His birth: in its self-sacrifice, utter detachment from the things of sense, in its profound contempt for the wisdom of this world, behold a sovereign, three-fold remedy for the sovereign, three-fold source of all evil. In His birth, He exhibits the lessons which He afterwards taught. He begins to reform mankind, the moment He comes among them. Faithful preacher and guide, He asks no man to do what He had not Himself already done from infancy.

In what light does all self-love appear, in presence of the self-sacrifice exhibited in the mystery of Christ's nativity?—self-love, which prompts a man to prefer himself to others, his passions and interests to all other considerations,— to even the just claims of others;—thence resulting all sins against justice: self-love, stifling all feelings of generosity, freezing the fount of sympathy and pity to the extent of not undergoing a slight sacrifice for sake of others;—thence proceeding all breaches of the golden law of doing as we would be done by. Who can do his neighbor wrong? who can fail to do him every good, when he beholds so much done for himself? Who can think about himself and his rights, when he beholds the Lord of heaven and earth voluntarily abandon all, and bring Himself to such utter forgetfulness of His character and dignity? How withering the condemnation of all self-seeking and self-love! How divine the commendation of self-denial and self-sacrifice! In what light appear all luxury and ease and self-gratification; all that men live for,—in presence of the Lord of all things in such utter destitution, deprived of even the comforts to which the humblest of men feel they have a rightful claim? What an insight is given to us into the truth of the words: "He that will come after Me, let him take up his cross and follow Me:" "He that loses his life, shall gain it; he that gains his life, shall lose it." There is need of suffering and mortification. There can be no true religion without it, —the royal way of the cross.

In what light is seen this sensible world with all those sensible objects that men pursue, in presence of the external circumstances of the birth of Christ? Man comes into life with his soul athirst for happiness; a thirst implanted in his soul to lead him to his last end. He looks around and finding not God, he seeks and fastens on some sensible object for his happiness. The veils of this sensible world hide from him the God for whom he longs and for whom he has been made. The demon sense tyrannizes over us and holds us in its iron grip. It begins its sway when first we open our eyes on the objects around us. It only relaxes its hold, when we close our eyes upon them forever. We are encased in a body of sense. We seek only the things of sense. Pleasure, traffic, honor, fame, are the husks upon which we would feed the spiritual cravings of our immortal heaven-destined souls tarrying for a little while on earth. Sense dominates us. We are too sluggish to force its iron grip, to break its fatal spell, to chase the foul illusion from us, and to rise to the eternal realities beyond this world. But how this veil of sense is rent in twain, in the study of the external circumstances of Christ's nativity! How real the future life and all the truths of religion, when He who best knew their value and reality, did not hesitate to appear in such humiliation to obtain them for us. How unreal this life and all that men live for, when He who best knew their worth, made so little of them in the circumstances of His birth.

As to the vices that sense creates in our souls, lust, sensuality, desire of display, greed of gain, love of honors, thirst of pleasure; how bitter the censure of all these, in the manner in which Christ is born! Who has the heart to seek the riches of this life, when he sees the Infinitely rich having not whereon to lay His head. What an insight do we not get into His teaching, "Blessed are the poor in spirit, for theirs is the kingdom of heaven"! We begin to understand the necessity of poverty, we begin to feel the danger of riches, we realize that His words are not an exaggeration: "It were easier for a camel to pass through the eye of a needle, than for a rich man to enter the kingdom of heaven."

Behold the contempt poured upon all human wisdom, in the humiliation in which Christ is born! Little would worldly wisdom have ordained that Birth in a stable, for the reclaiming of man and the conversion of the world. But such is the essential difference between the wisdom of God and the wisdom of men. What is folly with man is wisdom with God: what is wisdom with man is folly with God. Worldly wisdom is narrow and short-sighted. It extends not beyond its own horizon. It is made up of considerations altogether human. It makes little account of anything that does not affect the senses. It feels its self-sufficiency. It measures out all things in heaven and on earth by the narrow rules of its philosophy. It contemns that with which it agrees not; it laughs to scorn what it cannot comprehend. In the birth of Christ we see how Divine wisdom contemns every suggestion of this wisdom of man. We behold the lofty superiority of the intelligence of the Creator over the creature, and the essential difference between the Divine idea of how the Saviour of men should come into the world, and that birth which men would have deemed congruous. Human wisdom was not invoked in the accomplishment of the mystery of Christ's birth. Truly does He show His divinity, by turning what with men is folly, and weakness, and humiliation, into instruments of His wisdom, and power, and glory.

In his birth Jesus teaches us what men have ever sought to know and ever refused to learn; what men are continually taught, and yet continually contemn: the secret of human happiness. It does not depend upon external circumstances. Its home is built within the heart, where it may exist in spite of the most untoward and abject external circumstances. Felicity of soul in the midst of misery, is the lot of those who have learned the lesson of Christ's birth. Discontent of heart in the midst of worldly happiness, is the portion of those upon whom this lesson is lost. Whatever progress society may make, however the arts of life may advance, or the science of government improve, or the condition of the poor and destitute be ameliorated, it must always be that the greater part of men must labor and suffer. By the lessons of His birth, Christ teaches them how this condition may be borne with patience and resignation. He has compensated for its hardships, by making it meritorious of an eternal reward. By His own example, He has consecrated poverty: He has reversed the world's esteem of it. Before His birth, it was contemned and was the synonym of meanness: He has placed the poor in spirit above the rich of this world: ever since, voluntary poverty has been thought the higher state;—an evangelical perfection. The type of meanness has become the profession and glory of the noblest souls,—souls given entirely to God,—souls who seek to model themselves upon His divine example.

By being born a helpless child and in a stable, He wished to put His love for us in a sensible form. By that condition, He appeals most feelingly and powerfully to our warmed hearts. Although His incarnation was enough to show His love, yet if He had stopped at that, it would never have come home to the hearts and minds of most people; they might have reasoned and concluded that His love was infinite, but they would have never felt it; and religious truth to be efficacious must be felt. But when they behold the Eternal God born in the form of a little child, of a Virgin Mother, not having whereon to lay His head,—exposed to the cold of a winter's night, with the meanest animals for companions, conviction gives way to rapture, and we are overpowered by a manifestation of love which appeals so directly even to our feelings and senses.

The humility of the birth of Christ has shown itself to be a mystery of the power of God. Power! forsooth, the unbeliever may say, talk of power in that helpless infant who lies in a manger between an ox and an ass! Yes, I assert that Christ's lowly birth has been the Mystery of His power. St. Paul preached the cross and sufferings of Christ, as the Mystery of the power and wisdom of God. The lowly crib of Bethlehem has shown itself no less the Mystery of His wisdom and power. Behold the influence that has gone forth from that birth! See how it has revolutionized the world! How it has entered into and changed all the thoughts and sentiments and lives of men! What class, what sex, what age, what profession, what walk of life, has not felt this saving influence. Nor has this influence been of that human kind which lasts for a period and then disappears; but that which, beginning in obscurity, works imperceptibly, yet effectually and for all time; overcomes all obstacles; continually increases in power, and at length accomplishes its final purpose. It has proved itself to be one of the great moral forces, which, under the providence of God, and endued with His grace, has enlightened and exalted the human race. Such influences resemble nothing more than the great powers of nature.

The lessons of the birth of Christ are the very

essence of whatever is most valuable in our Christian civilization. All the great improvements of our race are to be traced to its heavenly and beneficent influences. The simplicity of that birth has confounded the wisdom of the world. Its self-denial has subdued the world's selfishness. Its love has won the hearts of men. And they have learned that He must be Divine Who shone with the virtues which belong to God alone. If the birth of Christ be not a mystery of power, then has Christ overcome the world by His weakness.

To-day Jesus Christ rules an empire of which the Cæsars, in their maddest ambition, never dreamed. They could command or kill the body, but over that which is noblest in man they had no control: that which is best was freest: but Jesus reigns supreme over an empire of souls. He is their first lisp, their consolation in life, their hope in death. To them His word is the word of eternal life. His life is their unceasing study. His death is their ransom from sin. His resurrection is the type and pledge of their own. He is the very God of their souls; and living and dying they bless His holy name. Was influence ever like to this! Was triumph ever more triumphant!

Whatever human wisdom may suggest, or however little to human eyes the facts may seem to warrant the statement, it cannot be doubted that Jesus Christ, according to His wisdom and in the manner which He proposed to Himself, has mastered the world. "Fear not, little flock, for I have overcome the world." This the disclosures of the last day shall make manifest. And how has He subdued it? There have been those who seemingly conquered parts of the world, but it has been by violence and bloodshed and by giving unbridled license to the passions. But Jesus has had resort to no such means. He is the God of peace, the God of love. His conquest has been by love and peace and good will,—by declaring a war to the death upon the strongest passions of the human heart. Others have won apparent triumph by yielding to the world. Jesus Christ has triumphed by compelling it to yield to Him, by teaching it to crucify the flesh with its concupiscences, by obtaining the assent of the mind to truths which it could not comprehend, and which in its pride it would naturally reject and contemn.

LOVE OF OUR NEIGHBOR.

And Jesus answered him: The first commandment of all is, Hear, O Israel: the Lord thy God is one God.

And thou shalt love the Lord thy God, with thy whole heart, and with thy whole soul, and with thy whole mind, and with thy whole strength. This is the first commandment.

And the second is like to it: Thou shalt love thy neighbor as thyself. There is no other commandment greater than these.

And the scribe said to Him: Well master, thou hast said in truth, that there is one God, and there is no other besides Him.

And that He should be loved with the whole heart, and with the whole understanding, and with the whole soul, and with the whole strength; and to love one's neighbor as oneself, is a greater thing than all holocausts and sacrifices.—St. Mark xii., 29-33.

THE passage which I have just read teaches us the lesson of brotherly love. It is the lesson which the Church so often places before us; the lesson which is laid down on every page of the Gospel and breathes from every action of our Saviour's life. "I give unto you a new commandment: that you love one another; as I have loved you, that you also love one another. By this shall all men know that you are My disciples, if you have love one for another." It hath been said, "Thou shalt love thy friend and hate thine enemy; but I say to you, love your enemy, do good to them that hate you, and pray for them who persecute and calumniate you." This lesson is the substance of all religion, the keeping of all law, the fulfilment of all justice.

The duty of loving our brother springs from, or rather is identical with, the duty of loving God. He who loves his neighbor does so because in him he sees the creature of God, made in His image, and redeemed with His blood. His love then flows from, or is one in fact with his love of God. He who loves God, loves his neighbor. He who loves his neighbor, loves God. If he loves not the one, he loves not the other.

Brotherly love is not a mere sentiment or emotion of the heart. It is not even the purest human sympathy. It is not even the most disinterested human benevolence. Human benevolence is a noble virtue, a mighty motive and one capable of vast results. It assists the needy, compassionates with the suffering, solaces the forsaken, and pours the balm of consolation into the wounds caused by grief and every manner of distress. Like human goodness, from which it springs, pure, disinterested benevolence is the choicest gift with which God has endowed our hearts. In the natural order, it would seem to be a reflex or emanation of God's own essential goodness. And yet, the purest human goodness and benevolence is not Christian charity,—this divine virtue is higher still. Human benevolence is destitute of an adequate principle to sustain it; it soon languishes and fails by its own innate unsteadiness and want of perseverance, or it is vanquished by the ingratitude and shortcomings of those who are its objects; or, founded as it is on a feeling of sentiment or even a transient conviction of duty which soon evaporates, it, too, evaporates with what was its source and support. Not so with Christian brotherly love. It has its principle and motives in the love of God. Every consideration it has for man is in and from the love of God whose image and creature he is. It is God, in the person of men, whom Christian brotherly love recognizes and serves. And in this service of God and the eternal reward thereto attached, it finds enough to sustain it, and to compensate it for any sacrifice, even of life itself, which it must make in its career.

The duty of brotherly love flows from the positive command of Jesus Christ: "A new commandment I give unto you, that you love one another." A "new mandate" it was, indeed. Such a virtue was unknown before Christ. It was His spirit, and He that first inculcated it among men. There may have been human sympathy and something of human benevolence in the pagan world. But Christian brotherly love was never dreamed of by the philosophers and sages of antiquity. It can only subsist among the worshippers of a common Father and God. Such worship is its principle and permanence. Polytheism knew nothing of the tenderness and strength of the ties of Christian charity.

It is not necessary that I should remind you of our common origin, common nature, common redemption, common heirship of the pardon and grace purchased by our Saviour, common weaknesses, common temptations, and common destiny, as so many arguments and inducements to the cultivation of this virtue. Nor should I prove to you the duty of loving your brother. No one needs proof to be convinced of his duty of loving God. No one requires demonstration of his obligation of loving his neighbor. He already knows it, and owns it. These are like the other duties and truths of religion,—admitted by all and practiced by few.

If, on the one hand, we consider how this duty of loving our neighbor is acknowledged by all, and, on the other, how few there are that practise it, we cannot but ask, how it is so widely and so generally neglected? It is chiefly because people excuse themselves from it on frivolous pretexts, which a little reflection will show to be such.

In looking about us and considering the various obstacles that charity encounters, we find the first and most fatal to be self-love and selfishness. Selfishness and charity are entirely incompatible, are in direct and positive antagonism. Self is necessarily fatal to what in its very nature is sacrifice of self. As well might light and darkness coexist, as generosity and selfishness, fraternal charity and self-love, in the same bosom. In every act of charity which we practise, there is necessarily an act of self-denial. If I give of my means to relieve the needs of my brother, I practise self-denial so far as to deprive myself of that which otherwise I would retain. If I check the risings of anger, or the promptings of ill-will against my brother, I practise self-sacrifice so far as to deprive myself of the satisfaction of gratifying my passion. If I drive from my heart rancor and bitterness towards my brother and supplant them with kindness and forbearance, I practise self-denial so far as to suppress one of the strongest passions of the human heart; that of hate. If I freely and from my heart forgive my brother the wrong that he has done me, and in patience and resignation submit to the injury and suffering thence resulting, banishing from my heart all resentment, and am even prepared to do him the good which, in charity, I am bound to render to another, I overcome the most ineradicable feelings of nature, and exercise a virtue which, in a manner, would seem too great for our human condition, but which God's grace has made possible and His law obligatory. Every act of brotherly love, then, implies self-sacrifice.

Charity is a union of hearts, a mutual communication of kind offices. No union can subsist without a foregoing of self on the part of individuals. No union can subsist while each member insists upon all the rights which, outside the union, he would have. Union implies the surrender of individual right. Advantages common to many must be purchased at the price of particular interests. Without this mutual self-sacrifice, no society or bond of charity could subsist. Now, it is manifest that selfishness and self-love, seeking itself in everything, unmindful of the claims of others, unwilling to practise self-denial in anything, is necessarily fatal to such union and harmony, and to the dictates of brotherly love. The human heart always seeks itself. It is only by restraint that it can be overcome. It is only by effort that it can practise disinterestedness. It is true, what you may say, that charity as known among men, carries with it very little sacrifice. Few give except what is superfluous to them. Fewer still what may be necessary. And who is the man that will put himself to any serious inconvenience or loss, for his neighbor's sake? True, indeed, charity as known and practiced among men carries with it very little sacrifice. But this only proves how rare charity is. Whether what I say may be in harmony with charity as its subsists among men, or not, it yet remains true that real charity in its nature is self-sacrificing.

If brotherly love does not imply self-sacrifice, why was it ever put under obligation? if it requires not more than inclination moves us to, or than may be agreeable to our natural propensity, or if it be but the experience of mere natural feeling, why was it ever made a matter of grave precept? It is not necessary to place the feelings of the heart under the constraint of law. Why was it declared the greatest of virtues, the first of commandments, the fulfilment of all justice, unless because of its intrinsic difficulty, and that he who fails not to discharge this duty, will overcome the temptations and obstacles in the way of the other virtues. For this it was, that immortal happiness was declared its just reward and eternal recompense.

Self-love must be destroyed in the heart in

which brotherly love would reign. What is it that engenders feelings of ill-will and hatred among friends? Self-love which prompts a man to seek offence or insult in the words and manner in which none was meant. What is it that breeds dissensions among the members of the same family? Self-love which moves each one to think that his rights are not respected, or his feelings not regarded or consulted. What is it that daily introduces disagreements and feuds in every pursuit and profession in life? Self-love which cannot brook rivalry, and accounts the success of another as an injury to itself. If, then, we would cultivate brotherly love for our neighbor, we must root out from our hearts this cursed love of self, this spirit of selfishness. We must assume greater self-forgetfulness, a more self-denying spirit; and a noble generosity should characterize all our actions to our fellow-men.

There are those who excuse themselves from the duty of brotherly love on the ground of the personal traits and forbidding qualities of their brethren; their ways are so unpleasant, their manners are so disagreeable, their methods of thinking and acting are so contrary to their own, and so unbearable. And in these personal dislikes and repugnances, they find reasons to relieve them from the duty of dispensing the offices of Christian charity. Can the bond of brotherly love be broken by such pretexts as these? is Christian charity then no stronger tie than that which springs from fancy, and the pleasure produced by the winning disposition and bland ways of our brother? What is it to us, of his personal characteristics and repelling defects! We are not bound to love his qualities, nor to love him because of them. The duty of brotherly love is a duty of the mind and will, a teaching of religion, a dictate of conscience. It sees in man the image of God, redeemed by His blood; a being of common origin and common nature, common hopes and common destiny, with ourselves. In all this, it recognizes the motives of its duty of brotherly love. Does our brother cease to belong to our nature, does he fall from his high destiny, is the image of God and the blood of Christ effaced from his soul, does he forfeit his inheritance of the grace and hopes of Christ, does he cease to be the child of God and the redeemed of the Lamb, because of his personal shortcomings and disagreeable qualities?

See what they put up with who hang on princes' favors, who solicit the bounty of courts; what humiliations and insults they endure, all for the sake of retaining the good graces of the king and of obtaining some temporal reward. Now God has staked our eternal happiness upon mortifying our personal dislikes, at least, so far, that they may not interfere with the fulfilment of the duties of fraternal charity. Is not salvation worth the self-sacrifice which men do not hesitate to endure for the sake of some end merely temporal?

But your neighbor has done you injury; he has ruined your good name and credit,—he has deprived you of your property. I admit it; and so far, he has sinned, he has done wrong. But will this relieve you from your obligations towards him? Will you do right, by doing him wrong? He has done you wrong. Will you permit him to do you the further wrong of depriving you of eternal salvation by the sin of your retaliation against him? This, surely, would not redress the grievance you have suffered. Will his dereliction break up the great system of fraternal charity under which God has placed all men? His malice has violated his duty to his fellow-man; are you therefore liberated from the great law of Christ? You act as if Christian charity were like a mere human contract, which, if broken by one side, ceases to be binding on the other. But this law is not of human origin. It comes from heaven. It is there that it has its eternal sanction. As it is to Christ alone it belongs to reward those who observe its requirements, so it is for Him alone to punish those who are unfaithful to it and who yield to the feelings and passions which it would govern and subdue. If, then, because of our brother's trespass, we refuse him the offices of brotherly love, our act redounds not to his disadvantage but to the offense and insult of God Himself, the author and bond of Christian charity. If we take vengeance on our brother, our act reverts to the contempt of Jesus, in Whose blood he has been redeemed, and of Whose body he is a member, and of Whose law he should be the beneficiary.

It is not permitted us to hate those whom God does not hate, to cast off those whom He has not cast off; to punish them whom God has not seen fit to chastise. They may not be in His favor, they may even exhibit some of the marks of the reprobate. Yet remember, that the sinner of to-day may be the saint of a time to come; and that he who at one time is covered with sin, and black with guilt, may, in the eternal counsels of God, be one of the elect. If we would hate, we may hate the devil and the damned, because they deserve God's eternal reprobation, and have received His eternal malediction. They are the fit objects of our hate and loathing and increasing aversion as His undying enemies.

You complain that your brother has shown himself ungrateful for all the past kindness which you have bestowed upon him. Was it, then, to put your brother under gratitude and to receive his thanks that you showed him the duties of brotherly love? Was a human reward the actuating principle of your charity? Instead of proposing to yourself the eternal recompense offered by Christ, you have substituted a human one, and you have deservedly lost both. How much better to have sought the reward of Him who has promised that not even a cup of water given in His name shall go without reward.

How shall we love our neighbor? What is the manner and measure of fraternal charity? I answer, the love of Christ for us. Behold the measure and the model of brotherly love. Even as He has loved us, so should we love one another. "A new mandate I give you, that you love one another, even as I have loved you."

What, you will say, must I die for my neighbor? Such may sometimes be your duty, if it be necessary for his eternal salvation. I do not say that such an obligation may occur often, if at all. But the fact that it can happen shows how sacred is the bond which binds us to our brother. See what Jesus has done for your neighbor and the price which He has thought fit to pay for him, and you will learn after what manner you should love your brother. Jesus, infinitely rich, and the Lord of all, became poor, and had not whereon to lay His head for him; surely, you should not be unwilling to spend some of your goods in supplying his needs and lightening his sufferings. Jesus, for his sake, has made Himself of no repute, a worm of the earth, an outcast from men and a reproach. Surely, you should not be so regardful of your name and reputation; injured, as you say, by your neighbor. The sufferings and death of Christ teach us that there is no forgiveness too ready and sincere, no generosity too profuse, no sacrifice too heroic, when the well-being of our brother needs it. Be charitable, then, to all: see yourself in those of every age, rank, condition, and claim; in every creature that bears the image of God. To the young contribute generously, that their hearts and minds may be formed to virtue, and while yet pliant early receive deep impressions of piety. Be charitable to the poor and needy, to the sick and suffering; for to you they represent Christ, and appeal in His name to your generosity. Be charitable to the sinful and unfortunate, whom wayward fortune, or perverse passion has not spared from those ills to which we are all subject, and from which we have only been saved by God's grace. Be charitable to the old,—do what you can to solace old age, to smooth its path to the grave; for on this earth there is nothing more worthy of veneration and love. Be charitable to your brother who has injured you, whether wittingly or unwittingly; for you have yourself injured your neighbor, if not purposely, at least through inadvertence, impatience, querulousness, or unguarded words; all which you expect him to overlook, because of the absence of evil intent and your general good disposition. Measure out to him the consideration that you would desire shown to yourself. While if you have not injured him purposely, you certainly have sinned wilfully and deliberately against God. For these sins you are a debtor to His justice. Yet you confidently ask and expect His pardon. Bestow then upon your neighbor the forgiveness and love you expect for yourself. "For with what measure you bestow justice and mercy, it will be measured unto you." The condition of Divine pardon to you, is your complete and absolute forgiveness of the wrongs done to yourself. Do all this, and at the last hour you will hear these words, "Come, ye blessed of My Father, possess the kingdom prepared for you from the foundation of the world; for I was hungry, and ye gave Me to eat; thirsty, and ye gave Me to drink; naked, and ye clothed Me; sick and in prison, and ye visited Me. Amen, I say to you, so long as ye did it unto the least of these my brethren, ye did it unto Me."

THE FORGIVENESS OF INJURIES.

Lord, how often shall my brother offend against me, and I forgive him? till seven times?

JESUS saith to him: I say not to thee, till seven times; but till seventy times seven times.

Therefore is the kingdom of heaven likened to a king, who would take an account of his servants.

And when he had begun to take the account, one was brought to him, that owed him ten thousand talents.

And as he had not wherewith to pay it, his lord commanded that he should be sold, and his wife and children and all that he had, and payment to be made.

But that servant falling down, besought him, saying: Have patience with me, and I will pay thee all.

And the lord of that servant being moved with pity, let him go and forgave him the debt.

But when that servant was gone out, he found one of his fellow-servants that owed him an hundred pence : and laying hold of him, he throttled him, saying: Pay what thou owest.

And his fellow-servant falling down, besought him, saying : Have patience with me, and I will pay thee all.

And he would not : but went and cast him into prison, till he paid the debt.

Now his fellow-servants seeing what was done, were very much grieved, and they came and told their lord all that was done.

Then his lord called him ; and said to him: Thou wicked servant, I forgave thee all the debt, because thou besoughtest me :

Shouldst not thou then have had compassion also on thy fellow-servant, even as I had compassion on thee?

THE FORGIVENESS OF INJURIES.

And his lord being angry, delivered him to the torturers until he paid all the debt.

So also shall My Heavenly Father do to you, if you forgive not every one his brother from your hearts.—St. Matt. xviii. 21-35.

ALL the commandments of God, all the precepts of His Church, all the laws ever made for the guidance of human society, are all summed up in the command of loving God for His own sake and our neighbor for God's sake. It is their substance and fulfilment. If we follow it in its various, in its multiform and manifold applications, we have no need of any other light or rule in our duties to God, our neighbor, and ourselves.

It is not my intention to speak to you to-day of the duty of brotherly love,—which springs from, and has its source in, the love of God, except in so far as it may concern the duty of forgiving injuries. I wish to direct your attention to merely one branch of Christian charity. Let me ask you to reflect with me on the duty of forgiving our enemies.

Nothing is more commonly contemned than this duty of forgiveness. It is seldom that we meet one who, from his heart, pardons offences done him. The desire of vengeance shows itself in various ways; sometimes in manifest violence, in taking life or in maiming the body. But generally it pursues meaner and more insidious methods. For, though vengeance pretends to be the prompting of courage, the manner in which it often seeks its object, reveals a cowardice, the most abject and contemptible. It will not resort to open attack, for that were bold though

THE FORGIVENESS OF INJURIES.

sinful; but by innuendo, hints, insinuations against his enemy's character, the aggrieved seeks to satisfy his passion. Calumny and detraction are the blows that vengeance strikes. Even with these injustices which, though grievously wrong, have this in their favor, that, as they specify a charge, they can be refuted, if untrue, vengeance is not content; but has recourse to that meanest of all calumnies which consists in implying that it could, if it would, injure its enemy's reputation; insinuating the existence of faults which, either do not exist, or if they do, not to the same extent as is implied. It has not the courage to strike, to do violence, to calumniate openly, to detract; because in all these defense can be made; but it tells us that if it wanted to speak it could, that it will say no more and such like, leaving the impression upon those that hear, that its enemy is guilty of some heinous fault. This kind of vengeance, the most cowardly of all, seeks in this manner to steer a middle course between conscience on the one hand, and vengeance on the other; "willing to strike, and yet afraid to give the blow."

There is scarcely anything harder to human nature than to entirely forgive the injuries received by us. So true is this, that in the Old law nothing was forbidden but manifesting unforgiveness by open violence. A better and more perfect law is the Christian. He Who said to the Jews that it was not only forbidden to commit adultery, but even to look after a woman to lust for her, also declared that not only vengeance, but even its desire was sinful. This Christian virtue was too much to expect from those who lived under the " weak and beggarly elements of the law."

And what is it to forgive our enemies? Many understand not the nature of this obligation; some making of it more than it is, others making it less. To forgive is to have for our enemy that love and to perform for him those kind offices which we would have shown him, had he never offended us; to reinstate him in our esteem to the extent of doing for him, without reluctance, whatever charity prompts us to do for any one else: to feed and clothe him when destitute; to prevent his misfortune or disgrace when we can; to succor him in all needs, both temporal and spiritual; in one word, to do for him under all circumstances whatever we would wish done to ourselves similarly placed. It will be seen that this does not forbid our remembering the wrong he has done us. It were well that we should have such control over our minds as even to forget it, but this is not always possible. So long as we do not consent to the thoughts of vengeance that sometimes arise from thinking of the injuries done us, we do not sin. It is like other passions; sinful only when and to whatever degree we yield to them.

As fraternal love does not consist in feeling, does not spring from fancy, cupidity, or from any other of those motives upon which mere human love rests, so neither are we obliged to have any sensible love for our enemy. We are to love him as ourselves, that is, with the kind of love, but not with the degree of intensity with which we can love only ourselves. As the love of God differs essentially from, and is incomparably superior to, the sensible love we may lawfully have for friends, so the love we ought to have for our enemies is different essentially from the love generated by mere sentiment. All such love languishes and perishes; it cannot survive the trials of life, the vicissitudes of time. But Christian charity is superior to all these. Founded upon the principles of reason, the teachings of revelation, prompted and fostered by grace, it outlasts all love that is merely the growth of emotion naturally short-lived. This is the solid, the enduring love we are to cherish for our enemies.

It is easy to see that the obligation of forgiving enemies comes from the duty of loving all men. If we are required to love all, to serve all, to perform charitable duties to all, we surely must begin by forgiving the wrongs they have done us. When God commands us to love, He necessarily obliges us to everything that love requires. Even though we should do good to our enemies, though we should exhibit all the other promptings of charity, unless we begin by forgiving them their offences, we are wanting in charity.

We are all subject to the same temptations and weaknesses; we are all hewn out of the same rock; we are all liable to offend; not one of us but has given offence at some time or other, if not wilfully, at least through inadvertence, selfishness, want of consideration, fault finding, or other forbidding defects. People are so different; their ways are so contrasted; like the human face, no two alike, that we can scarcely avoid giving offence from time to time. Yet we expect pardon for these faults. We complain of our brother, if he be not willing to overlook them; we justify ourselves on the ground that we did not mean to offend, that our goodness of heart and amiability of temper would not allow us. Should we, then, be slow to forgive the faults committed against ourselves? If we look for pardon for ourselves, should we hesitate to give it to others? Do we justify, by our own unwillingness to forgive, the reluctance of those who are unwilling to forgive us? Has our brother no goodness, no amiability? Can we see nothing in him inviting our forgiveness? "If thy brother sin against thee, reprove him: and if he repent, forgive him. And if he sin against thee seven times in a day, and seven times in a day turn to thee, saying: I am sorry: forgive him."

Let us bear in mind always that though we forgive not, yet God can and, perhaps, has already forgiven our enemies. They may have already approached the sacrament of reconciliation with the necessary dispositions; they may have already repented of the offences committed against thee, and they may have been again restored to God's grace. If He has pardoned, should we refuse them pardon? If the satisfaction offered to God's sovereign majesty has been sufficient, should we deem it insufficient for us? Are we of greater account than God? Is our dignity and importance greater than God's eternal majesty? Is our pride greater than God's mercy? Are we to spurn whom God has embraced? Should we not rather imitate the goodness of God? Should we not try to propitiate God's anger against our own sins, by freely and generously pardoning the faults committed against ourselves and which He has been pleased to cancel? In doing so, we should but imitate God, and call down upon us His choicest gifts and blessings. When we were all lost, He sent His Only Son to redeem us; to redeem all, just and unjust; those under the law, those outside the law; those who crucified Him, as well as those who believed in Him; all men without distinction. Should we not be equally lenient with our enemies?

Again, God does not limit His favors to His friends, but extends them to those who offend Him daily, even hourly. He makes His sun to shine, and His rain to fall upon all. If He were to take vengeance, He would at once destroy the world; but no; He bears with the innumerable outrages momentarily offered to His sovereign majesty. He seeks no vengeance, and if He does, it is a father's vengeance—not vindictive, but salutary and corrective—looking to His child's reformation; a vengeance prompted by His immeasurable love. Whom He loves, He chastises. Should we not imitate our Father's goodness? If He can afford to pardon, we should long to pardon for our Father's sake, and in conformity with His example.

The wrongs we suffer from our enemies are not inflicted upon us without God's permission. Our enemies would have no power to injure, if God did not give it to them. All things happen with at least God's permissive will. Nothing takes place in the world, not even sin, without His allowance. He tolerates all sin and suffering, all misery and calamities, all the evil under the sun, and all the wretchedness that men endure, for the sake of the elect. If, then, we suffer from enemies, let us remember that they may be but the ministers of God's vengeance, or the dispensers of His mercy. It may be an act of the greatest love, on the part of God, to allow misfortune to befall us. Sometimes the greatest blessings come to us in the guise of calamities. God looks down upon us and sees us prospering in all things: amassing riches, acquiring fame, enjoying the world's vanities; the fear and love of God, the remembrance of the end for which we have been created, all the truths of religion are forgotten; we begin to love the world instead of God; we are pursuing a career that will assuredly entail our eternal misery; and then God, in His loving mercy, sends some accident to awaken us from our lethargy, to snatch us from the awful precipice on which we are standing; to remind us of the emptiness and perishableness of all human things; to wean us from undue attachment to ourselves; to make us fix our minds and hearts upon eternity; to create a longing for Himself, by infusing into us a disgust and loathing for all else; and for this purpose, He permits our enemies to prevail against us.

THE FORGIVENESS OF INJURIES.   285

Instead, then, of seeking vengeance on God's instruments, we ought to thank them; instead of resenting these visitations of His mercy, we ought thankfully to embrace them; we ought to kiss the hand that strikes us; we ought to invoke blessings, on whom passion prompts us to summon curses; we ought to give God thanks, and converted ourselves, we ought to beseech Him to enlighten the minds, to touch the hearts of those who have injured us, in order that they, too, may be partakers of the mercy which God has vouchsafed to pour down upon ourselves.

The wrongs we suffer cannot injure us, except in so far as we make of them occasions of sin, and consequently, of our eternal perdition. What can they deprive us of, except some temporal goods,— riches, property, name or pleasure? But, we must one day lose all these; we must leave them all behind. It makes therefore little difference, whether we part with them now or then, sooner or later. It is true we ought not to be indifferent to our good name, St. Paul counsels it; yet for its sake we ought not to harm our neighbor. Our enemy can do us no harm that can possibly justify our doing him harm, and thus imperiling our souls. The loss of temporal goods cannot stand in comparison with the loss of eternal happiness. Of this we can be deprived by no one but by ourselves. "Fear not those who can only kill the body; but fear Him who is able to plunge both soul and body into hell." If we resent, with revenge, the wrongs done us, we offend Almighty God, we become amenable to His justice; and thus, of these wrongs we make an occasion of losing our immortal souls. Injuries then can harm us only in so far as we make them occasions of our sin.

Men speak of their honor,—must they not defend it? What will men think of them, if they bear with patience the insults offered to them? Will it not pronounce them cowards, as of poor blood, as lacking spirit and honor? If they are injured should they not injure? if calumniated should they not retort with calumny? if insulted should they not repel it with indignation? blow for blow? This is the wisdom of the world; always opposed to the wisdom of the Gospel, as the shadow attends the light. No, says the Gospel, "Do good to them that hate you, pray for them that persecute and calumniate you." "Be not overcome by evil, but overcome evil by good." "If thy enemy be hungry, give him to eat; if he be thirsty, give him to drink." Vengeance pretends to courage. Its seeker thinks himself brave; but he is the meanest, the most despicable of cowards, because he has not character enough and force of will to contemn the world and its esteem. He is, indeed, a poltroon who prefers the world to God; its opinion to His law; his passion to his soul; who prefers his neighbor's injury to the loss of some little of this world's honor. But he truly gains the sincere esteem of men, who forgives his enemy; whose love for his fellow-creature is greater than his love for himself. He is always sure to gain the world's praise, who despises it. Vanity contemns its votaries, honors those who are above its influence. If we would be popular, let us contemn popularity. Jesus contemned the world, and the world has honored Him with a glory which it has never decreed to another. The world honors the saints who despised it. Virtue, if not always, frequently has its reward even in this world. I understand not what honor can be purchased with eternal ruin. I cannot see that there is any honor in preferring the world and its corrupt maxims, to God and His eternal law. I can never understand what honor can accrue to a man for being unreasonable; or rather, for acting like one destitute of reason. Man's true nobility is to be found in placing himself in harmony with those laws that God has given for our guidance and which are necessary to our own happiness and the welfare of society. Yet, we must not wonder that the world's votaries seek vengeance; for they are in darkness. "He that hateth his brother, is in darkness, and walketh in darkness and knoweth not whither he goeth, because the darkness hath blinded his eyes." "He that hateth his brother, is a murderer."

If those persons who seek vengeance, who are unwilling to pardon their enemies, were themselves without sin for which they expect and ask forgiveness, there would be something which, if it did not justify, would at least extenuate their malice; or, if they did not seek forgiveness for their own sins, they would be consistent. But, how a person covered with sin, guilty of hundreds, thousands, even, it may be, millions of sins, can have the audacity to ask God to pardon him, while he nourishes hatred to his own enemy, is something I cannot understand; how he can have the effrontery to approach the sacred Tribunal and there even confess his reluctance to forgive his enemy, while he implores God's forgiveness on himself, is one of the many contradictions into which one blinded by perversity can fall. How can he, with any show of reason, ask God "to forgive him his trespasses," while he is not willing "to forgive those who have trespassed against himself?" He repeats the Lord's prayer; and, taking his words literally, he asks God to forgive him, as he forgives others, that is, not at all; he begs God then not to forgive himself. Of course, he does not mean this. Will he not remember that God will not forgive those who are themselves unwilling to forgive? that to forgive one's enemies, is the indispensable condition of obtaining pardon for one's self? Upon what conditions has God promised to hear our prayer for mercy? hear: "If you will forgive men their offences, your Heavenly Father will forgive you your offences. If you forgive not, neither will He forgive you." "When thou shalt stand to pray; forgive, if thou hast aught against any man; that also your Father who is in heaven may forgive you your sins." "Love your enemies, do good to them that hate you." "If thine enemy be hungry, give him to eat; if thirsty, give him to drink; thus you will heap coals of fire upon his head." "If you offer your gift at the altar, and remember that you have aught against your brother, go first and be reconciled to your brother, and then come and offer your gift at the altar."

Let us then forgive all, love all; those who have injured us, those who have tried to injure us; let us forgive, and we shall be forgiven. Let us pray for all without distinction; for those in the Church, that they may persevere; for those outside, that as we all have a common Creator and common Redeemer, so we may all, in a common Church, meet in the Unity of Faith; and thus there may be but "One Lord, one Faith, one Baptism." Let us imitate Jesus Christ, Who, on the Cross, amidst His awful agony, His cruel dereliction, prayed for His persecutors, "for they knew not what they did." His action is for our edification. For us He shed His blood. For us He left that sublime example for which the world has had no parallel, and which alone proclaims His Divinity. It was only a God that could die imploring pardon for those who were putting Him to death. We are His disciples; let us study our model. Let us remember that we all need mercy and the glory of God. No one of us is without sin. "He is a liar and the truth is not in him, who says he is without sin." We have offended God thousands of times; we can have no hope but in His mercy. Without it, and in justice we are lost. If then, we would obtain mercy for ourselves, let us bestow it upon others with no parsimonious, begrudging hand. A time will come, at the hour of death, when we shall have need of all the mercy which our own can now purchase for us. Let us remember that awful moment, when, stretched on the bed of death, with eternity before us, and God, the all-merciful and all-just, about to judge us with the judgment with which we have judged, and the mercy with which we have shown mercy, our only hope will be His boundless mercy, His all-forgiving goodness. Let us now forgive, if then we would be forgiven.

THE NEW YORK
PUBLIC LIBRARY

ASTOR L
T

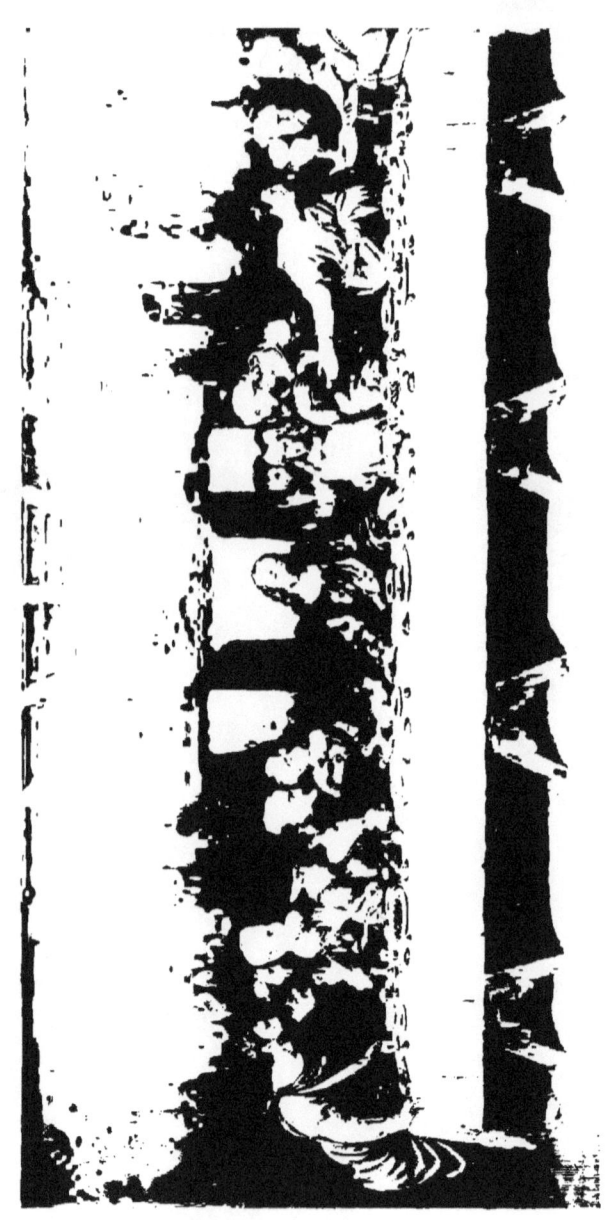

THE LOVE OF JESUS IN THE BLESSED SACRAMENT.

When you come, therefore, together into one place, it is not now to eat the Lord's Supper.

For every one taketh before his own supper to eat. And one indeed is hungry, and another is drunk.

What! have you not houses to eat and to drink in? Or despise ye the Church of God; and put them to shame that have not? What shall I say to you? Do I praise you? In this I praise you not.

For I have received of the Lord that which also I delivered unto you, that the Lord JESUS, the same night in which He was betrayed, took bread,

And giving thanks, broke, and said: Take ye, and eat: this is My Body, which shall be delivered for you: this do for the commemoration of Me.

In like manner also the chalice, after He had supped, saying: This chalice is the new testament in My Blood: this do ye, as often as you shall drink, for the commemoration of Me.

For as often as you shall eat this bread, and drink the chalice, you shall shew the death of the Lord, until He come.

Therefore whosoever shall eat this bread, or drink the chalice of the Lord unworthily, shall be guilty of the body and of the blood of the Lord.

But let a man prove himself: and so let him eat of that bread, and drink of the chalice.

For he that eateth and drinketh unworthily, eateth and drinketh judgment to himself: not discerning the body of the Lord.

Therefore are there many infirm and weak among you, and many sleep.—St. Paul's I. Corinthians xi., 20-30.

IN placing before our devout contemplation the life, sufferings, and death of Jesus Christ, we may with profit close our eyes to the many other considerations which they suggest, and fix our attention exclusively upon the marvellous love which they disclose. In doing this, we cannot but ask ourselves, why God has loved us after so wonderful a manner? He could have saved us at a far less price. One word of His had been enough to blot out the sins of ten thousand worlds, and Infinite Wisdom could have found other means for our redemption without the shedding of blood. Why, then, did not Christ save us without this prodigal expenditure of His blood?

It was to show us His love. Without His incarnation and death, we should forever have remained ignorant of His love. His power we should have beheld; for the works that were made from the beginning gave testimony of it. His justice we should have felt; but we should never have been able to realize that God is a God of love. So true is it that Christ became man to manifest His love, that many Fathers of the Church tell us that even if man had never fallen, yet Christ would have become man as the result of His infinite love. Why God should have shown us so amazing a love, is, indeed, beyond our comprehension: but we must remember He is God: when He acts, it is in the manner of God. We could never expect a man to make such a sacrifice for man: it is not in human nature. However, we must not think of God as we think of man; as in all things else God shows His infinitude, so we must expect that He will also show it when He comes to proclaim His love.

Considering the unspeakable love of Christ in becoming man and dying, we are not at all to be surprised at the love which he displays in the Sacrament of the Altar. On the contrary, it is something like what we might expect. Belief in the one leads us on, I may say, to anticipate the other. It could never have entered the mind of man to believe that God would become man: but after the fact, I say that Christ's Real Presence is only in harmony with the love of the Incarnation. The two truths fit into each other so, that, far from being surprised at Christ's remaining with us, it is something like what we might expect. Birth in a stable, finds a fitting sequel in the institution of this Divine Sacrament, in which He gives us His body to eat and His blood to drink. No wonder then, that, the night before He suffered, He devised a means by which He would forever abide with men to feed and nourish their souls. He loved those of His generation, but not more than those of all other generations. He would not leave us bereft of His Divine Presence.

In this Sacrament, His love brings Him to the utmost limit His power could go. One would think that in the unutterable condescension of His birth, and still more, in the untold agony and sufferings of His death, He would have done enough for man; He would have exhausted Divine love; but no! where we think it ought to end, it is there that it begins! so far are God's ways above ours, so far greater is Divine love than we could imagine, or have any right to expect. Not content with the love shown in His lowly birth at Bethlehem, His illimitable love and wisdom have established this Sacrament by which He is given a still lowlier birth daily, in the unworthy hands of His priests. Not content with a residence of thirty-three years among men, He shows us that, indeed, His delight is to be with them, in that He has ordained this Mystery in which He is perpetuated for all time among them. Not content with the all marvellous love disclosed in the inconceivable agony of His passion, and in the excruciating torments of His death, He has willed to die daily, in this Sacrament, by the symbolical separation of His soul and body. Theologians love to dwell upon the thought that the Church, His mystical body, is a continuation or extension of the Incarnation. How much truer to believe that the Eucharist is such a continuation, since it is His real body. For what is the Blessed Eucharist but the perpetual abidance of Jesus Christ upon earth? He is as truly in the world in this Mystery, as if He had never gone to His Heavenly Father.

As then His mortal career was drawing to a close, as He began already to feel in His soul the anguish of Gethsemani, as there was vividly present to His mind the death and dereliction He was to suffer, His divine wisdom revealed a still more marvellous disclosure of His boundless love, His unconquerable thirst for souls. He then determined to remain with men, but in a different manner: in a manner far more transcendent than that in which He had come into the world. He would not only remain with men, but He would become their food and drink, the spiritual nourishment of their souls. Accordingly, the night before He suffered He instituted this Sacrament.

It is not my purpose to expose to you the proofs of our Lord's Real Presence. It does not suit the occasion,—which is for devotion rather than for argument. I wish to draw your attention to the wondrous, the amazing love of Jesus Christ, in giving us His body to eat and His blood to drink, in this stupendous Mystery.

True love always seeks to show itself in act. What we do, is the expression and measure of our love. When we love anyone we long to manifest it to him. Love diffuses itself between the loving and the loved. It reveals itself in the performance of kind deeds, in the expression of good-will, in supplying, in anticipation, that which we believe will be agreeable to him whom we love. Sometimes it may be that love is expressed by the performance of only some trifling favor; but that is because circumstances do not allow of our exhibiting it in a more marked manner. When it is in our power, if we fail to render signal service to Him whom we profess to love, our love is not worthy the name: it is not true love. Doing for another all that he desires, and even more, is the test and measure of our love. In proportion as we do this, do we love. When we are loved by one possessing great resources, we expect great favors from him. If he loves us ardently, he will show his love in a generous, munificent way. If we are loved by a prince or a king, we expect it to be shown in a princely or kingly manner. If we should be loved by God, we would expect it to be shown in a God-like manner. As His love would incomparably surpass that of creatures, so the manifestation of this love should as far surpass any human exhibition of love, as God's resources and power are greater than those of creatures.

In this great Mystery, Almighty God suspends the laws of nature: He does violence to His own creatures, by performing a series of the most resplendent miracles, any one of which is far greater than any elsewhere known to us. St. Thomas calls it, "The compendium of all miracles." It is assuredly God's greatest work: greater far than the mystery of Creation, or that of the Incarnation. It is miraculous that the bread and wine are changed into the Body and Blood of Christ: miraculous that the Body of Christ is found, not only under the form of bread, but also under that of wine: that the Blood of Christ is found, not only under the form of wine, but likewise under that of bread: miraculous that the Soul of Christ is present under each form: miraculous that the Divinity of Christ, forever and indissolubly united to His Body, is present under each form: miraculous that One and the Same Body is present in all the hosts throughout the world, and in every particle of the host, at least when divided: miraculous that being His Real Body, and therefore material, It is endowed with a spiritual mode of existence: miraculous in that It has no extension: miraculous in that It is insensible and impalpable: miraculous in that the appearances of bread and wine remain subsisting detached from their substances, and yet endowed with all the force of substances, and subject to all the vicissitudes of substances.

Here, then, is a series of the most prodigious, the most resplendent miracles, far eclipsing in splendor all the other miracles which God has wrought. Great thing it was that God condescended to create the world; greater, that He made man to enjoy and rule over it; greater still, that when man had fallen, He brought Himself to the amazing condescension of becoming Man for his redemption: but infinitely beyond compare with these mysteries, is this, in which we receive God Himself: the Omnipotent Creator, the Sanctifier of souls, the very Body that He took when He became Man, united with His Divine Personality. This Mystery contains all the excellences of those three mysteries. It is their crown and complement. It is the extension and fulfilment of the love and wisdom begun in the act of creating the world.

The production of Christ's Body in the Eucharist as far transcends the creation of the world, as the Body of Christ is more precious than the world. It as far surpasses the graces conferred on man for his restoration, as the source of graces transcends the graces it bestows; as the sun is greater than the rays it diffuses. It so far surpasses the Incarnation, as in the Incarnation Christ became man but once: in this Mystery He is daily, hourly incarnated; and as it is itself only an extension of the Incarnation, made more glorious, by the addition of all those surpassing miracles, which His Sacramental Presence necessarily supposes.

If God were to create ten thousand worlds, infinitely more perfect than this, He would not do as much for us as He has done in this Mystery of inexplicable love. Why has He done so much for us? To manifest to us His love. Love is to be measured by what it does. What, then, must be the immensity of Christ's love for man, which has moved Him to perform all those wonders which I have just endeavored faintly to narrate? How can we begin to understand the munificence, the exuberance of Divine love? Who can tell why God should love us with such a profusion, such a prodigality of love?

What are we to say of the awful self-abasement of our Lord in this Mystery? How are we to begin to understand the unutterable humiliation which He suffers in this Sacrament? Does it not stagger credibility that God, the Maker and Lord of all things, the Omnipotent, the Omniscient, thé Eternal, should come into this world, and put Himself under the form of bread and wine, in order to become the nourishment of our souls and the pledge of their immortality? Yet, it is true. Out of sheer love He strips Himself of His glory, relinquishes His throne at the right hand of His Father, and in a manner, annihilates Himself. If, as the Apostle says, "Being made man He humbled Himself to the condition of a servant, and became obedient even unto the death of the cross," what are we to think of His amazing condescension in becoming our food and drink? Great as was Christ's humiliation in His incarnation, immeasurably greater is it in this Sacrament. In becoming man, inconceivably lowering as it was of Himself, yet after all, it was taking upon Him the nature of the noblest of His beings, the greatest work of His hands, in the natural order. He had the stature and form of a man and accommodated Himself to the circumstances and needs of a man. But in this Mystery, He takes upon Him the form of the commonest elements, than which, we are more familiar with nothing. In it, although the parts of the body are truly present and not at all confused, yet they observe not the order in place which belongs to other bodies; wherefore He is neither visible nor palpable; discernible alone by the sense of hearing through the word of faith; wanting in all the appearances, yet endowed with every attribute and faculty and sense, of a human person. "My substance is as nothing before you." He is reduced as it were to nothing. In the Incarnation His humiliation was but once; but here it is daily, never ceasing; there He was born of the chaste womb of an Immaculate Mother; here He is born daily, hourly, in the unworthy hands of His priests; abandoned in the tabernacle, exposed to insult and profanation, continually entering into sinful hearts: hearts filled with hatred, envy, impurity; sacrilegious hearts,—hearts seething in crime, black with a perfidy worse than Judaical.

He is, indeed, a God humiliated, hidden, stripped of every vestige of His glory, "trembling, as it were, on the confines of annihilation." Yet, all humbled as He is in this Mystery, He proclaims to us the dimensions of His love: its height, its depth, its breadth. The depth of His humiliation is the depth of His love. The more He has humbled Himself, the more He deserves our love. We must raise our hearts high in order to love Him above all things. Do our best, we can never love Him as He has loved us. He does not expect it, we cannot hope for it; yet we are not exempted from loving Him as much as we are able; to the utmost limit of our capacity. Love is to be repaid with love. We can testify our love only by our actions. Let us love, not in word, but in truth and by work. If He has done so much for us, what ought we not to do for Him? What poorer, and yet, what greater return is it in our power to make, than to pass our lives in the service of Him Who has loved us with so marvellous a love: always testing our love by the rule He Himself has given us: "If thou lovest Me, keep My Commandments."

What is there that Jesus does not give us in this Divine Sacrament? What more can He give us than Himself! His Sacred Body! His Precious Blood! His Whole Being! God and Man indissolubly and forever united! What is there more precious in heaven or on earth than the Body of Christ? Would you prefer some great grace? But He gives the very source and fountain of all grace! Would you prefer some earthly gift? But He gives us the very excellence and beauty that you prize in such a gift! The beauty, goodness, loveliness, and all other perfections that you admire in the works of God, must be contained in their fulness in Himself, the Maker and Model of all things. St. Augustine says that: "Christ in giving us His body has exhausted His love." He can go no farther. Even God, infinite in wisdom, could do no more, to manifest to us His love. He has placed a limit to His power: inexhaustible, He has drained it, as it were, to the last drop.

Love seeks for union, delights in the converse of the object of its love. What union closer could Christ have devised, than that in which we abide in Him and He in us? By that chemical combination which subsists between the body and its nourishment, food becomes one with the body, becomes the body. Christ in this Sacrament is made one with us, and changes not Himself into us, but changes us into Himself. For this celestial food, while its union with our body is as close as the union of corporeal food; yet, over such food possesses this wonderful excellence, that we who are nourished by it are changed into it: transformed into Christ. "He that eateth My flesh and drinketh My blood, abideth in Me and I in him." "Unless you eat the flesh and drink the blood of the Son of man, you shall not have life in you. He that eateth My flesh and drinketh My blood hath everlasting life, and I will raise him up on the last day. For My flesh is meat indeed and My blood is drink indeed." "As the living Father hath sent Me, and I live by the Father, so he that eateth Me, the same shall live by Me. This is the bread that cometh down from heaven; not as your Fathers did eat manna, and are dead; he that eateth of this bread, shall live forever." Thus we see that Christ is incorporated into us by the closest possible of unions. In the Incarnation, Christ had indeed by the most marvellous and unspeakable of all unions, united Himself to our humanity. We can only fall down and adore, when we are told that God has stooped to our nature and united it to His own by His Divine Personality. In this union effected at His incarnation, it is God Who comes down to us and becomes our brother in the flesh; but in the Holy Eucharist we are lifted above our proper condition, we are placed even above the angelic, and are made partakers of Christ's Divinity; and human nature is exalted to the highest pitch of glory, by its union with the God-head.

But you will remind me, perhaps, that I have said that this Sacrament changes the receiver into Christ; and you will ask, how is it then that Catholics, being so much like other people, give so little evidence of this union?

But, to answer this question, let me ask of what Catholics do you speak? Of those, doubtless, who seldom or never receive this life-giving food. What wonder that it has no effect upon them who never receive it; being like the rest of men, and never receiving this food, only proves what I say: they are like them because they do not receive it. How can it affect those Catholic men who never come to Communion, or, at most, come once or twice a year, through custom, human respect, or to put an end to the solicitation of their wives, and who have no appetite, no hunger or thirst for it? Even ordinary food taken without desire or appetite is useless. So it is with this food, it must be received with a longing, an earnestness, a greed.

Look at the devout frequent communicant and see the wondrous effects it produces in his soul! See how seldom such persons stain their souls with mortal sin and how frequently they are free from even venial! See how lust is quenched in the soul by this wine that germinates in virgins! How the heat of all passions is cooled by the heavenly dew that falls from this celestial food upon the soul! See how it increases it in detachment from the world and unites it closer in union with God! How it reconciles itself with the crosses of life, and in all things conforms itself to the will of God! See how the conviction of the shortness of time, the emptiness of life, the all importance of the great hereafter, grows upon and sinks deep into that soul, giving a character, and a shape to all its being and actions! See, in one word, how frequent and fervent Communion transforms the soul, until as far as human imperfection and our condition here below permit, it becomes true to say that it is no longer the man that lives, but Christ that lives in him!

Could Divine love go farther? Could Divine wisdom devise any means by which He would be more intimately and absolutely ours than He is in this Sacrament? Love is lavish and prodigal of itself; but it is only the love of God that can go the length that Jesus does in this Mystery. "With desire have I desired to eat this Pasch with you." With vehemence, with burning ardor, with anxious longing did He desire to eat this Pasch, to give us His body to eat and His blood to drink. During the years of His infancy, during the labors and privations of His manhood, during the fastings and prayers and other works of His three years' missionary life, during the bitter sufferings of His passion endured in anticipation, with Gethsemane and Calvary always present before Him; during all this and in spite of all this, did He yearn to eat the Pasch with them that He might give to men the last and greatest pledge of His love.

In the manner of giving, in the ease with which we can all partake in this Divine Banquet, we see, too, the marvels of His love. He gives Himself most absolutely: becomes our daily bread, places Himself under the most ordinary elements, imparts to an untold number of priests the power of consecrating His body. Great mercy and love it had been, had He but given this transcendent power to one, and that, only at stated times; even as it was permitted of old to enter the Holy of Holies but once a year; and if the material of which the Sacrament would be wrought should be the rarest and most precious. But no; He wishes to be the food and nourishment of every man who is born into the world! hence the mat-

THE LOVE OF JESUS.

ter must be the most easily obtainable, ten thousand altars must witness unto the awful sacrifice— "the clean oblation that is offered to His name, from the rising to the setting sun," an uncounted number of priests, good, bad, and indifferent, must possess a power denied even to the angels: the sublime power of consecrating the Body of God, and distributing It to His faithful.—All this because He is to be our food, the nourishment of our souls, even as corporeal food is that of our bodies. As without such food we would languish and die, so without this spiritual food, the spiritual life of our souls would run out and finally be extinguished. "Unless you eat the flesh of the Son of man, and drink His blood, you shall not have life in you. He who eateth My flesh, and drinketh My blood, hath everlasting life: and I will raise him up on the last day. For My flesh is true food, and My blood is true drink. He who eateth My flesh, and drinketh My blood, abideth in Me, and I in him. As the Father Who liveth sent Me, and I live by the Father, so he that eateth Me, the same also shall live by Me. This is the bread which came down from heaven. Not as your fathers ate the manna, and died. He who eateth this bread, shall live forever." Where is our gratitude to repay all the riches of the love poured out so profusely in this Sacrament! Truly "His delight is to be with the sons of men."

We see, too, the insatiable love of Jesus in giving us this Sacrament when we call to mind the circumstances under which it was instituted, and the sin and sacrilege which He foresaw would be forever inseparable from His Real Presence on our altars. He gave it to us on the very eve of His passion,—a time when, considering the ingratitude that was shown Him, and the ignominious suffering and death He was about to undergo, He would have been well justified in denying to us this design of His mercy. It was the day before He suffered, the very night of His agony, in the garden of Gethsemane: His death and dereliction was vividly before His mind: He was about to be betrayed and abandoned by His disciples: Judas had but just dipped his hand in the dish, the sign of him who was to betray his Master. Peter who had sworn that he would never deny Him, was soon to foreswear Him thrice at the voice of a maid-servant. All the apostles were about to flee at the approach of the soldiers sent from the High Priest: Peter and James would alone remain, and they would not be able to watch even one hour with Him. The people for whom He had done so many good works, whose friend He had ever shown Himself, are about to rise against Him and demand His blood, with the curse of it upon their heads and their children's; the priests whose ordinances "He had not come to destroy, but to fulfil," are actively engaged in compassing His death; and for this purpose are soliciting false witnesses. Yet, it is in the midst of this ingratitude,—this base, this black ingratitude, this perfidy worse than satanical, that Jesus Christ bestows upon men His divinest gift! His Body and Blood! the earnest and assurance of their immortality! Man nor angel can fathom the wondrous depth of such love! We are surprised, amazed at it; but comprehend it, we cannot; reciprocate it fully, we never can!

Nor was He deterred from His purpose of love by the foreknowledge, which He always had, of what He would have to suffer in this Sacrament. There was present to His divine foresight the future of His Church. He saw that the unbelief of men would surpass His love; that His very love would be to many a rock of scandal: that there would be men to call in question His Real Presence; that there would always be some to say with the Jews, " How can this man give us His flesh to eat? or with the disciples, "This is a hard saying, and who can hear it;" that men's incredulity would seek to explain away the clear and unequivocal words by which He established it. He knew, too, that even many of those who would believe in His Real Presence, would have but a theoretical faith,—a faith which would not dare to doubt its truth, but yet would fail to realize it: which would not penetrate the veils of His Sacramental Presence and bring it home to the mind and heart with the eyes of faith as a living reality, this abidance of God with men; that they would regard His dwelling among them, if not with aversion, with at least coldness and indifference; that if they received Him at all, it would be with tepidity; that it would require the threats and anathemas of the Church to force men to partake of this Sacrament, the nourishment of their souls, the energy of a future resurrection, the pledge of a glorious immortality.

No, this dreary, this chilling prospect of coldness, of ingratitude, of unbelief, was not enough to deter Him from becoming our food and sustenance. He would win us, draw us to His love. He would melt our frozen hearts with His burning love. He would expose Himself to profanity, contumely, unbelief, sacrilege even, for our love. Nothing could deter Him, nothing could intimidate Him; He seems to court them for our sakes. To abandon Himself to such evils, to subject Himself to such indignities, to suffer all this and more that I have not dared to express,—does it not show an all consuming thirst for the souls of the children of men? Who will measure the height and depth and breadth of such love? Should we not exclaim with St. Paul, "Who then shall separate us from the love of Christ? tribulation? or distress? or famine? or nakedness? or danger? or persecution? or the sword? For I am sure that neither death, nor life, nor angels, nor principalities, nor powers, nor things present, nor things to come, nor might, nor height, nor depth nor any other creature shall be able to separate us from the love of God, which is in Christ Jesus our Lord."

We cannot begin to fathom the depth of the Divine love displayed in this wonderful mystery. We can only say that God is infinite, infinite in all His attributes: infinite therefore in His love. Nor man nor angel can compass the love of Jesus. For the preacher to attempt to describe it would be to collect the waters of the ocean in his palm; would be as a child lisping its first accents, or writing its first letters in the sand. We have read of the marvels of a mother's love: our hearts have melted with compassion as we learned of the heroic acts of self-denial and self-sacrifice, even unto the shedding of blood, which loving mothers have so often endured for the children of their womb. We have heard, too, of the power of pure human love: the noblest traits of our nature have come to light under the influence of this strongest and noblest of passions. We are overcome at the impetuosity of the love that filled the hearts of the martyrs and nerved them to face death in its most dreadful forms. We contemplate with emotion the sublime deeds of Christian heroism which history records: of St. Paul wishing himself an anathema from Christ for the love of his fellow-men; of St. Vincent de Paul selling himself into captivity to redeem a captive; but these and all other instances of love,—of the sublimest, most disinterested love, fail to give us any idea of the love of Jesus in giving His body to eat and His blood to drink. Not the maternal love of the parent, not the loftiest transports of pure human love; not the unconquerable love of the martyrs, not the divinest form of heaven-born Christian charity in saint or martyr, which nothing but the love of God could inspire, can convey to the mind the faintest image of the amazing, unutterable love of Christ in this Greatest of all mysteries.

It was then to overcome us by His goodness

that Christ came into the world. We have but a faint idea of what goodness is. We understand it in the abstract; in the concrete we experience and see but little of it. It is the greatest attribute of God, as it is of man. In proportion as men are possessed of it, do they resemble God: goodness in the human soul is the reflection and emanation of God Himself. It is His impelling motive in all that He has done outside of Himself. Creation, Redemption, the Holy Eucharist,—all His works find their motive in His goodness. God wanted creatures for no other purpose than to make them sharers of His goodness and witnesses of His glory.

Jesus Christ really present in this Sacrament is, indeed, the soul of the Church, and the continual Sacrifice of propitiation between the uplifted anger of God and the sins of men. Remove it, and the Church at once is, what the world would be, if you were to blot out the sun in heaven; and the anger of God at once falls upon the children of men: you would undo the work of Redemption carried on by the Church, and paralyze all the energies set in motion and sustained by the Holy Ghost dwelling within her for the salvation and sanctification of souls. Belief in this Mystery is a foretaste of the happiness of heaven; it fills even the material temple with something of heaven's majesty. It is this most consoling of truths, which, letting down heaven to earth, gives perseverance to the contemplative to pass his life before this God to the senses hidden, but to the light of faith made manifest.

From it flows the martyr's constancy, the virgin's chastity, the missionary's courage to leave father and mother and sister and brother and all things else, to spend his life and shed his blood for those for whom Christ did not hesitate to die. In this Sacrament Christ is not only the life of the Church, but the life of each individual soul; its daily supersubstantial bread. Honor then and love to Jesus in this Mystery of invincible and unutterable love.

The saints who now see Him face to face, were once compelled to worship him as we do now: as a hidden God: by their fervent faith, their ardent hope, their burning charity. If we would one day behold Him as they do now, we must be content during our mortal pilgrimage to worship Him as they did, by an unshaken faith that will realize His presence, an assured hope that will know no faltering, and an undying love which will stop at no sacrifice that His honor and glory may demand.

And having thus known Him in His Sacramental Presence here on earth, we shall come to enjoy His Manifested Presence; and to see Him face to face in heaven where we shall forever be partakers in the love and adoration of the Blessed Spirits whom St. John saw serving night and day before the Throne of the Lamb Who was slain; to Whom be all praise, and honor, and glory, and power, forever and ever. Amen.

THE NEW YORK
PUBLIC LIBRARY,

ASTOR LENOX AND
TILDEN FOUNDATIONS.

NECESSITY OF A TEACHER IN RELIGION.

Now an Angel of the Lord spoke to Philip, saying: Arise, go towards the south, to the way that goeth down from Jerusalem into Gaza: this is desert.

And rising up, he went. And behold a man of Ethiopia, an eunuch, of great authority under Candace the queen of the Ethiopians, who had charge over all her treasures, had come to Jerusalem to adore.

And he was returning, sitting in his chariot, and reading Isaias the prophet;

And the Spirit said to Philip: Go near, and join thyself to this chariot.

And Philip running thither, heard him reading the prophet Isaias. And he said: Thinkest thou that thou understandest what thou readest?

Who said: And how can I, unless some man show me? And he desired Philip that he would come up and sit with him.—Acts of the Apostles viii. 26-31.

WE have the same need of a teacher to-day as the eunuch had who could not understand " unless someone showed him." Widespread ignorance of religious truth and obstinate unbelief are as common in many places to-day as they were at the time mentioned in the Acts. However, we have a teacher at hand: Jesus to-day teaches from the See of St. Peter as truly as He formerly taught the Jews during His life. Let us beware lest we show ourselves as slow to understand and believe as they did.

One of the principal characteristics of our age, and more particularly of our own country, is every one's self-sufficiency. It shows itself in every-day life, in business affairs, in literary pursuits; it extends itself even to religion: reason is his only guide in these things which, from their very nature, are above its power. He is impatient of all restraint; he cannot endure the idea of authority. This is no doubt owing to the influence of our institutions; but its principal source is to be traced to the influence of Protestantism, to the pride of the human heart rising in rebellion against the divinely established authority of the Church.

No sect has maintained with greater fidelity, and with greater pertinacity, the proper office of reason, than the Catholic Church. Knowing it to be the gift, the work of God; recognizing in it the relative perfection to be found in all His works, she has ever sought to maintain for it its rightful dignity; not overrating its importance, nor elevating its scope beyond that for which it was designed; nor degrading it below its true rank, its due province. While Protestantism has at one time exaggerated its office in religion and at another has degraded it, the Catholic Church has ever assigned to it its definite well-fixed limits. She claims that it is the prelude to faith; its office is to consider the extrinsic motives of religion, to determine the fact of a Revelation, and who are its divinely appointed custodians and teachers;

to lead us to, not to invade, the sanctuary. She maintains that any apparent contradiction between it and the truths revealed, is but apparent, not real; that it arises not from these truths being opposed to reason, but from being above and beyond the ken and scope of reason. Reason and Revelation have both the same author; therefore, there can be no contradiction in His works. Hence, we should not seek to test the reasonableness of what God teaches, for we know beforehand that it is reasonable and must be reasonable. She claims that reason is not a sufficient guide in matters of religion, that it is insufficient to discover any save a few of the elemental truths of religion: it must be assisted by a divine teacher: its horizon should blend into and form one with the horizon of Revelation, by which it is to be elevated, illuminated, and strengthened.

Faith is a Divine virtue which inclines the mind to assent to a doctrine as true, which we do not see, which we cannot prove; because God, who cannot lie, says it is true. And since God does not in person propose to us the truths to be believed, but commissions His Church to do so, faith is exercised when we believe in the teachings of the Church, because she is God's authority or messenger upon earth.

Faith is one of the theological virtues. It is a gift of God. Without His grace we would be unable to elicit an act of faith. "It is the beginning, the root, the foundation of justification." "Without faith it is impossible to please God." As without it, we cannot be saved, God grants it to all who seek for it with humble and docile hearts. It is an act not merely of the intellect, nor merely of the will; it is the act of both. The will, moved and directed by grace, inclines the intellect to accept the truth of what is proposed: not because of its intrinsic credibility, but because of the authority and truth of God, Who can neither deceive nor be deceived.

The holy virtue of which we speak is not opinion. Opinion is the result of doubt: but faith is immeasurably removed from all doubt. We do not think or opine the truths of revelation to be true; in that there would be no real faith; we are certain of their truth with a certainty greater than that of any human demonstration. The certainty of the truth of faith is the certainty of the truth of God.

Nor is faith to be confounded with conviction. Conviction is the result of argument and of investigation. But faith is the result of the unerring word of God. We may be convinced of the truth of a doctrine, and yet not believe it. We often know what we ought to do, and yet we fail to do it. Many are convinced that the Catholic Church is the true one; and yet they do not believe in it. Such people need, and must pray for, grace to move their will.

Faith from its nature is entire in its scope. It is the authority of God that induces us to accept any truth revealed; we have the same authority for all. To believe part and reject part is fatal to the very conception of faith. He who would reject one truth, and believe another, would do so because the one would have for him some intrinsic credibility which would be wanting to the other. The word of God, pledged for the truth of both, would not be sufficient for him; hence, he would make shipwreck of his faith.

Faith being the acceptance by the heart and soul and mind of whatever God reveals because of His truth and authority, is necessarily the firmest of assents. It is most decided, positive, immovable in its nature; it admits of no doubt; it is shaken by no difficulty; it is the result of no demonstration. It is founded on the word of God; the same yesterday, to-day, and forever. No possible difficulties, however great or numerous, though they seem to our minds to possess an overwhelming force, can dislodge or disturb it. They may be explained away, or given up as inexplicable; but faith, having its everlasting foundation in the truth of God, remains forever. Thus we see what faith is, and its constituent elements. The act of the mind by which we accept and believe the truth revealed, is the act of faith; the object of faith is what is revealed; the motive that leads us to believe, is the authority and truth of God.

Human society could not exist without what may be called natural faith. No one is sufficient for himself. We must believe one another in many things which we are not able, and have not the time, to investigate for ourselves. The scholar must believe his master. He cannot test for himself the accuracy of his master's teaching. The scientist cannot investigate every branch of knowledge. If he would advance in knowledge, he must rely for much on the authority of those who have gone before him. Every man even unconsciously exercises this natural faith. We believe the world is round, we believe in the discoveries of astronomy, we believe that China exists; who knows those things from his own personal experience? No one can examine everything for himself, and no one will think of doubting anything simply because he himself has not examined it. Human society would be dissolved without faith: knowledge could never progress, the relations of men would cease, commerce could not be thought of, the most ordinary and necessary duties of every-day life would be impossible. If, now, faith is necessary in the affairs of this life, how much more so in the affairs of the life to come? If we have not the time and ability to investigate for ourselves matters of this life, which fall under our senses and are within the scope of our reason, how much less competent are we to investigate, for ourselves, the eternal truths, which are so far removed from our senses, and which so immeasurably transcend the power of our reason? If we must accept the authority of others for what we are so familiar with, how reasonable that we should accept the authority of God for the impenetrable mysteries of religion, that are infinitely beyond the grasp of our finite comprehension.

The necessity of faith is shown, too, from the waywardness of our reason. Reason infallible in itself, is anything but infallible in man,—subject as he is to passion, blinded by prejudice, misled by his feelings, prone to error. Consider how few subjects there are either in politics, or science, or literature, or art, in which there are not the most opposite views. How little of unanimity there is on any of these things on which we should naturally expect the greatest accord. See, too, the persistency, the stubbornness with which men maintain their conflicting opinions on these subjects. See the wild, lamentable antagonism continually raging in the world of politics. See the untiring energy, the fearful pertinacity exhibited by political factions in the espousal of their respective views. See how nations will go to war and shed the blood of millions of their subjects, and exhaust millions of their wealth, to maintain some opinion or to defend some theory. History is but a record of battles lost and won,—battles brought on by the perversity of human reason. The most powerful nations, the most enlightened peoples of the world have shed blood in torrents, for the assertion of some theory or principle to which all could not, or would not subscribe. If, now, in science, in politics, in matters with which we are familiar, which are, so to speak, on a level with reason, there exists so mighty, so stubborn a conflict of opinion, how can we expect unanimity on subjects religious, and so far above us, so little within the domain of reason? If we cannot agree in our opinion of a book, or on a point of science, or on a principle of politics, or on a theory of government; what hope can there be that men will agree on matters that so far transcend the intellect of man, as the truths and mysteries of Revelation? Here we see that reason is inadequate to interpret and preserve the truths of Revelation, even when revealed. Some teacher divinely taught, and capable of exacting faith in his teachings, is a necessary part of Revelation: without it, Revelation would be incomplete; without it, Revelation would not accomplish the end for which it was vouchsafed. To those who have substituted reason or private judgment, for the living voice of a Divine teacher, nothing remains of the Revelation of Christ save fragments and rationalism; they are even drifting into Atheism. Such is the fatal, undermining process when reason assumes wanton, unrestrained license with supernatural truth. All this shows the need of Divine Faith to guide human reason, even after Revelation has been disclosed to men.

Faith and reason are both gifts of God. Faith perfects reason, and introduces it to a knowledge of truths which of itself it could never reach. It is an act of the highest reason to yield to faith and to accept its teachings. It is the very genius of reason to pay to God the homage of our understanding, and to believe, on His authority, what we cannot comprehend.

While then there should be no opposition between reason, which discovers truths of the natural order, and faith, which accepts the supernatural truths disclosed by Divine Revelation, yet, as reason is obscured and perverse in fallen man, there is deadly conflict between them. Its natural proneness is to doubt and scepticism; nor can it be otherwise, when, forgetting its proper office, it dares to scrutinize the intrinsic nature of supernatural truth. This tendency is all the greater when revealed truth seems to contradict its light and dictates. Hence, when Revelation came into the world, reason at once assailed it. Philosophy and heresy have always sought to quench its Divine light. Every point of Revelation has in turn been subjected to the scrutiny of unregenerate reason. It has only been by the Divine, infallible authority of the Church, exacting an immediate and unflinching faith, that Revelation has been preserved in its original purity and integrity. Nothing short of such authority is equal to the task of repressing the inherent and irresistible tendency of reason to doubt and unbelief. Faith, then, is necessary to protect Revelation from the assaults of reason.

Nor can it be said that the Spirit of truth will illuminate the mind of the reader of Holy Scripture so as to teach him its true meaning. The Holy Ghost cannot teach contradictions. Consider how the Word of God is read and understood by private judgment, and you will see that God could have never intended private judgment as a standard or rule of faith. Some relying on private judgment in their interpretation, think that the Holy Scriptures do not warrant the belief, the most fundamental of the Christian Faith and received by all who have any claim to orthodoxy, that there are Three Persons in One God. The very corner-stone of Christianity, and the very soul of the Mystery of Redemption, is that Jesus Christ was true God and true Man, and that He offered Himself as the divinely appointed Victim and Atonement for our sins and salvation. Many while believing in the Word of God, yet interpreting it by the light of their private judgment, claim that it contains no proof of His divinity, nor of any redemption or salvation wrought for us by His sufferings and blood. All Catholics, not to speak of others in heresy or schism, believe that the words by which Our Lord instituted the Eucharistic Sacrifice evidently express the Real Presence of His body and blood: others who claim to be no less but even more His faithful followers, teach that such an understanding of His words is absurd and idolatrous; a manifest perversion of what was obviously a symbol or figure. Can, then, God, Who came to teach us the truth, to reclaim us from error, Who willed that there should be but One Faith, as there was but One Lord and One Baptism, have given us as the foundation and rule of our faith, and for our guidance in the all-important matter of our eternal salvation, a principle so fatal to truth, so fruitful of contradictions and error, so subversive of the very foundations of Christianity!

But let us see if they who object to belief in mysteries, do not believe in mysteries themselves: nay, in mysteries far greater than we are called upon to believe, and let us ask if they find anything unreasonable in so doing. The man who objects to faith in things incomprehensible is either an infidel or a Protestant. If the former, he believes that God created the world; let him explain how God could, by a single word, or by any other way, bring forth from nothing the immense and marvellous universe of which this our world is but an atom. Yet, perhaps, he will deny that God created it at all. How then came it to exist? How could the world exist and have no cause? It could not cause itself; it cannot have existed from everlasting. Who could explain the absurdities and mysteries inseparable from the idea of an everlasting world? What mind could reconcile the contradictions involved in the thought of making God and the world identical? Let then the infidel explain these mysteries of which that of creation is but one, which he himself never thinks of doubting, before he carps at the mysteries of the Christian Religion. He believes mysteries far greater than any which we Catholics are called upon to believe.

But the Protestant scoffs at Catholic Mysteries, while he himself believes implicitly mysteries harder to be believed than any the Church proposes. He believes in the Trinity; let him explain how God can be Three in One. He believes in the Incarnation; let him explain the unfathomable mystery in the thought of God becoming Man. He believes in the transmission of original sin; let him explain the manner in which this sin is diffused, and let him show the justice which decrees that the child inherits the sin committed before it was born, and in which it could have had no personal participation. Does the Church call upon us to believe mysteries greater than these? They scoff at the thought of God being confined in a little tabernacle. If they lived in the time of

Christ, they would have derided the thought of God being born in a stable. They would not have been of the number of the wise men who followed the star till it led them to find their Redeemer, lying in a manger, with an ox and an ass for His companions. They talk of the irreverence to which He is liable in the Divine Sacrament. Are they forgetful of the insults which in the flesh He suffered from His creatures? Do they forget the details of the Passion? the mockery, the haling to and fro, how He was spit upon, crowned with thorns, made a fool of, done even unto death, by those for whom He shed His blood? His blood may be spilled, they say, in this Sacrament. But was it not spilled on the Cross? Is it exposed to any profanation greater than that which it suffered on the way to the hill of Calvary? They who are scandalized or astonished at the sacrileges to which the Body of Christ is exposed, in the belief of His Real Presence,—if they had been present on the day of the Crucifixion and followed the Saviour through His bloody journey, might have seen even the streets of Jerusalem reddened with His sacred blood, as it fell from His torn and mangled body! And yet even this did not hinder Him from consummating the great Sacrifice which He had come into the world to make, nor extinguish the love which filled His heart. What incongruity, then, in believing that, for the same love, He has placed Himself in this Sacrament, and again exposed Himself to ignominy, outrage, sacrilege?—that He is willing to enter into hearts filled with hatred, anger, black with perfidy?—that He is willing to suffer the passion even all over again for our sakes?

I have explained to you the nature and necessity of Divine Faith. Now the question offers itself: What are we to believe? The answer is: All that God has revealed. But how are we to know what He has revealed? Has He established any means by which we may learn it? As it has pleased God to exact from man belief in truths far beyond the reach of the human mind, it was necessary that He should establish some authority by which the fact of Revelation might be unerringly determined; by which its sense might be infallibly known; by which its integrity and purity might be forever preserved. Such an authority has God, in His wisdom, given to us in the Church which He has set up on earth, and made the depositary and guardian and teacher of His Revelation. This Church endowed with inerrancy, promised the perpetual and unfailing light of the Holy Ghost, and in which He dwells teaching her all truth and guarding her from all error, is to teach us what we have to believe and what we have to do in order to salvation.

It is only by the prompt, immediate, unhesitating submission and unflinching adherence of the mind to such an authority, divinely instituted and divinely taught, that we can be safeguarded from the distressing perplexity and chaos of doubt in which the mind is lost, when, with its limited powers, it presumes to match itself with the infinity of God and to comprehend things incomprehensible. It is only by this same submission to the Church, that we can be preserved in unity of faith; that we can escape being "tossed about by every wind of doctrine;" that the truths of Revelation can be protected against the incredulity and scepticism of the human mind. It is this principle of submission to authority, which separates us from the countless sects and uncounted innovations of those who have cast it off, and have arrogated to themselves the right of interpreting the Scriptures, every one for himself, in spite of the admonition of the Apostle: "that no interpretation of Scripture is to be made by private authority, as there are many things therein hard to be understood, which the unwary and unwise wrestle to their own destruction." By this same principle over 300,000,000 of men, differing widely in race, nationality, language, customs, feelings, and sympathies, are brought to partake the same Sacraments, join in the same Worship, acknowledge the same Head, and believe the same Truths. They are assured of their belief; it is like Him on whom it is built, "the same yesterday, to-day, and forever, and its record is from generation to generation."

It was by this principle of exacting submission to her teachings, that the Church was enabled in all ages to withstand and to control the wild scepticism of the human intellect and the stubborn pride of the human will. By the same means she was enabled amidst the vicissitudes of human events, and the assaults directed against her, to preserve Divine Revelation in all its primitive wholeness and unstained from the defilement of heresy. By this means has she been able to bring home the truths of Revelation to all men : to the millions who are unable to read the Scriptures, as well as those who, although able to read them, are yet utterly unequal to the task of rightly knowing or determining their meaning. It was the Will of Christ that the Gospel should be made known to every creature. Submission to a teacher divinely taught, is the only adequate means for this end. This submission to the Church is explicitly enjoined by Christ. It was not the dead letter of Scripture, but the living, energizing voice of an Unerring Teacher, that He introduced into the world to teach and enlighten men, and to impart to them the graces of Redemption.

While we should with the liveliest feelings of the deepest gratitude, thank God for the inestimable gift of Faith which He has bestowed upon us, yet we should never forget that faith alone is not sufficient for our salvation. Though we should have faith to move mountains, it will avail nothing, unless accompanied and animated by charity. Our faith must be a living, an operating faith; a faith instinct with charity. As the body without the spirit is dead, so faith without good works is dead. A faith barren of good works will serve rather for our condemnation than for our justification. Our actions must correspond with our belief, which should be the informing principle of our daily life and character. " He that doeth the will of My Father, Who is in heaven, he shall enter into heaven."

THE IMMACULATE CONCEPTION OF THE BLESSED VIRGIN MARY.

And the Lord God said to the serpent: Because thou hast done this thing, thou art cursed above all cattle, and beasts of the earth: upon thy breast shalt thou go, and dust shalt thou eat all the days of thy life.

I will put enmity between thee and the woman, and between thy seed and her seed: she shall crush thy head, and thou shalt lie in wait for her heel.—Gen. iii. 14-15.

The Church honors the saints because they are the work of God. It is a true principle to honor the artificer in his work, for there is nothing in it which comes not from his hand. Every perfection which it possesses, and every purpose for which it serves, is to be ascribed to the wisdom and power of the mind that conceived it and of the hand that made it. In this way we can honor the great Creator, in things the most insignificant that He has made. The vilest insect that we trample under foot, becomes a fit subject in which to find His praise. We can, indeed, praise the Lord, and in all His works.

Yet, in our admiration and praise of the works of God, we must be careful that we rest not in the work itself. We must praise the Lord, truly, in His work. To adore the creature without reference to its Creator, would be idolatry. As in the great law of Christian charity we are to love our neighbor not precisely for his own sake, but because of God whose image and likeness he is; so, in like manner, we are to praise the creatures of God because they manifest His wisdom and power, and reflect, in some degree, His own divine perfection.

The Church honors the saints because they are the noblest work of God in the supernatural order, the very masterpieces of His grace. Of themselves they are nothing. They were men of like passions with ourselves; hewn out of the same mass of our fallen humanity, subject to the same temptations, and, left to themselves, would have fallen into the same sins. It was God's powerful grace that made them what they became. Hence, in honoring the saints we honor God Himself. We recognize His power and wisdom just as truly as we do when we admire His works in the natural order. The higher character of the object does not diminish the worship.

This principle of honoring God in His saints, as far as it goes, justifies the honor and veneration which the Church offers to the Blessed Virgin Mary, the Mother of God, the Queen of Saints and the most supreme work of Divine grace. As the greatest of the saints, she is entitled to their worship; and as Mother of God, she is entitled to something immeasurably greater. All the honor the Church claims for her is for the sake of God Incarnate, Whose mother she is. All the gifts which she received from the hand of God, were given to her that she might be not unworthy to be His mother; all the Church's recognition of these gifts proceeds from its wish to honor God Who has conferred them. The Church's love of God is so exuberant and overflowing that it loves not only Him, but all who had any relation with Him; and the closer the relation, the greater the honor it bestows. It is because of Mary's intimate relations with the great mystery of the Incarnation, that the Church claims for her all her great prerogatives. It is because she was the Mother of God Incarnate, and that, in the words of the prayer of the Mass of the Immaculate Conception, she might be a worthy tabernacle in which He might dwell, that the Church claims for her the sublime gift of an Immaculate Conception.

It is well that we should understand clearly what is meant, when we say that Mary was conceived immaculate. Like so many other of the doctrines taught by the Church, it is sometimes misunderstood, and even misrepresented by its enemies.

You are aware, of course, that we are all born in sin, "born children of wrath." We all sinned in Adam, we all died in Adam. Our race is fallen. We have all shared the curse once uttered against our first parents. We are defiled with original sin. Mary is the sole exception to this universal law. "She is our tainted nature's solitary boast." This is what is meant by her Immaculate Conception. She enjoyed immunity from this curse. She was never stained with this original sin. Theologians distinguish between the active, and passive conception of a human being. The active conception is that by which the human body is formed and prepared for the indwelling of the soul. The passive is the union, or infusion of the soul into the body. With Mary's active conception the doctrine of the Immaculate Conception has nothing to do. Her body was formed in the same way as that of the rest of the children of Eve. The body of Jesus alone was formed by the miraculous interposition of the Holy Ghost. Her Immaculate Conception regards her passive conception, and means that when the soul was formed in the moment of its union with the body, it was formed free from original sin.

Was she not redeemed? She was redeemed as truly as any of the children of men. But the manner of her redemption was different. We are redeemed from original sin, after having once incurred it. She was redeemed from it, before she had incurred it. She was preserved from it, in the words of the prayer of the Feast, because of the merits of Christ foreseen and applied in anticipation to her soul. The grace of Christ was beforehand with sin, and claimed as its own, the soul of her of whom God was one day to be born Man. She was, then, redeemed.

Remark well, that we say, she was free from original sin, in the first moment of her conception. There were not two moments, in one of which she was conceived in sin, and in the second, or thereafter, cleansed therefrom. This would have been sanctification in the womb; a transcendant privilege, surely, but far below that which we

THE IMMACULATE CONCEPTION. 333

claim for the Mother of God. In the instant in which her soul was created, it was created in entire innocence of all original sin.

Is this truth divinely revealed? We answer that it unmistakably is. Here let us state that there are several ways in which a truth may be revealed in Scripture, or in Tradition. It may be declared explicitly, as when it is enunciated in so many words. Thus the unity of God is declared in the words uttered by Moses, " Hear, O Israel! the Lord our God is one God." Thus the Incarnation, in the words of St. John, " The Word was made flesh and dwelt amongst us." Truths may be declared virtually or implicitly, as when they are contained in Scripture, not in so many words, but in their meaning, or by logical analysis or necessary consequence. Thus the Council of Nice declared the consubstantiality of the Word as virtually contained in the scripture proofs of Christ's divinity. Christ Himself reasoned the resurrection of the dead from the words, " I am the God of Abraham, of Isaac, and of Jacob." He is the God of the living, not of the dead. Thus also were deduced, by logical consequence, the procession of the Holy Ghost from the Father and the Son as from one principle; the existence in Christ of two wills and of two operations; not to speak of many other doctrines. Of these truths thus virtually or implicitly made known, some are revealed manifestly, some obscurely.

Now, the truth of Mary's Immaculate Conception belongs to this latter class. It is implicitly, though obscurely, revealed. It is revealed by implication in the fact of Mary's being the Mother of God. Once granted that the Eternal God has become her child, and we at once infer her freedom from all sin. And this out of reverence to the Lord, and because we must believe that He prepared her to be a Mother, not unworthy of Himself. An Immaculate Conception must have been one of the graces which He bestowed upon her, to prepare her for this sublime vocation. If we claim exemption for Mary from all actual sin because she was the Mother of the Most High, for the same reason, we must believe that never, for an instant, did the stain of original sin defile her soul. Of this argument we shall have more to say before the close of our discourse.

We find Mary's Immaculate Conception virtually contained in, and logically deducible from, the promise of mercy and reconciliation which Almighty God made to our first parents after their fall, and contained in the Third chapter of the book of Genesis.

Scarcely was man created when the devil sought to accomplish his destruction, and in him, that of all his posterity. He tempted Eve. She yielded to the temptation. She tempted Adam. Adam yielded to the temptation, and all men sinned in him. Thus the race, in its very origin, was involved in a dreadful estrangement from its Creator.

But God determined to save man from the effects of his sin. He pitied him because he had been circumvented and foiled by the stratagem of the evil one. He promised him future reconciliation with Himself, and future triumph over the seducer. He will destroy the enmity which the devil has sought to introduce between man and his God. He will retort this enmity upon the head of the devil himself. He will raise up a seed that shall crush the head of the serpent, and so undo his treacherous work. "And I will place enmities between thee and the woman, between her seed and thy seed, and she shall crush thy head, and thou shalt lie in wait for her heel."

Nothing diviner and nothing more according to the order which Divine providence is pleased to adopt in other things, than that the instruments of man's subversion should serve for his restoration. The evil one made use of the woman, as the instrument for the destruction of the human race. God made use of the woman for its redemption. The devil employed a lying friendship, that he might seduce Eve and afterwards enslave her. God employed the hostility of the second woman to Satan, that she might never be his friend or his slave. The devil by his triumph over Eve, the mother of all men, subjected to himself the whole race. God restores to Himself the whole race, in the triumph which the new woman, by her seed, wins over the evil one. That He may thus overcome the evil one by his own arms, it is necessary that God should raise up another woman who should never be bound to him in friendship, nor enslaved by sin; but who, by reason of the eternal hostility to him in which she would be conceived, and by reason of the hostility of her seed, would pursue with undying hate, and would thoroughly rout and destroy him, rescuing the human race which he had seduced from God and enslaved to himself.

If this was God's plan for the conquest of the seducer, and the redemption of mankind, it was necessary that the new woman,—the divinely appointed instrument of that restoration, should never be the friend or the slave, by sin, of him whose head she was to crush. No stain or consequence of that primal sin should pollute or degrade the new Eve, who was to be the very antithesis of the first. Mary's original integrity and innocence should be the first-fruits of the divinely appointed conquest of Satan, and the destruction, through her and her seed, of the dark dominion of the prince of this world. As the defeat and disgrace of the first woman had entailed upon her posterity the loss of untold blessings, so the triumph of the second woman should be the triumph of all her children, and should restore to them all the blessings which, through the first woman, they had lost. Mary, the mother of the living, taking the place of Eve, the mother of the dead, and united in the most intimate and indissoluble union with her seed, should never have been the victim of the tyranny and slavery which she was to destroy; but should have been conceived in the innocence and freedom from sin which she was to bring among men. As Christ Himself, the seed of the woman, so she, in whom He was formed, and who was made one with Him in his warfare against Satan, and whose hostility

THE IMMACULATE CONCEPTION. 337

to Satan was identical with His own, should never have been obscured by sin or involved in its consequences.

The woman in her seed, is to overcome Satan by virtue of the hostility that shall exist between them. What is the nature of that hostility? I answer that it is an hostility proper to the woman; perpetual and peculiar in its own nature. It belongs to the woman alone. It is not the property of any other of the children of men, for the article "the" points out some distinguished woman. The manner of speech indicates that it is proper to the woman alone; no other person is mentioned, which would not happen, if the hostility belonged to others as well as to her mentioned. The intimate union between the woman and her seed indicates that the enmity of one to the evil one is the same as that of the other. But this enmity of her Divine Son could not be shared by others. The hostility spoken of is perpetual. As it is identical with that of her Son, it must have been from everlasting in the Eternal Mind. The closest union exists between the woman and her seed. They are, so to speak, knit closely together for the conflict with Satan. The arms that they shall employ, is the one identical hostility, not two several kinds. When God says that He will place enmity between Satan and the woman, the construction of words indicates that there shall be no previous friendship, afterwards to be dissolved, between the woman and the serpent; but that the hostility will be before all friendship. If it were a question of separating the woman already in friendship with the serpent, God would say that He would place enmity "between the woman and between the serpent." If He wished to make the division before such friendship was contracted, He would say that which He actually does say, "between thee and the woman." Enmity "between thee and between the woman" would apply to those justified even in this life, and to those sanctified in the womb; enmity "between thee and the woman" means more; it means not rescued from sin once incurred, but saved from incurring sin. Mary's enmity, therefore, to the evil one was not a friendship broken up; it was a friendship debarred, one that never existed. It was a perpetual hostility, even as that of her Divine seed. Never was she held in the yoke of original sin. No friendship between Mary and Satan was possible, from the moment that God decreed that He would place enmity between the serpent, and her whom He would raise up to be its vanquisher and the restorer of the race. Therefore, in God's mind, Mary was exempted from original sin, in the day when He proclaimed this future reconciliation of men to be wrought through her and her Divine seed. From the bitter antagonism between the devil and his seed on the one hand, and the woman and her seed on the other, it is obvious to believe that Mary could never have belonged to the hostile camp,—could never have been of the seed of the serpent; but all conceived in original sin are of the evil seed. Behold Mary side by side with her God, in this first promise of future redemption and reconciliation, made by Him to the estranged sons of men. Behold her united to Him in the closest possible union, made one with Him, made consubstantial with Him in His human nature, even as a mother is with her son. Reconcile, if you can, with such a union, the existence of the least stain of sin in her soul and the least friendship for Satan; deny, if you can, that Mary's hostility was perpetual, even as that of her Son. As the hostility spoken of is personal to Mary, as it is confined to her alone, and as it is perpetual, it is easy to learn what the nature of it must be. It is not the enmity which exists between the devil, and those who have cast aside his yoke in baptism; it is not the enmity which comes from abstinence from all actual sin; it is not the enmity which is implied by sanctification in the womb. These different hostilities are common to many; but Mary's, confined as it is to herself, and perpetual in duration, is not any of these. It is nothing less than that primordial hostility which resulted from the destruction, in the first moment of her conception, of the friendship implied in original sin.

Besides the literal sense in Holy Scripture, which is the direct, obvious meaning of the Divine word, there is as well a spiritual signification, equally intended by the Holy Ghost. It is rather the things signified, than the direct ideas expressed by the words. It is the result of the fecundity of the Divine mind, its Author. In this spiritual sense, we find much reference to the Mother of God in the Old Testament. Thus, according to the Fathers of the Church, the Temple, the Altar, and the Sacrificial victims, are to be taken as figures or emblems of the Blessed Virgin. Among the Jews there was nothing holier than the Altar and its Victim; no profaned hand was allowed to touch them; but once a year the high priest entered the Holy of Holies. How pure, then, and how free from all possible defilement, should she not be whom these types prefigured, and of whose sanctity they were the emblem?

We come now to consider the words of the Archangel, addressed to Mary, "Hail, Mary, full of grace, the Lord is with Thee." The Greek word which is rendered "full of grace" properly means, full to overflowing, full to surfeit, laden with grace. Such a salutation as this had never before been addressed to any of the children of Eve. Angels had been often sent as messengers from God to man, to Abraham, to Jacob, to St. Joseph, to St. Peter; but never has such a greeting been recorded. No wonder that Mary was alarmed, as Origen remarks. For she was familiar with the ancient Scriptures and Prophecies, and was aware that no such words had ever before been heard. This unheard-of salutation is the angelic recognition of the unparalleled gift of Divine grace which adorned the soul of her alone, to whom alone of all the children of Eve it was addressed. This gift is that she possessed grace in all its fulness, even before she had conceived God Incarnate. What does this mean but her unstained origin, her Immaculate Conception?

Bellarmine, in his Catechism, tells us what is meant by "full of grace." The grace of God works in the soul, especially, three effects. First, it destroys sins, which as stains contaminate the soul. Second, it adorns the soul with gifts and virtues. Third, it supplies it with strength, that it may be earnest in meritorious works, particularly pleasing to the Divine Majesty.

Our Lady is full of grace. She was infected with no stain of sin, either original, or actual, or mortal, or venial; she had all virtues, and all the gifts of the Holy Ghost, in the highest grade. She performed works so pleasing to God and meritorious, that as regards body and soul, she was worthy to transcend all the choirs of angels. She was, indeed, full of grace, and blessed among women.

The truth of this surpassing privilege of the Mother of God is likewise contained in Divine tradition. The lofty conception that the Church has always entertained of Mary's sanctity, and the cherished belief of the faithful, have been such as to virtually include the persuasion of her Immaculate Conception and to exclude anything contrary thereto. All Christian antiquity venerated the Mother of God, as a new creation upon earth, absolutely unlike the rest of mankind, and immeasurably superior to the greatest of the saints, in her ineffable graces and exalted spiritual endowments. Her holiness was not merely that of the saints, yet incomparably greater in degree; but of a new order and kind from that which had ever before been known on earth, or conceived by the human mind. New expressions and phrases were sought to adequately designate this new sanctity which had come among men. Before her transcendent and incomparable holiness, the glory of the seraphim and of the angels sinks, even as the light of the stars before the rising sun. "She is a paradox of grace, a mystery and a miracle." St. Ephraem salutes her, as "The plenitude of the graces of the august Trinity." St. Thomas says that, "She received so great a plenitude of graces as to come as near as possible to God." St. Bonaventure, "Mary is one greater than whom God cannot make." In a word, the Fathers teach that in her dwells the fulness of divine grace;" that "her purity merited for her, because of the graces given to her, the rank of Mother of God;" that "she is dearer to God than all other creatures;" that "her holiness is second to that of God only; that "her excellence can never be sufficiently celebrated." The persuasion of Catholic tradition that Mary's holiness was of a rank and of a degree to preclude any defilement, actual or original, is shown in the words and titles by which the Fathers of the Church sought to give it adequate expression. Of these, some deny to her every possible defect or sin; others claim for her every possible degree of purity and sanctity. She is called "the faultless," "the immaculate," "the undefiled," "the unadulterated," "destitute of the least admixture of aught that stains." Not content with this praise, they declare her "altogether unspotted," "completely and entirely immaculate." And St. John

Damicene salutes Mary, " Thou art the seat of the Divinity, O! completely and entirely immaculate." The Council of Basle declared that, " Belief in the Immaculate Conception was pious, and in harmony with ecclesiastical worship, Catholic faith, right reason, and Holy Scripture ; and to be approved, held and embraced by all Catholics." The Council of Trent declared that, in its Decree on the transmission of original sin, it was not to be understood to mean to include the Blessed Virgin Mary.

In the Acts which record the martyrdom of St. Andrew, we read in the Discourse spoken by him in presence of the pro-counsel Egeus : " And, therefore, because the first man was created of immaculate earth, it was necessary that of an immaculate virgin should be born that perfect man, by whom the Son of God (who first formed man) was to restore that eternal life which men had lost." Origen says, " Mary was not infected by the breath of the poisonous serpent." The Greek menologies saluted Mary, as " free from blemish ; " as " she who was formed pure from all eternity." St. Jerome, " Mary was never in darkness, but always in light." St. Augustine, " Except therefore the Holy Virgin Mary whom, through respect for the Lord, I will not suffer to be named when there is question of sin ; for do we not know that, in order to conquer sin entirely, a fulness of grace has been conferred on her who merited to bear Him, Who it is certain had no sin ? " St. Cyril, " All men, except Him Who was born of a Virgin and the Virgin herself, were born in original sin." St.

Ildephonse, "It is certain Mary was exempted from original sin." St. John Damicene, "To Mary, the serpent had no access." St. Peter Damian, "The flesh of the virgin received from Adam, admitted none of Adam's guilt." *

The comparison which the Fathers of the Church continually make between Mary and Eve, indicates more clearly than even explicit words (if anything could be more explicit than this antithesis) their belief in her Immaculate Conception, and her unapproachable rank in the plan of man's Redemption. St. Paul declared that, "as in Adam we all died, so in Christ we were all made to live." The Fathers adopting this suggestion, declare Mary to be the mother of the living, as Eve had been the mother of the race fallen from grace and dead in sin. She is the source of life, while Eve is the source of death. She is the faithful child of the Most High, while Eve is the slave of the evil one. From Eve came the poison that has contaminated the race and destroyed it. From Mary comes the purifying and restoring medicine that shall cure,— the healing balm that shall extinguish the sin and restore mankind. As with Adam and his disobedience, they contrast Christ and His obedience unto death; so with Eve's pride and prevarication, do they contrast Mary's humility and fidelity. Mary with her seed is the source and instrument of humanity regenerated and restored,- even as Eve had been the instrument of its fall. Continually do they compare Mary, with Eve yet

---

* The authorities consulted in this discourse are chiefly Passaglia, Wiseman, and Lambruschini.

innocent and the faithful daughter of the Most High. And the similarity is the strongest for which they can find expression. Continually do they contrast Mary always innocent, with Eve guilty,—the slave of sin and of Satan. The contrast or dissimilarity is the fullest and completest they can conceive, or that any words at their command can declare: as opposite as light and darkness, as virtue and sin, as God and His enemy, as salvation and perdition; the antagonism is as great, as extremes the most opposite can declare. As the archangel Michael was unlike Lucifer, as the angels that stood faithful were unlike the faithless that fell, as Christ was the antithesis of Adam, so was Mary the opposite of Eve. The condemnation of the race, and the punishments inflicted upon it, brought about by Eve, never reached her,—the contagion of Eve's sin never contaminated her soul. She was never seduced by the arts of the evil one, never for a moment yielded to him; nor was separated from, nor wavered in her loyalty to, God: that is, never incurred original sin.

We should not omit to mention that the truth of the Immaculate Conception of the Mother of God, was always believed by the faithful in the Church. The universal belief of the faithful in a doctrine, is a far greater proof of its divine revelation, than would be at first supposed. Such universal belief can only come from the guidance and illumination of the Holy Ghost. The permission of so universal an error could, with difficulty, be reconciled with Christ's gracious promises to His Church. If the gates of hell were never to prevail against it, it was that the belief of the faithful should be forever preserved pure and undefiled. Patavius, one of the profoundest theologians, of unrivalled gifts and wondrous erudition, declared that he believed in the Immaculate Conception, because it was the universal belief of the faithful.

When we say that it was universally believed, we are not to be understood to mean, that it was believed absolutely everywhere, and without any exception. Opposition here and there only showed that it was not yet defined. Such exceptional opposition is in the very nature of things, until the doctrine is formally and explicitly enunciated. From St. Augustine, declaring that he would tolerate no mention of Mary when there was a question of sin, to the Council of Trent, enunciating that, in teaching all men to have incurred original sin, it was not its intention to include the Blessed Virgin, the voice of antiquity, the intimate persuasion of the faithful, and the unanimous opinion of the Fathers of the Church, and the teachings of theologians, all declare for Mary's immunity from the defilement of original sin.

Even if Holy Scripture were less explicit, even if Divine tradition were less full and decisive, yet the Immaculate Conception of the Mother of God would flow, as a necessary consequence, from truths and principles already revealed. The relation of Mary to the Adorable Mystery of the Incarnation would bespeak her Immaculate

Origin. She was the Mother of God Incarnate. She who was thus united in the closest of all unions with the God of all holiness, could never have lain under the shadow of sin.

From all eternity, God decreed to become man. The Lamb was slain in God's eternal counsels before the foundations of the world. The creature to whom was reserved the unspeakable privilege of being His mother, must have been pre-elected from everlasting. This, surely, was assigning to her a great part in the plan of the Incarnation. Great privilege it was to have been elected from all the daughters of Eve, from the glorious women of the Old Law, and the more glorious still of the New,—virgins and martyrs who spent their lives in pondering every incident in the life of the Redeemer, loving hearts, souls burning to shed their blood for His sake; inexpressibly exalted, then, was the dignity of Mary. It, surely, carries with it the presumption that She who was thus exalted, was conceived without sin. God could grant such a grace: therefore He did grant it. What is fitting God always does. God the Father could not permit His Son, the very "figure of His substance and splendor of His glory," to be born of one subject to the devil, His fiercest enemy. Ill would it become God the Son, to be indebted for His human nature to one from the seed of hell or the ranks of His enemy. God the Holy Ghost could not conceive in her, over whose soul sin had ever cast its darkened shadow. He who had the effrontery to tempt the Lord, when hungry, by offering Him, as if his, the kingdoms of the earth, would have reproached Jesus with such a mother.

Destined to be the Mother of God, with what sanctity, must She not have been furnished. Greater, certainly, than ever given to another child of Eve. For Her office was incomparably higher than any ever before assigned to the creature,—greater certainly than ever given to angel, or archangel, or seraphim; for, why are they pure, except to be worthy to approach God. How infinitely purer and holier should She not be, who is not merely to approach God, but to be His very Mother! So great should She be, to use the words of antiquity and the unanimous voice of the Fathers, as God could make Her. The first principle of this greatness is an Immaculate Conception.

In the Old Law, the Tabernacle, the Altar, and everything pertaining to the Worship, were made of the rarest and most precious material; and this, that they might be worthy of the Sacrifices, which were only types and figures. Jeremiah, probably, and John the Baptist, certainly, were sanctified in their mothers' wombs, that they might be worthy,—the one to pre-announce, and the other to prepare the way of, the Lord. In the New Law the Altar and the Chalice and the Hand of the priest, are anointed and consecrated with a wondrous consecration that they may be, in some sort, not unworthy to touch and to handle the body of Christ. How pure from all possible defilement, and with what sanctity should she not be adorned, in whose womb was to be conceived,

THE IMMACULATE CONCEPTION. 349

whose arms would fondle, whose breasts would nourish Jesus Incarnate. Gifts and graces vouchsafed by Almighty God, are always in keeping with the rank and duty assigned.

Finally, in our own day, the voice of the living Church illuminated and directed by the Holy Ghost, after profound discussion and exhaustive analysis lasting through centuries, has unerringly enunciated and drawn up in formal definition the truth, of which it had always been instinctively conscious ; but which now had been investigated to its foundations : that Mary, in the first moment of her conception, by the singular privilege of Almighty God, in view of the merits of Christ anticipated and applied to her soul, was conceived without the stain of original sin. This teaching made known by the Church divinely taught—the proximate rule of our faith—is sufficient for all Catholics. In proposing to our belief this prerogative of the Mother of God, the Church proposes nothing strange to our minds or abhorrent to our feelings. She but explicitly enunciates that which has always been virtually believed, of which the faithful were always deeply convinced, and which they ardently desired to see formally defined.

As of all other doctrines subsequently defined, the Church was, at first, conscious of this truth, and the faithful recognized it without formal teaching. Intimate persuasion of a truth may exist without the desire, or even the ability, to analyze it and to explain the arguments that support it. This was the state of the belief of the faithful in reference to the Immaculate Conception. Afterwards, the Church undertook to analyze this consciousness of the truth of Mary's Immaculate Conception, and to investigate its relations with other revealed doctrines. This began about the Twelfth Century. The Feast of her Immaculate Conception had been already established by the Roman Church, and was a manifest sign of its belief; for, as St. Thomas says, the Church cannot celebrate but what is holy, and the very object of the Feast, was the Immaculate Conception. During the controversies in Catholic schools on this privilege of the Mother of God, the Church remained silent; after long years, by encouraging the devotion and enriching it with Indulgences, she showed the leaning of her mind. She forbade that either side should censure the other, and, finally, threatened with gravest penalties those who wrote against the belief, or left objections to it unanswered. Centuries before its formal definition, it was unlawful to call it in question. The Council of Trent re-affirmed these censures, and declared that Mary was not included in its Dogma upon the diffusion of original sin.

The thought of the Mother of God, and the purifying influence that goes with it, were never more needed than at the present time. The spirit of impurity is everywhere. We breathe its atmosphere, continually. It pervades society, literature, art, and the noblest productions of genius; through these it stains the imagination of the young, and defiles the character of the more advanced, while it contaminates the consciences of all. The sacredness of marriage is no defence against its unhallowed influence. This spirit shows itself, not merely in gross shocking indecency, which is not the most dangerous, for it becomes impotent by its very vulgarity; but in a more subtle, insidious manner which appears under the cloak of delicacy of sentiment and refinement of taste. It is the more effective, because dexterously concealed. The faculties of the mind and heart are stimulated to effort, undeterred by any appearance of obscenity or fear of guilt. The very idea of Mary and her purity, is enough to banish this corrupting influence, even apart from her supernatural influence. Her name and example are enough to correct this disorder. In her presence and in her remembrance every unhallowed suggestion disappears, and we are raised to a plane of holier thoughts and emotions.

It is our duty to think of her, to imitate her, and to invoke her. God has seen fit to assign to her a high place in the Mystery of our Redemption; He has honored her by permitting her to co-operate with Him. As in the physical world, so in the spiritual, He makes use of second causes. Even as He has made use of her, so should we invoke her intercession that we may be saved. She has been given to us at the foot of the Cross as a mother. The children of men have, in the person of St. John, been placed in her custody. With what filial confidence and love the child runs to its mother, so should we have recourse to her. Our true devotion to her will be shown, by our true love of her Son and the faithful observance of His law; according to the sense of His own words, more blessed is she who keepeth His law, than she who would be His mother.

THE HOLY GHOST IN OUR SOULS.

By whom He hath given us very great and precious promises that by these ye be made partakers of the Divine nature : shunning that corruption of lust which is in the world.—II. St. Peter i. 4.

But if the Spirit of Him who raised up Jesus from the dead dwelleth in you; He Who raised Jesus Christ from the dead will also quicken your mortal bodies, because of His Spirit who dwelleth in you. . . . For whoever are led by the Spirit of God, they are sons of God. For ye have not received a spirit of bondage again in fear, but ye have received a spirit of adoption of sons, in which we cry Abba (Father). For the Spirit Himself beareth testimony to our spirit that we are children of God.—St. Paul to the Romans viii. 11, 14, 15, 16.

WHEN the Holy Ghost is said to dwell in our souls, it is not to be understood in any mere spiritual or metaphorical sense ; nor, that He dwells in them as He does in all creatures, by His ubiquity or immensity. This would be merely saying that, as He is everywhere, He is necessarily in our souls. But we claim for Him a special indwelling, or, if you will, a local habitation in the inmost recesses of our being. Nor does it express the truth to say that the Holy Ghost is present in our souls as by a consecration or dedication. In this sense, the material church is devoted or the altar is anointed for His service: but it is not in this manner, that our souls and even our bodies are said to be the very temples in which dwells this Divine Spirit. The dwelling of the Holy Ghost in our souls is real and true. By the gift of Sanctifying grace which He confers upon us, He unites Himself so closely to us and us to Him, that it is perfectly true to say that in Him " we live and move and have our being." He takes such entire possession of our souls that, if it were possible for Him to cease to exist elsewhere, He would still continue to exist in them. He is the very life of the soul, even as the soul is the life of the body; as the body without the soul dies, so the soul loses its life if the Divine Spirit be withdrawn. There is a life of the soul as truly as there is a life of the body; there is a spiritual world within us and around us as truly as there is a physical world. The Sanctifying grace of God is the vital principle of the soul; and this Sanctifying grace is the efficient cause of the life of the soul, while the soul is the formal cause of the life of the body. As man's physical life becomes remiss and languid, if the soul's energy or activity be anywise impeded; so his spiritual life becomes remiss and languid and may even perish, if grace be lessened, or obstructed, or destroyed in his soul.

This union, abiding and life-giving, of the soul with the Holy Ghost by means of Sanctifying grace, makes of it a very temple of God and exalts it as of incomparable excellence over all other creatures, in the eyes of God. By this indwelling, the soul, already like to the Adorable Trinity by its threefold powers of will, memory and understanding, becomes even a more perfect likeness of the Holy Ghost and a more perfect image of the Divine nature. By this mysterious union the soul becomes even a partaker of the nature of the Holy Ghost, according to the words of St. Peter, 2d Epistle, 1st chapter: "By whom He hath given us very great and precious promises: that by these ye may be made partakers of the Divine nature: shunning that corruption of lust which is in the world." By this union through grace with God, the soul is said, in some sense, to partake of the Divine nature. Indeed, according to some Fathers of the Church, the Holy Ghost subsists in our soul not merely by the gift of Sanctifying grace, but even substantially and in His own proper person; in this sense, while they declare man to be a compound of soul and body, they declare a Christian man to be made up of body and soul and of the Holy Ghost.

The Holy Ghost enters the soul particularly by Baptism and Penance; which, as they pre-suppose the soul dead in sin, are called Sacraments of the dead. By Baptism we are again born of water and the Holy Ghost into a new life of grace and immortality, from which we had fallen in the fall of our race; we are again admitted into the supernatural order, and there is again opened upon us the same prospect of immortal blessings which, by that primal sin, was in the beginning closed; we are again restored to our divine inheritance, and grafted as members upon the mystical body of Christ. As in the old Adam we all fell, so in the new Adam humanity is restored. As by one man sin entered into the world, and by the sin death, so by one man, Jesus Christ, came grace and justice; and by His obedience came life. Mankind lost in Adam, is restored to life, and to life more abundant in Christ Jesus, the Author and Restorer of the spiritual order, and of grace in the souls of men.

When through temptation, or the perversity of the will, or the darkness of the mind, or the proneness of the flesh to sin, we forfeit the Sanctifying grace of the Holy Ghost by mortal sin, we are again restored to spiritual life by this Divine Spirit. He pours into the soul the true sorrow and unshaken purpose of amendment which, in His gratuitous goodness and sacred promises, will insure us by the reception of Sacramental penance forgiveness for our sins. Thus, as by Baptism He inaugurates His spiritual life within us, so by Penance He restores it when interrupted by sin; and, in the end, finishes His work by conferring upon the soul the grace of final perseverance.

By Sanctifying grace the soul is made pleasing to God, no matter how numerous or how black in their nature the sins may be which have been committed and which have murdered it. The Sanctifying grace of the Holy Ghost makes them as white as snow, destroys them as if they had never been, and restores to new life and grace the soul. It is able to overcome the fury of the strongest passions and the most downward tendency to sin. It can turn the mass of corruption into the vessel of election, or the divinest exemplar of virtue; it can produce purity from impurity, and create a saint, the fervent and life-long penitent from a Magdalen. It can transform the proud and lustful king into a David, the model of repentance. It can create the foundation of the Church and the Supreme Teacher of the faithful out of an irresolute, vain-hearted, and impetuous Peter. It can make the intrepid Apostle and Teacher of the Gentiles and the vessel of election out of the zealous persecutor of the Church, breathing vengeance upon the faithful, and send him forth to proclaim the glory and divinity of Him whom he had persecuted. It can produce the noblest types of virtue and sanctity out of the most loathsome sinfulness. By it an Augustin seethed in impurity is transformed into the great Doctor of the Church and the teacher of all time. In every country and in every age it has wrought the holiest embodiments of godliness out of the gross and sinful mass of our lost humanity. It can, in very truth, out of the very stones raise up children to Abraham. When Sanctifying grace is poured into the soul, it irradiates it with a light and glory and joy which reach even heaven, where we are told "there is joy upon every sinner doing penance." The light of sun and stars pales before the light of Sanctifying grace. The glory of a sanctified soul is not surpassed even by the glory of Cherubim or Seraphim; the sanctification of a soul is a greater work in the supernatural order, than the creation of a world in the physical; it is, indeed, a masterpiece of God's power, the work of His own right hand.

The Holy Ghost is the sustaining principle of the sanctity of the soul; He is the unfailing source whence the grace of God, weakened by continual assaults of temptation, is continually renewed and replenished; He is the salient, living fount that nourishes and supports our supernatural life. Without Him, continually assailed by the inroads of sin and the attacks of the flesh, the world, and the devil, it would soon be quenched and destroyed.

Sanctifying grace makes the soul like to God; nothing among creatures can resemble more the Divine Life than the union between the soul of man and the Holy Ghost by Sanctifying grace. Even life itself, be it rational or sensitive or merely vegetative, in its simplest element, is an image, howsoever feeble, of God and of His Divine Life. Life is motion; under the idea of a first mover, philosophy has ever formed the idea of a First cause. First motion could not proceed from a cause outside the Creator. He must possess it in His own nature. Life proceeding from itself, manifests a Being eternal in duration, infinite in power, and in all perfection; there can be but one such Being. The life possessed by the creature, being the nearest approach that can exist to this primordial life of the Creator, has ever been taken as the fittest emblem of the Divine Life. All things that God has made He has made in His own image. Hence, mere life in its simplest element is a figure of God Himself. But how incomparably more excellent and how infinitely nearer to the life of God, is this supernatural life of the soul, whose Author and Sustainer is the Holy Ghost. If man is a microcosm in that by his natural faculties and endowments he sums up all created nature, by this indwelling of Divine Grace he is the most exalted of creatures and the adopted son of the Most High.

Sanctifying grace in the soul raises man to the highest pitch of glory; it makes him, in a manner, a partaker of the Divine nature. The mysterious bond which Sanctifying grace creates between his soul and the Holy Ghost makes him, indeed, but little less than the Angels, and unites him in a most unspeakable manner with his first beginning and last end. "Whoever," says St. Paul, "are led by the Spirit of God, they are the sons of God, for ye have not received a spirit of bondage again in fear, but ye have received the spirit of adoption of sons in which we cry 'Abba,' Father. For the Spirit Himself bears testimony to our spirit that we are children of God, and if children, heirs also, heirs indeed of God, and joint heirs with Christ, yet so if we suffer together that we may be also glorified together." (Rom. viii.) "And because ye are sons, God has sent the Spirit of His Son into your hearts crying: 'Abba' Father; therefore now he is not a servant, but a son; and if a son, heir also through God." (Gal. iv.) "But ye are not in the flesh but in the spirit, if however the Spirit of God dwell in you, but if any man hath not the Spirit of Christ, he is not His. . . . But if the Spirit of Him Who raised up Jesus from the dead dwelleth in you, He Who raised up Jesus Christ from the dead, will also quicken your mortal bodies, because of His Spirit Who dwelleth in you." (Rom. viii.) " I said to you, ye are gods and ye are all sons of the Most High."

Jesus Christ, even according to His humanity, became not the adopted, but the natural son of the Eternal Father; and this, because without the Divinity, the human nature of Christ never, for one moment, subsisted. When, by the ineffable motion of the Holy Ghost, the Sacred Humanity of Christ was conceived in the womb of His Virgin mother, in that same moment and simultaneously with the act of conception, the Divine Person took possession of that body and made it His own forever; as, then, that human nature never subsisted without its hypostatic union with the Second Adorable Person, it became the true and natural Son of the Most High. In some such way, but at an infinitely greater distance, our human souls united with God by the Sanctifying grace of the Holy Ghost become not, indeed, the natural, but in very truth, the adopted sons of God; according to the words of St. Paul which I have already quoted.

In the moment of the conception of God Incarnate, His human soul and body, by reason of their personal union with the Divinity, received all the riches of Divine wisdom and grace. The soul of Jesus was anointed with the sevenfold gifts of the Holy Ghost. He was constituted the heir and partaker of all the treasures of the Godhead. While union by Sanctifying grace with the Holy Ghost is far from being the hypostatic union of our humanity with Jesus Christ, yet, because of the intimacy that it admits us to with the Godhead, and because of its ordaining us as the adopted sons of God, we, too, receive, according to the measure of creatures and the purpose of God, the treasures of His wisdom and of His grace. "He Who has not hesitated to ordain the incarnation and death of His Adorable Son for our salvation, and Who has sent the Holy Ghost into our hearts for their sanctification, cannot stop short of making us possessors of all the riches of His wisdom and goodness."

Jesus Christ as man, because of His union with the Godhead, is forever placed on the Throne of God, as the Mediator and Intercessor of the race which by His blood he has rescued from sin and Satan. He is anointed forever as the great High Priest, always at the right hand of His Eternal Father, where with groans unutterable He makes unceasing intercession for the souls which he has ransomed by His sacrifice and blood. We are the members of His mystical body, we are His brothers in the flesh, we are the fruit of His spiritual loins; in Him we have received life and grace. Where He is, there, also, we shall be; He is there to prepare a place for us. We are united to the Holy Ghost by the closest possible union; by His grace He is the very life of our souls; we are the adopted sons of the Most High; by the Blood of Jesus Christ which has saved us, and by the Grace of the Holy Ghost which has sanctified us, we are forever made acceptable and precious in the sight of God, Whom, by the inspiration of the

Holy Ghost, we call our Father. We, too, then, are the priests of the Most High, "the royal priesthood, the elect people" ransomed by His blood from every tribe, and race, and nation.

The supernatural life of the soul manifests itself by action; any form of life is shown by its motion and productiveness. The act of reason evinces the existence of rational nature; the act of growth demonstrates the existence of vegetative life: a spiritual life must show itself in acts conformable with its nature. Works of which mere nature is evidently incapable, and to which it even is opposed, must proceed from a higher life and energy. Vital actions prove the existence of life; acts which are clearly spiritual are as clearly the operation and fruit of the supernatural principle. These actions which are at once the result and the evidence of the supernatural life, are the very pulsations of the Holy Ghost within us; they are the operations of that supernatural life under the influence of His actual grace. By His light He teaches us what we ought to do, and by His grace He gives us fortitude to perform it. It is by His light that we receive faith, and are enabled to incline the mind to accept Divinely-revealed truth. The absence of this Divine light renders faith impossible. From the Holy Ghost in Baptism the soul receives the germ of faith; it is for this reason that we find faith so easy to practise. It is because they have never received the light of the Holy Ghost during life or in Baptism, that many find faith so impossible. Those who by faith already know what they are to believe, the Holy

Ghost enlightens as to those truths which are the very foundation and support of a Godly life. He keeps alive in their minds the vanity of life, the shortness of time, the certainty of death, the malice of sin, the Sacrifice that was made for our souls, and the all-importance of the life to come. As the light of the Holy Ghost is as necessary to have faith in religious truth, as the light of the sun is to discern the objects that surround us; so, also, the light of the Holy Ghost is as necessary to live a life of virtue, as physical beings are necessary to support our physical life. Having taught us the truths which we are to know, and the manner of life that we are to live, the Holy Ghost gives us inclination and fortitude to be faithful to this light, and to live this life. He enables us to overcome all obstacles, to surmount all difficulties, to triumph over all temptations, to rise superior to all weaknesses, to overcome the suggestions of the flesh, the fascination of the world, and the assaults of the devil.

There can be nothing more precious than this Sanctifying grace of the Holy Ghost. Nothing that is in the sea or in the earth, nothing in those objects that men pass their lives in pursuit of, and die without attaining, can for a moment be compared with it. The loftiest human genius, or its divinest production that may have immortalized its author, is as nothing to it. The most exalted human distinction and glory that man has ever reached, or in his boundless ambition has ever aspired to, is but dust before it. No work of God on earth, or in heaven, can be placed in the balance against this emanation of His nature, this gift of Sanctifying grace. Seraphim or Cherubim, deprived of it, would lose all their glory and be as nothing before its Giver. Take away, if it were possible, from the Blessed Mother of God the gift of Sanctifying grace, and the privilege of being the Mother of God would count for naught; because she was more blessed in keeping His word, than in being His Mother; the observance of His law, of which Sanctifying grace is the result, is more precious in His eyes, than the transcendent privilege of the Divine Maternity.

The spirit of the Holy Ghost is essentially opposed to the spirit of the world. What can there be common between holiness and sin, between God and the evil one, between the love of God, and the hate of Him which fills the souls of those who are the followers of the prince of this world? "You cannot serve God and mammon; no one can serve two masters, for he will hate the one and love the other." He that will save his life hereafter, must lose it here below. If we try to unite this twofold service of God and man, we shall find that our labor will be languid and indifferent. In the end, tired of the effort to serve both, we shall abandon God and become the abject slaves of sin and Satan. The flesh, the world, and the devil, are the fortresses behind which lie intrenched the enemies of our salvation: self-denial, detachment from the world, and the grace of Jesus Christ, are the means by which we are to conquer them and come off victors in the conflict.

The Holy Ghost speaks to our souls by the inspirations, the illustrations, the holy suggestions with which He is ever trying to gain entrance into them, shut against Him by sin. In the exercise of our free will, we can, if we will, resist these gracious visitings and suggestions of His grace; He places no compulsion upon our free will; He gives us abundant grace, if we but correspond with it. Yet we may by our perverseness resist His holy influence, we may shut our eyes to His light, close our hearts to His invitations, steel our consciences to these compunctious visitings of His mercy; or, as the Scripture says, "grieve the Holy Spirit of God, and put Him before men to an open shame." Such are they who are continually admonished by the Spirit of God; by interior inspirations, and by the ordinary means of the preaching of the word of God which He employs, to return from sin and to seek their Lord and His mercy while they may be found.

There are others, who have, indeed, received the Holy Ghost in their souls by either Baptism or Penance; He abode with them; for a season they enjoyed the delights of His presence; they felt the hatred for sin and the disrelish for the world which He is sure to inspire; but, little by little, they began to feel the attractions of sin and the inroads which temptation made upon them; careless, at first, in little things, growing indifferent to smaller sins, cultivating ease and self-gratification, seeking to combine what they regarded as reasonable gratification with the law of God, they, finally, succumbed to greater temptation and fell into mortal sin. In that moment they drove the Holy Ghost from their souls; the Spirit of God and the spirit of sin could not co-exist, and the house divided could not stand. The evil one once exiled from that soul, returned with tenfold fury. When the temple of the Holy Ghost was profaned by the stain of mortal sin and this sacrilegious intrusion, He could not remain. These, too, have grieved the Holy Spirit of God and put Him before men to an open shame.

There are others, in whom the Holy Ghost may have dwelt even for a long time; but they tired of the loyalty of heart which His presence necessarily enjoined; they chafed under subjection; they longed for the freedom of sin; they rose, even as the angels rose against God, in the full light and knowledge of the malice of mortal sin. They felt the caressing voice of passion, it suggested the delights of sin. As in the beginning, the evil one whispered in our first parents' ears that they should by no means die, that they should be as God, that the forbidden fruit was an inexhaustible source of life and pleasure; so, also, he put it in their hearts that the years of life were many,—too many, perhaps, to pass in the pain of privation, in hope of a future life which after all, may be, was but a shadow, a dream, and an illusion. They made up their minds to prefer the world to God, sin to self-denial; like the Jews of old, they determined to prefer Barabbas to Christ; what they could touch and taste and handle to what they could only believe in, hope for, and love from afar. These, too, have grieved the Holy Spirit of God, and, by deliberate act and wilfulness most obstinate, driven Him from their souls. They have set up the abomination of desolation in the holy place in which He had dwelt so long.

There are others, who do not belong to any of these classes: who have not forced the Holy Ghost from their soul by sin, who have not resisted His knockings for admission into their hearts; who, in a word, have by no serious or deliberate act done despite to the Spirit of God. They have, indeed, admitted Him into their hearts; He still abides there; but they correspond not with Him calling them to a still higher life,—to a still more intimate union with Him. The Holy Ghost is not satisfied with the sacrifice of self and the surrender to Him which they have already made; it is the property of Divine love never to be satiated, but to draw the soul closer and closer to Him Who is at once the object and inexhaustible source of Divine charity. They are unmindful that the soul already sanctified, should advance from faith to faith, and from grace to grace, until it reaches, as far as its human condition permits and the will of God ordains, the highest Christian perfection. They yield not to the influence of the Holy Ghost urging them to a loftier faith, an intenser hope, and a more burning charity. They should not be content with these divine virtues in that degree which may be sufficient for salvation, but which is not sufficient to realize the purpose of the Holy Ghost in their regard. It may be that he urges them even to the profession of evangelical perfection; to utter detachment from the goods of this life, to complete denial of the inclinations of the flesh, to an entire surrender of their own will. It may be He is heard whispering in their souls, "If thou wilt be perfect, go, sell what thou hast, and come and follow me;" and, like the young man in the Gospel to whom these words were addressed by Christ in person, they may be "sorely grieved, because he had great possessions;" or they may have great attachment to the little which they do possess, or they may live in the hope of one day coming by such temporal goods. They turn a deaf ear to the voice of Christ: "He that will come after me, let him take up his cross and follow me;" "He that loses his life for my sake shall gain it." They are content with what satisfies the great bulk of even those who live to save their souls. They may melt with love and compassion in reading the lives and heroic actions of the martyrs and saints of God, who followed wheresoever the voice of His blood and the influence of His grace would lead them; but they have not the resolution or inclination to imitate their example. They pass their lives in what seems to them, in their moments of illumination, as a sort of half or faint-hearted service of Almighty God. These, too, grieve the Holy Spirit of God, in not following resolutely wheresoever He would lead them. "He that followeth Me, walketh not in darkness."

There are still others, who are as truly given over to a reprobate sense, as the world before the coming of Christ,—" without God and without hope."

If they believe in God, they live as if they believed not; and if they could, they would willingly destroy Him. He is neither in their hearts, nor, so far as they can make it, in the world at all; they would willingly forego Him, for sake of the years of pleasure they can enjoy in this life; they would willingly barter their souls for eternity, for sake of the short lived gratification that the prince of this world can bestow; they are the invincible slaves of sin; they are the foresworn enemies of Christ; they are irrevocably enrolled under the banner of the evil one; they jeer at religion and mock its holy ordinances; they turn the word of God calling them to repentance into ridicule; they would willingly efface the traces of God written in their conscience and heart; they would seem to be those in whom some of the fallen angels lingering on earth have taken up their permanent abode; they seem to be confirmed in iniquity; obstinately steeled against all influences of grace; they are the blind who cannot see the truth and the obdurate who cannot follow its suggestions. These, too, have grieved the Holy Spirit of God and driven Him forever, it would seem, from their souls. It may be that they have incurred the guilt of that sin against the Holy Ghost which we are told shall never be forgiven, either in this life, or in the life to come.

Behold the rank and dignity in the scale of His creations, to which Almighty God has exalted the soul and even the body of man, by this Divine gift of Sanctifying grace! To what greater height could he be raised? what more precious endowment, what diviner glory short of His manifested presence, could even God bestow? What royal diadem or kingly sceptre could, for a moment, be compared to this supreme Gift? How true it is that they whose souls it illustrates, are made "a chosen people, a royal priesthood." They are ennobled even to the level of Cherubim and Seraphim. All human glory, all human riches, all that God has made in this world, and which the heart of man most madly pursues, pales before the glory and transcendent lustre of this Sanctifying grace. If we could imagine the loftiest spirits in heaven destitute of it, they would envy the lot of the sons of men who possessed it. How true it is that "man has been made but little less than the Angels, and has been crowned with glory and honor." How even truer is it, that he has been made equal to the Angels by the possession of this inestimable boon of Sanctifying grace. It is in a manner scarcely to be marvelled at, that man as having been once the heir of this Divine gratuity, and having, even in his fall, an aptitude for it, moved the compassion of the Lord of heaven and earth to become man, to suffer and to die, that he might come again by its possession. No wonder that the Angels in transports of admiration, behold this Divine grace restored where it once belonged; no wonder that the splendor of the soul rising from the foulest depths of degradation and sin, and enriched again with this Divine treasure, sends a triumph and jubilee to heaven that make the Angels rejoice more than over the n.nety-nine who never lost it and therefore needed not its recovery.

The Sanctifying grace of God is more valuable in itself, and in its fruits, than any other of the works of God. The glory of the sun and moon, the ineffable wisdom and harmony which God has bestowed upon the illimitable works of His hands which the heavens show forth, are as nothing compared with the excellence and beauty of this Divine emanation. In the words of St. Thomas, the least Sanctifying grace is more precious, than all the good to be found in created nature; even the human soul considered in the natural order, and apart from this Divine grace, while the noblest of God's works, is as nothing before this Divine gift, which gives it all its real life and immortal value. Countless are the treasures which the wit of man has discovered in the bowels of the earth, or drawn forth from the depths of the sea; still more countless are those that therein lie, and which man shall never reach. We know not what may be the riches of Divine wisdom and power that are spent in the unnumbered worlds and universes of worlds that roll in space. But we do know that all this and ten thousand times more could never equal the incalculable value of Sanctifying grace as conferred upon a single human soul. We know, or, at least, we have some faint conception of the matchless wisdom and boundless power which the heavens, as the handiwork of God, proclaim; and of the manifest evidence of God's omniscient, all-compassing intellect which is disclosed in the smallest element of matter. And, yet, we know that all this infinite wisdom and power of God's creations are nothing compared with the wisdom and power displayed in the renovation of the soul from sin and its blightful effects, by Sanctifying grace.

A cup of cold water is the least gift that man can confer; and, yet, this gift conferred in the name of Jesus Christ, and viewed as the inspiration and result of Sanctifying grace dwelling in the soul of the giver, exceeds by far all that the most princely generosity and the most lavish munificence could bestow; it may be indeed the purchase-money of the salvation of a soul, nay, even of many souls. In God's sight it is more precious than a fortune sacrificed from some motive merely human; more precious than even kingdoms granted from considerations merely temporal. Ten thousand kingdoms, untold fortunes, the world itself, if it were possible, given away, but not for God's sake, would be nothing before this cup of cold water bestowed in the name of Jesus Christ, and by a soul truly animated with His spirit. It is this principle of Sanctifying grace actuating all our works that gives them their real value; with it they are acceptable to God and worthy of Him; without it they are but refuse and worthless. "If I speak with the tongues of men and of angels, and have not charity, I am become as sounding brass or a tinkling cymbal; if I have all faith so as to move mountains, and have not charity, I am nothing; if I give my goods to feed the poor and my body to be burned, and have not charity, it profiteth me nothing." In these words, St. Paul clearly shows that he realized to the full the unapproachable excellence of this unspeakable Gift. No wonder he exclaimed, "Cursed be he who loveth not the Lord Jesus Christ;" no wonder that he declared that "neither persecution, nor nakedness, nor fire, nor the sword, nor might, nor height, nor things present, nor things to come, nor any other creature, could separate him from the charity of God which is in Christ Jesus."

Consider the felicity of which this Divine gratuity is the assurance and inception,—which is its fruit and reward. This Sanctifying grace is the germ which will develop in immortal happiness. Even in this life its possession constitutes the only real happiness of the soul. Other objects men may pursue and in them seek to satisfy the cravings of their heart; but, sooner or later, surfeited with the goods of this life, or disappointed in their attainment, they turn to God, acknowledging that He alone can fill their souls and satisfy their desires. The soul is made for God, and can be only truly happy when united with Him in the life to come. The soul's happiness in this life can only be in possessing God in that way which here below is possible, that is, in its union with God by Sanctifying grace. This truth so clear to the light of reason, and so consonant with the teaching of Revelation, is brought home to the mind and heart of every one by the universal experience of mankind. All human experience would have to be reversed and belied before any son of Adam could declare to be untrue, what the wisest of men has taught as the result to him of unlimited gratification in all that passion could suggest, or wit devise, or wealth procure: "Vanity of vanities, and all is vanity, except the love and service of Almighty God." What is even the happiness secured for us in this life by Sanctifying grace, compared to the immortal bliss which this same Sanctifying grace shall obtain for us in the life to come, and of which it is the necessary condition and Divine assurance? If without grace during life the soul is miserable, how miserable would it be forever without it in the life to come? If the soul which during life is possessed of this Divine gift, rises superior to all human misfortune and trial and disappointment and enjoys a lofty serenity and unbroken bliss, how great must not be the happiness that it shall insure the soul in the life to come, and of which all human happiness is but the merest foretaste and presentiment! Sanctifying grace dwelling in the soul and persevered in till death, is the guarantee of everlasting union with God hereafter. The soul united to God in this life is united with Him forevermore. The soul disunited from God in this life is disunited from Him forever. "Eye hath not seen, nor ear heard, nor hath it entered into the heart of man" to conceive the glory and felicity which this Sanctifying grace shall procure for us in the life to come.

Nor can we feel that the choice of this everlasting bliss is supererogatory; a choice which we may make or not make, a preference to which we may or may not incline, a happiness which we may or may not covet, which we may neglect, and yet be in no worse condition than we are here below. This choice is absolutely necessary: if we fail to make it, we not only fail to obtain an unending bliss, but we sink into everlasting misery; positive punishment is the consequence of spurning positive happiness; we are not free not to choose everlasting felicity so as yet not to choose, or to avoid everlasting suffering; to decline the one is to incur the other. In such an issue, our freedom is the freedom of sin, and eternal misery or eternal bliss is the alternative before us. If we are not sharers of God's Sanctifying grace, we are sharers of God's withering and eternal curse, which entails upon us punishment and sufferings without end. Our eternal destiny hangs trembling in the balance of our possessing, or rejecting, Sanctifying grace during the days of life. A blessing and a curse I place before you, choose ye.

The unceasing care and tireless assiduity and unswerving perseverance to be employed in obtaining and retaining this Divine gift, should be proportionate to the eternal consequences which depend upon it, and to its own incalculable value. As this Gift of the Holy Ghost is so precious that the mind cannot conceive it, nor words declare it, and as undying bliss or unending woe is the issue which depends upon it, one would think that man's efforts to obtain it and to cherish it, would be continual and unlimited; one would think that no sacrifice could be too much, that no life could be too long, to spend in its acquirement; one would think that man would value it above all the objects of human ambition, above all the interests of this world, above all the treasures of this earth, above all the concerns of time. It should certainly be manifest that as eternity alone can suffice to proclaim the value and necessity of Sanctifying grace, so the few years of time would be but too little to spend in its acquisition. As immortal happiness is to be purchased,—and must be purchased by this Divine gift; as eternal misery is to be avoided,—and can only be avoided by the same Divine gift; so our lives should be employed for no other end than to attain it; nothing else should stand in its way, or, much less, usurp its place. This is the teaching of good sense and sound judgment. Yet the fact is that there is nothing which men regard as less valuable, or cheaper, or of less account, than this Sanctifying grace; they barter it for every, even the least, gratification. A temporary gain, an hour's pleasure, a night's revelry, a beastly gratification, a vengeance gratified,—these and countless other sinful acts are accounted by most people as more valuable, and always to be preferred to this Divine gift of which we speak. Such is the contradiction between man's soul illuminated by grace and freed from sin, and man's soul destitute of heavenly light, filled with the darkness of sin and passion, and enslaved by the tyranny of Satan.

What can we do but pray that this Divine Spirit, Whose presence and operations in the soul we have endeavored to describe, may come to the rescue of all who are so minded ; that the spirit of darkness may flee before His light, that perversity of the will may be rectified by His grace, that the power of temptation and passion may be slackened by His influence, that hearts obdurate with sin may be softened, and led to the practice of virtue; that all may come to manifest, by the manner of their life and the improvement of their character, the appreciation of this Divine gift, and of the eternal felicity that it leads to, which they express by their faith and outward profession.

THE PASSION OF CHRIST — THE LESSONS OF THE CROSS

But Jesus turning to them, said: Daughters of Jerusalem, weep not for Me, but weep for yourselves, and for your children. For behold the days are coming in which they will say: Happy are the barren, and the wombs that never bare, and the breasts that never suckled. Then will they begin to say to the mountains: Fall upon us: and to the hills: Cover us. For if they do these things to the green tree, what will be done to the dry? St. Luke xxiii. 28–31.

THESE are the words which Our Blessed Lord addressed to the women of Jerusalem, whom He met weeping for His sake, as He ascended the Hill of Calvary. And the same words may to-day be addressed to every Christian congregation: children of the Church weep not for me, but for yourselves; weep for the sons of men.

It is not my purpose to-day to seek to excite your sympathy or compassion for Jesus suffering and put to death. It was not to move the pity or draw the tears of men that Jesus suffered and died on this day. And the preacher who undertakes to preach Christ crucified, will do well to propose to himself some other end than that of a transient feeling or passing tear. Discourses descriptive of the sufferings of Christ may be useful, yet it is to be feared that they too often produce but a momentary impression, and leave no lasting fruit. I would then to-day seek rather to inform your minds than to move your feelings; to impart to you solid food for thought. I would ask you even to look beyond the sufferings and death of Christ, and contemplate the truths to which these sufferings give such fearful expression and portentous meaning. I would ask you to meditate upon the lessons of the Cross of Christ. This Cross is a great book in which we can well learn all that it most behooves us to learn. As profane books are the mirrors in which are reflected and by which we come to know the secrets of nature, so the Cross of Christ is an open book, in which we may read and come thoroughly to understand the great truths of religion. It is intelligible to all. It requires no painful effort of the mind, no long-continued application. It is no elaborate argument, no recondite dissertation, no subtle process of reasoning. It is level to the meanest capacity. It is worthy of the devout meditation of the highest genius.

Let us, then, draw nigh to the Cross of Christ, and in its light contemplate some of the truths which it so wonderfully teaches.

Fix the passion and death of Christ well in mind. Fix your mind upon any stage or circumstance of the passion which brings home to it most forcibly, most vividly the idea of a suffering, dying God. Let it be, if you wish, the agony in Gethsemane, where Jesus went to pray the night before he suffered; let it be there where our Lord may be said to have abandoned Himself to Himself; where the agony which He endured was, in a special and true sense, self-imposed: where by His own act He withdrew from Himself the consciousness of innocence, which to every just man suffering is a source of consolation and support, and which has often nerved the martyr's heart to meet death in its most awful form; where He felt Himself to be what, but in seeming, He could never be: a criminal black with the guilt of all the iniquities of men; contemplate Him in that garden when shutting off the support and glory of the Godhead from His soul, there rushed in upon it that fearful agony which issued in the mysterious sweat of blood. Or, if you prefer it, behold Him abandoned to the Jews, fallen a victim to the cruelty of men, crowned with thorns, lashed at the pillar, mocked, spat upon, haled from court to court, treated as a fool, covered with every manner of insult and contumely. Or, finally, look upon Him to-day raised upon the Cross, offering Himself a victim between the uplifted vengeance of God, and the sins of men; and accepted as such, the Eternal Father lets fall upon Him the last blow of Divine Justice resulting in the mysterious cry, "Lord God! why hast thou abandoned Me?" Consider, I say, our Blessed Lord in all or any one of these circumstances which will give you the best idea of a suffering, dying God. And having done so, try to give a meaning, and a value, and a sufficiency to those sufferings, by remembering that they are the sufferings of a God, endured, indeed, in his human nature; yet, by reason of that nature's personal union with Divinity, in very truth, the sufferings of a God; and as such, of an infinite value. It is the Eternal God Who agonizes in Gethsemane, Who suffers at the hands of the Jews, Who is to-day raised upon the Cross. Let us come now to learn the lessons which we have said the Cross discloses: some of those truths of which we hear so much, and think so little, and which are so imperfectly understood, because so little reflected upon.

I ask, first, why this amazing fact of a God, suffering and dying? Alas, it is an old story; one which we have often heard, but which cannot be repeated too often. Adam had sinned and fallen. In him we all sinned and fell. In him we stood. He was the moral head of the human race. His fate was its fate. His destiny was its destiny. He fell from the supernatural order. He forfeited his supernatural destiny. He could not transmit his supernatural inheritance to his children, any more than a king justly bereft of his kingdom, can transmit it to his offspring. Thus was the whole race estranged from God, and condemned to hell.

This fall was in itself irreparable. Adam's sin was in itself irremediable; there was an essential and invincible malice in it. It was not the mere eating of the forbidden fruit, but the violation of the Divine law which forbade it. It was the effort of the creature to rid itself of the duty of obedience and submission which it owes to his Creator. It was the rebellion against the Creator of the creature endowed with free will; the first exercise of its sovereign faculty. There was an infinite malignity in it, because aimed against an infinite God. Hence, it was inexpiable. Man could offend, but could not appease, God. Not all men offered up as a holocaust would suffice to atone for sin; not all the angels and blessed spirits incarnated, and suffering, and dying, could satisfy the justice of God for sin.

The pagan sacrifices of expiation and mediation betrayed the consciousness of the original fall of our race, and of their own insufficiency to propitiate God. The Jewish sacrifices bespoke the same consciousness of guilt; and confessed this same insufficiency, in looking forward to the One Great Sacrifice which they prefigured. The psalmist gives the reason: "No man can pay the price of his soul." In vain did men seek to propitiate heaven by the blood of sheep and oxen and goats. If an atonement was to be made, if a ransom was to be offered, that atonement should be of infinite efficacy, that ransom should be of priceless value. Nothing short of an infinite sacrifice could suffice: a God-man should be that atonement:—God, that the atonement might be infinite and thus equal the malice of sin; man, that this atonement might be reputed the satisfaction of the race that had offended.

God, then, should suffer, or man be irretrievably and hopelessly lost. Christ offered Himself as the necessary Atonement, the all-sufficient Sacrifice. "For it is impossible that sins should be taken away by the blood of bulls and goats. Therefore coming into the world, He saith: Sacrifice and oblation Thou wouldst not have: but Thou hast fitted to Me a body. Holocausts and sacrifices for sin did not please Thee. Then I said: Behold I come: at the head of the book it is written of Me, to do Thy Will, O God." Heb. x. 4-7. "For God so loved the world, as to give His only begotten Son, that whosoever believeth in Him may not perish, but have life everlasting." John iii. 16.

The Eternal God came upon earth, and shed His blood worth more than hecatombs of sheep and goats; worth more than the blood of all the sons of men. Because of the charity with which He loved the world, He did not hesitate. We are bought truly at a great price: not of corruptible gold and silver, but with the blood of the Immaculate Lamb. The All Holy takes upon Himself the sins of men, and for their sake becomes before His Eternal Father the criminal upon whom falls the justice due to their guilt. By His blood is blotted out sin and its entailed punishment. How can we believe that such unutterable mercy has been shown us, without tears of sorrow, without the profoundest emotions of gratitude and love?

How mysterious the truth that here presents itself! God dies to satisfy the justice of God! God dies as an expiation for sin! Nothing less required for man's Redemption, than the shedding of the blood of the Incarnate God! The Creator dies that the creature may live! God must die that sin may be destroyed, and yet destroyed in such wise that Divine justice and majesty may remain inviolate. Sin is of a nature so incomprehensible, that He to Whom it is offered, must for its expiation assume the appearance of the sinner, and bear the load of his malice. The Second Divine Person, charged as He is with the sins of all men, becomes, according to St. Paul, an execration or curse from the Father, and a reproach and outcast among men.

While thus as an innocent victim He bore the full torrent of Divine vengeance; while it penetrated to the inmost recesses of His soul; while His whole being was plunged in sorrow and distress and pain, as in a sea, God was in Him, reconciling the world to Himself; for, in Him he had placed the power of reconciliation. By His vicarious sufferings were the sins of men no longer imputed to them, but forever blotted out.

That the Creator should die for the creature; that the offended God should become the victim of propitiation, while the sinner man should become His executioner, is a mystery which is not given to mortal intelligence to understand. God could not suffer; and, yet, the sufferings endured in His human nature derive their infinite efficacy from its union with the Divine. Immortality and death, the Divine and human, entered into an alliance to restore the relation of the creature to his Creator, subverted by sin. Man fell by pride and refused to serve; Christ humbled Himself to become a creature and became obedient even unto death. Man had rebelled; heaven closed, hell opened: by the incarnation and death of Jesus, heaven was opened and hell closed. The creature aspired to freedom from

God. God became captive in the hands of men. The Lord of all makes Himself a worm of the earth and an outcast from men, that the outcast man may be restored to God and the worm of the earth may become an inhabitant of heaven. He suffered death that man might live. He was reputed a sinner, that by His justice sinners might be justified, and that His obedience might be imputed to all. The Sovereignly rich strips Himself of all, and has not whereon to lay His head, that men may, through His poverty and destitution, be eternally enriched.

That Christ, in His sufferings and death, was the victim of expiation for mankind, is the very essence and soul of the mystery of Redemption. His prayer, in the Agony, that "this chalice might pass from Him," His cry, upon the Cross, "My God, My God, why hast Thou abandoned me," would show that His Sacrifice was expiatory in the highest sense, and compensatory to the Divine justice outraged by sin. This is the stumbling block of the Jew; this is the folly of the Gentile. These are the things of the Spirit of God which the natural man cannot receive. This is the mystery of Godliness which flesh and blood, "unless drawn by the Father," cannot receive. "O! the depth of the knowledge and wisdom of God, how incomprehensible are Thy judgments and how unsearchable Thy ways!" Man had become a debtor to Divine justice, and a slave to Satan. God alone knew how to punish him, and to devise a plan of Redemption by which man was rescued from sin and its eternal consequences, ransomed from the slavery of guilt and Satan, restored to the freedom of innocence and the children of God, by which sin was forever destroyed, and death made of no avail; and yet, all this, so as Divine justice was satisfied, sin avenged and its malice exhausted, and the Divine Majesty and all the Divine attributes remained inviolate.

Now we begin to feel the malice of sin that calls for such an Atonement. What are we to think of the nature of sin which crucified the Eternal God, put Him to an open shame, made of Him a very worm of the earth and an outcast from men? What are we to think of the deep-dyed guilt, black malice, foul enormity of sin which was satisfied with nothing less than the shedding of the blood of the Incarnate God? How are we to imagine the bitter malignity, the intense evil of sin, which stops at nothing short, I had almost said, of the annihilation of the God-head. Yes, my brethren, it is in meditating upon the suffering and dying Christ, as the Divinely appointed expiation for sin, that we can best understand its true nature, its deadly malice, the hatred that God bears it, and the ruin which it brings upon our soul. Now can we understand the justice of God which, for one sin, flung the Angels from their high estate down to bottomless perdition, "unrespited, unreprieved, ages of hopeless end." Now can we understand something of the mysterious nature of the sin of our first parents; a sin which cursed, with an everlasting curse, not only them, but all their posterity, and which brought into the world the intense, horrid, wide-spread evils of which all history is but the record, and of which we ourselves have daily experience: evils which are still festering in our souls; evils that endure after the Sacrifice of the Incarnate God; evils that will only cease when God Himself will come to judge the world.

Now we begin to apprehend the justice of eternal punishment. In the sufferings and death of Christ, viewed as the only sufficient Atonement for the sins of men, we read such a lesson of Divine justice as prepares us to believe in the existence of punishment infinite, if not in intensity, at least, infinite in duration,—nay more—to see the fitness of it. When I look upon Jesus crucified, when I reflect upon this fearful exhibition of Divine justice, I am no longer surprised that He has created the great pit and filled it with the cries of deathless souls. What must be the justice of God which spared not His Only Begotten Son? if He spared not the Creator infinitely great, will He spare the creature infinitely vile, a worm of the earth! If He hath done such things in the green wood, what will He not do in the dry? If His justice required the sacrifice of His Son, will it not require the eternal sacrifice of the sinner? Eternal punishment is the just sequel of infinite love despised. Eternal anger is the fit consequence of eternal mercy refused. A God who could only satisfy his love by becoming man and dying, can only satisfy His justice by damning the sinner to hell.

Sin is the act of the creature, turning his back upon the Creator, and refusing the mercy and pardon so freely vouchsafed. God wishes no one to perish, but to repent; He wills not the death of the sinner, but that he be converted and live. He opens heaven to all and induces all to enter. "Jerusalem, Jerusalem, thou that killest the prophets and stonest those who are sent to thee, how often would I have gathered together thy children, as the hen doth gather her chickens under her wings, and thou wouldst not. Behold your house shall be left to you desolate." Then He announces the desolation that shall overtake it, because of its stiff-necked incredulity to His word and blind obstinacy and resistance to His grace. If, in spite of all, he is lost, shame and confusion to the sinner. "O Israel! thou hast destroyed thyself." "So I let them go according to the desires of their heart: they shall walk in their own devices." Ps. lxxx. 14. Such perversity of will, such a contempt and turning away from God, such a renunciation of Divine goodness invokes the Divine justice upon the head of the sinner. " Dost thou despise the riches of His goodness, and patience, and long suffering! Dost thou not know, that the benignity of God leadeth thee to penance! But, after thy hardness and unpenitent heart, thou treasurest up for thyself wrath on the day of wrath, and revelation of the just judgment of God, who will render to every man according to his works. Rom. ii. "And as the Lord rejoiced over you before, doing good to you, and multiplying you; so He will rejoice in destroying and bringing you to nought." Deut. xxviii. 63.

It is a reckless and unblushing contempt of the

power of God, and a malign attempt to obliterate the intrinsic relation which necessarily subsists between the creature, and the author of his being. God is the absolute Lord and Creator of man: by every conceivable right and title does he belong to Him; his submission and loyalty should be as profound and unshaken, as the Lord's authority over him is indefeasible. The clay cannot dictate terms to the potter. We can conceive no law more absolute, than that which binds man to his duty to God. He sometimes fears those who can kill the body; but his fears should be reserved for Him Who can cast both body and soul into hell. God, by a just decree, makes him feel the weight of the power which he contemns. Thus the sinner's pride is crushed, and disturbed order is restored. "Because thou didst not serve the Lord thy God with joy and gladness of heart, for the abundance of all things, thou shalt serve thy enemy, whom the Lord will send against thee, in hunger and thirst, and nakedness, and in want of all things: and he shall put an iron yoke upon thy neck, till he destroy thee." Deut. xxviii. 47–8.

It is rebellion against the government which God has set up for the temporal and eternal welfare of human society. The laws whose observance God requires, are founded in the very nature of things as they exist, and in their mutual intrinsic relations to one another. He who violates these laws, violates the order and harmony which the All-wise Creator has inscribed upon them. Moral and free agents should freely and by choice obey those ordinances which brute and inanimate nature follows by the necessity of their nature. Man's free wish should be coincident with their enforced tendency. While he, in his freedom, and by sin, may oppose himself to God's providence in one order, yet, by his disobedience, he becomes amenable to another order of the same providence, which he cannot escape. Inevitable compulsion follows freedom abused, and perverted to his destruction. The harmony disconcerted by sin, and the disturbed relations of the Creator and creature, are restored by the punishment which Divine justice inflicts: and, thus, from evil God draws good, and compels sin to serve to manifest Divine justice, and so to further His general providence. "If ye will not hear Me nor do My commandments, . . . I will set my face against you: . . . I will chasten you seven times more for your sins, and it will break the pride of your stubbornness; and I will make to you heaven above as iron, and the earth as brass; . . . I will go against them with fury, and I will chasten you with seven plagues for your sins."

Yet, in this justice of God there is nothing forbidding, nothing to drive us to despair. He tempers His justice with love. He blends one into the other; while He astonishes us by His justice, he melts us by the display of his love. He is not justice to the exclusion of love. He is not so inexorably just, but that He is at the same time inconceivably loving and merciful. We are such strangers to any feeling of love for God, we are so filled with ourselves, deeds of disinterestedness are so foreign to us, that it seems extravagance to talk of God dying out of very love for His creatures. Yet, if humanity could have ever doubted that the great Creator, of Whose justice we have so far spoken, could be wanting in love for His creatures, we have, this morning, but to contemplate the spectacle which Calvary presents,—a spectacle, of which it is nothing to say that for it the earth has no parallel,—a scene which the human mind is utterly inadequate to conceive,— a sight upon which the Angels look down in transports of wonder and amazement. Sacrifice is of the very essence of love; love is to be measured by what it does, gives, and suffers, for its object. There is no real love without self-sacrifice. It is the test of the depth and tenderness and strength of love. What can we do but fall down in silent adoration of the unutterable Self-sacrifice which the Hill of Calvary to-day affords. The Lord of Infinite Holiness and Adorable Majesty at Whose sight heaven and earth do tremble, and the Angels hide their heads, dies the death of a malefactor! Jesus, the All-holy, takes upon Him the form of a sinner and offers Himself as a sacrifice to the Eternal Father for the sins of all men.

Why this uncounted expenditure, this extravagant profusion of the charity of God? Could man have been ransomed at no less price? Would nothing less have sufficed for our redemption than this astounding self-sacrifice of the Incarnate God! Why did it not please Him to require the sacrifice of a man, or the blood of all men? Or why did not an Angel or a choir of Angels assume our nature, and die; and thus save the shedding of the blood of the Only Begotten Son of God? Such a sacrifice would not have been sufficient, it is true; yet, it could have been accepted, as such, by Almighty God. Or, if Divine justice did require the shedding of the blood of the Incarnate God, why was it not satisfied with one stroke of the scourge, one puncture of the thorn-crown, one moment of the agony, one drop of that Sacred Blood, which would have sufficed to atone for the sins of ten thousand worlds? Why drain out that agonizing heart? Why endure a passion of such untold agony and grief? Why die a death of such inconceivable suffering, such unutterable woe? We cannot say why God should love us with so amazing a love. We cannot begin to comprehend the motive of such lavish, such unbounded love. God's ways and wisdom are so far above ours, infinitude so far surpasses what is finite, God the Creator, is so far above man, the creature. We can only say that God is infinite; infinite in all His attributes, infinite therefore in His love. What He does, He does in an infinite, God-like manner. It was to manifest this love that He became man; that He endured the awful agony of the passion, and the ignominy of the cross.

What can we, in return, do, but spend our lives in the love and service of Him Who hath loved us with so absorbing, so consuming a love. A man who lays down his life for another, performs an act of goodness so unheard of, that we shall long search history in vain for such an example. The man who dies for his country, secures for his name an immortality on earth and is forever enshrined in the hearts of men. What are the Divine and eternal claims of Christ Jesus upon our gratitude! And we need go no farther to find a motive for Christ's love. He wished by His prodigal display of love, to excite us, in return, to His love. He loved that He might be loved. He would kindle our love by the fire of His own. And in this love consists, St. Thomas tells us, the perfection of human nature. It shall find its glory and bliss in eternal union with God in the life to come. Here below it shall find its perfection and happiness in that union which, in this life, alone is possible; the union with God by faith, hope, and charity.

Faith makes the truths of religion as real, by the sense of hearing, as visible objects are, by the sense of sight. Not because we see an object is it any truer, than if made known to us by those who have knowledge of it. Hence, St. Paul designates faith as the substantial realizing of what we hope for. Owing to the merits of Christ, and His gratuitous promises, and our performance of the conditions required, we come to live in the unfailing hope of one day entering into the possession of what faith discloses. Seeing that our eternal bliss is to consist in union with the Godhead, which union must be wrought here below, if wrought at all, we come to be united with our Beginning and Last end, by the bonds of charity; so that we can in truth feel, "what can separate us from the love of God in Christ?" Upon this foundation of faith, this assurance of hope, in this union of charity, the man of God passes his life; and upon it is constituted his sanctity and true happiness here below. And this, because it is the nearest he can get to the Eternal union, for which he has been made, and is an indispensable condition thereto.

THE PASSION OF CHRIST.

(*Continued.*)

Now I begin to put a value on my soul when I see the price paid for it. When I consider the wondrous plan of the Incarnation to which Divine wisdom had recourse; when I consider the marvels of wisdom shown in the Redemption; when I consider the love and blood poured out in the sufferings and death of Christ, to redeem man from sin, yet so as not to leave Divine justice unavenged, I begin to realize the boundless value of a human soul. He who best knew its worth, hesitated not to shed His blood for it. That soul must be spiritual in its essence, which the Incarnate Word purchased with His blood; a gross material being, destined to corruption, could never invoke such a ransom. That soul must be immortal in duration, for which the Immortal God did not refuse to die; immortality would never have made such a sacrifice for a being whose duration would be confined to the limits of time. That soul must be capable of enjoying infinite bliss, or enduring undying woe, when there was such a Redemption, to regain for it the one, and to rescue it from the other; such a price would never have been paid for a deliverance from transient suffering, or for obtaining temporary joy. Boundless, endless in its hopes and aspirations must the soul be, when God's love for it was so great as to exhaust the fountain of Divine Charity and to constrain the Son of God to become man.

Christ suffering and dying teaches me, too, this important lesson: that self-denial is the only means of salvation; that the road to heaven is the road to Calvary, the royal way of the Cross. True happiness would be in a return to the state in which man was created, which is no longer possible. The nearest approach to that state, and even to the felicity of the life to come, springs from the subjection of the passions to reason, enlightened by God's holy law, and the submission of reason to God's will and revelation. This was the felicity of our first parents, constituted, as they were, in original justice and sanctifying grace. When they fell they lost it. Ever since it has been exiled from earth. Never again shall we enjoy it until we return, as far as may be, to that original state. To come to, once again, that lost happiness, to hold passion under the control of reason, and reason in harmony with God's sovereign will, has, ever since, been the aim of every Saint, the summit of Christian virtue, the scope and purpose of all religion. For this did Christ set us the example of suffering. "Did it not behoove Him to suffer, and so enter into His glory?" For this did the Saints imitate Him; for, those whom He predestined to glory, He predestined to be made like unto the image of His Son. There is no religion without suffering.

The Saints thought it a small thing to lay down their lives joyfully, and to pour out their blood, like water, for salvation. We hesitate to make the least sacrifice; has salvation become cheaper? We are the children of the Saints; we have inherited their example; are we faithful to it? Are we walking that path, narrow, and steep, and difficult on every side, which leads to Calvary, and through Calvary to glory? or are we, Judas-like, betraying the cause of Christ, and treading that broad, and downward, and facile path so easily found and so generally pursued? Does it not behoove us to suffer, and so enter into glory? There is no salvation, without that degree of suffering which is required to bring every passion into subjection to reason, and reason to the truth of God.

Study the suffering and self-sacrifice disclosed on the Cross. Let the avaricious man who lives for nothing but to aggrandize himself and family, look upon Jesus Christ dying, naked upon the Cross, and destitute of all things; and does he feel no sinking of his love of the things of life, when he beholds the Sovereignly rich, for our sake dying poor? Let him who blasphemes Providence for the wrongs which He permits, and who resigns himself not to His gracious dispensations, ponder the lesson which the Cross teaches of God's permission of the blackest wrongs, and of the Saviour's meek submission. Let the vindictive man who refuses to forgive, and who seeks vengeance as his due, and as the recognized right, listen to Jesus: "Father, forgive them, for they know not what they do." Let him who wallows in passion, who breathes impurity with his every breath, behold the Lord suffering in every nerve, mortified in every feeling, and dying amidst torment and agony. Let the proud behold the Lord humbled to the condition of a worm of the earth, and become an outcast from men; "Who, although He thought it not robbery to be equal to God, yet humbled Himself to the death of the cross;" and what a lesson should we not learn of self-abasement? By contemplating these, and other virtues as illustrated and inculcated in the suffering and dying Lord, Whom to follow is not to walk in darkness but in light, we shall learn how to live.

As Jesus in His life taught us how to live, in His death he teaches us how to die. He gives us an example of every virtue, an exemplification of all He had ever taught. By His mildness, meekness, patience, resignation to the will of His Father, suffering for justice's sake, submitting to an undeserved death in its most disgraceful form, He shows us that death should have no terrors for the just who have conformed themselves to His example; He shows us that we, too, are to be ready to meet death, if God and the salvation of our souls require it.

Who does not shudder at the certain prospect of death, the extinction of life? Who does not cling to life?—life, which has charms even for the beggar of ninety, who has lived destitute of all that would make it desirable, or at least endurable, no less than for him who has enjoyed all that it affords. Who does not shrink from the grave? to decay, to rot, to be as if we had never been, or rather worse; for, having tasted life, the deprivation is greater than if we had never known it. Who can submit with resignation to the infliction of the primal curse, "Dust thou art, and into dust thou shalt return." What a withering, chilling prospect! Well thought on, it stops the blood and paralyzes all our feelings. Who can bear the thought of the sundering, even for a time, of this soul and body, mated together for an eternal alliance? But all this has been reversed: our doom has been blotted out: in the grave of Christ we are reborn to life, to incorruption, and to immortality. There we learn that they who are dead, shall live. To gain our real life, we must lose this. The portals that close on this, open on our eternal life. We enter on the reality when we have passed from the shadow. Our eternal birth is coincident with our temporal death. Death, then, shall not have dominion over us. His death has made ours of no avail. "He died for our sins, and rose again for our justification." "He rose the first fruits of them that sleep." By His death, He has purchased for us the grace which is the pledge of our own resurrection. If we endure the separation of soul and body, if we sink into the earth, we shall only follow the example of Him Who has sanctified death and robbed the grave of its horrors.

Who does not feel the loss of the objects of

this life; its riches, honors, pleasures? Who does not feel the pang of leaving forever relatives, friends, companions? But Christ consoles for these losses, by teaching us, that all which we prize in the world, is but the faintest reflex of the reward which He has prepared for them who love Him and keep His commandments;—is but as the shadow to the substance, the figure to the reality; that to our relatives and friends we shall again be united in the day and world where "there will be neither marriage, nor given in marriage, but where we shall be as the Angels of God."

Who does not tremble at the thought of the judgment which it is appointed to every man to undergo: "Once to die, and after death be judged;" "Man shall render an account of every idle word." Who knows which of the dread alternatives, resting upon this judgment, eternal bliss or eternal woe, shall be his? But Jesus has deprived that tribunal of its terrors, and has disarmed the justice of God. He endured in his own person, the punishment which of right was ours. If we are still liable to the adverse sentence and to eternal misery, the responsibility is with ourselves; it is our own doing, it is our own perversity and free choice. As in Him we have all been made to live, it rests with ourselves, by our manner of life during this probation, whether we shall hear the sentence of consolation, or be consumed with the dire malediction.

The future life, which till Christ was dark, deep, and mysterious, is no longer so. Its darkness is dispelled by the light of the truth, the primal curse is blotted out. Its depths have no terror for those who are supported by the power of God. "When thou shalt pass through the waters I will be with thee: and the rivers shall not cover thee: when thou shalt walk in the fire, thou shalt not be burnt; and the flames shall not burn in thee."

The bondage of Adam is become the freedom of Christ. His death has been our deliverance. The future is not deprived of God, and sunk in misery. Nor is our destiny annihilation. The words, "Dust thou art, and into dust thou shalt return," have become, "O grave, where is thy victory, O death, where is thy sting." Its mysteriousness is illumined by the words of Christ: "For the hour cometh in which all that are in the graves shall hear the voice of the Son of God, and shall come forth, some unto the resurrection of life, some unto the resurrection of judgment." "I am the resurrection and the life. He that believes in Me, even though dead, shall live; and every one that lives and believes in Me, shall not die forever." "He that eateth My body, and drinketh My blood abideth in Me and I in him, and I will raise him up at the last day." "For if the Spirit of Him Who raised Jesus from the dead, dwells in you, He Who raised Jesus from the dead, will resuscitate your mortal bodies, because of the Holy Ghost dwelling in them." "This corruption must put on incorruption; this mortal must put on immortality."

In the Mystery of the passion and death of Jesus Christ, there was a hidden virtue and power capable of drawing to Him, "all whom the Father had given to Him:" "For no one cometh to the Son, save the Father draw him." To all such, the Cross of Christ has proved itself the potent instrument of salvation.

The Divine virtues and holiness which the Saviour exhibited in every stage and circumstance of His passion and death, manifested His Divinity: He was, indeed, "predestined the Son of God in holiness." His patience under calumny and insult, His resignation to the will of His Father, when the anguish of His soul forced from Him the prayer that the chalice of His agony might pass away from Him," His meekness and constancy under contumely and bodily suffering, His praying, even in death, to His Eternal Father for His executioners and those guilty of His blood, "for they knew not what they did," His spirit of fortitude, in suffering without complaint or resentment, the basest outrages, the most lying calumnies, and excruciating torments, when He had at His command "twelve legions of angels,"— these were the unmistakable evidences of the virtues of a God made Man.

He was charged with perverting the Jewish nation, although He had declared "that He had not come to destroy, but to fulfil;" and when they would make Him King, He had fled: He was charged with counselling not to give tribute to Cæsar, when He had commanded that "to Cæsar should be rendered what belonged to him, and to God what was His." He was charged with being an evil-doer, when, truly, He had performed every manner of good work, and when He had openly challenged any one "to accuse Him of sin." Pilate bore witness to His innocence, declaring "that he found no cause of death in Him." But the Jews, upon whom He had showered uncounted benefits and miracles and blessings, were resolved that " His blood should be on themselves, and on their children." Submission under such calumnies, and when vindicated by the voice of authority, was not the submission of a character merely human. He alone, Who was conscious that His condemnation, sufferings, and death were the Divinely-appointed sacrifice for sin, and the redemption of mankind, in the ordering of a Divine providence of which the Jews were but the instruments, though guilty, could be capable of so ready a resignation to injustice, and so profound a willingness to suffer and die.

In the Apostles demanding that fire be sent from heaven to destroy the people of Samaria, who had not received them, and in Peter's drawing his sword and cutting off the ear of Malchus, the servant of the High Priest, we see what human nature, when stung by insult, or exasperated under wrong, is capable of. In Christ's reproof of the Apostles, that they knew not of what spirit they were, in commanding Peter to put up his sword, for all who take it perish by it, in remaining upon the Cross, in spite of the jeers and taunts of his enemies, to consummate the work of redemption, when He could incontestably have descended uninjured,—in all this we see a virtue and holiness All Divine. His descent from the Cross would as little have convinced the Jews, as the resurrection of Lazarus from the dead (a greater miracle), and which had served as the occasion of His apprehension and trial and death.

The great prophecies, which had kept alive in the minds and hearts of men the promise made by Almighty God, on the day when man fell, of a future redemption, had been fulfilled by Christ. Daniel's seventy weeks of years that should elapse "From the going forth of the word to rebuild Jerusalem, unto Christ the Prince," expired at the end of the Saviour's career. He was slain at the middle of the last week, or in the four hundred and eighty-seventh year from the going forth of the command to restore the Holy City. The prophecy of Jacob, that "The sceptre should not pass away from Juda till He come Who is to be sent," was verified when Jerusalem fell before the Roman arms in the very generation of Christ, and in obedience also to His own prediction. The second Temple, which was to be yet standing when the Messiah would come, and Whose presence was to be its glory and to render it even greater than the first, to which, materially, it was incomparably inferior, has long since passed away; it was destroyed in the conflagration incident to the fall of Jerusalem, and in spite of the efforts of the Roman generals to save it.

In every circumstance and incident of His passion and death, Christ fulfilled to the letter, all that had been foretold, by Moses and the prophets, concerning Him. His iniquitous condemnation, His barbarous treatment, the unrestrained cruelty of His passion, and atrocious death, together with every detail attending each, had been clearly preannounced. His continual remark, "How then can it be fulfilled which was spoken by the prophet," indicates that He had, indeed, come "to fulfil the law," and the consuming desire, that He should discharge His mission. "The man of sorrows," "He Who was acquainted with infirmity," "He Who was wounded for our iniquities, and bruised for our sins," "He of Whom a bone would not be broken," "Upon Whose vesture they would cast lots," "Who would be sold for thirty pieces of silver, to be spent for a potter's field," was as real to the vision of Isaiah and Jeremiah and the other prophets, as He was seen on Calvary by the Jews and by his executioners, who unconsciously fulfilled their predictions.

Jesus Christ Himself uttered prophecies, which even in His own time, and since, have been gloriously fulfilled. Thus He showed that He possessed that intimate knowledge of the hearts of men and of future free events, depending upon the free actions of contingent persons and causes, which is the property of God alone. To know the future, belongs to Him alone with Whom there can be no past, nor present, nor future, but before Whose all-seeing, all-comprehending vision, all things are naked and open. "The Son of Man," said He to the Apostles long before any action against Him by the Jews was meditated, "must go up to Jerusalem, and suffer many things, that all written concerning Him may be fulfilled; die, and the third day rise again." No fewer than four times was this prediction uttered. And the Son of Man went up to Jerusalem, suffered much from the hands of the Jews, died, and the third day rose again, and all written of Him was abundantly, and to the letter verified. "Why this waste?" exclaimed Judas, when Mary Magdalene poured the ointment upon His feet, in preparation, as it proved, for His death and burial, "it could have been sold for much and given to the poor;" as if the treacherous and money-loving heart of him who afterwards sold his Master for thirty pieces of silver, could have had any regard for the poor. "Amen, I say to you, that wherever this Gospel shall be preached, that also which she hath done, shall be told as a memorial of her." And to-day, from the rising to the setting sun, the story of Mary's love and constancy is narrated. "An evil and adulterous generation seeketh a sign, and a sign shall not be given it, but the sign of Jonas in the whale's belly. For as Jonas was in the whale's belly three days, so shall the Son of Man be three days in the bosom of the earth." And the Son of Man was three days in the bosom of the earth, whence He rose glorious and immortal the third day. "Destroy this temple, and in three days I will rebuild it." And they destroyed that temple of His body, and in three days He rebuilt it with increased beauty, and transcendent endowments, and eternal glory. "Amen, I say to you, that one of you is about to betray me." And Judas forthwith dipped his hand in the dish, giving the sign of him who was to betray Him. "Al-

though all should be scandalized in thee, yet not I," exclaimed the impetuous and over-confident Peter. "Amen, I say to thee, that this night, before the cock crow, thou wilt deny me thrice." And that night, before the cock crew, Peter denied his Master. "He went out and wept bitterly remembering the word that Jesus had spoken." The morning found him shedding those bitter tears, which he never ceased to shed, and which eventually furrowed his cheeks. When thou shalt have risen from, and done penance for, the fault into which thou art about to fall, "confirm thy brethren:" and from then till now, Peter, in himself and in his successors, has not failed to confirm his brethren in the faith; his own being made secure by the efficacy of Christ's prayer. "When I shall be lifted up, I will draw all things to myself:" and He has drawn all things to Himself, either unto His love, or unto His condemnation. "He is set for the fall and rising of many in Israel." He foretold the ruin of Jerusalem, even before His generation should pass away, in words than which nothing more feeling or pathetic is to be found in all literature. He described the dire distress, the heart-rending scenes, the harrowing details that should accompany it, and declared it to be the just retribution for all the innocent blood which the Jews had shed, from the blood of Abel the just even unto the blood of Zachariah and His own. And while His blood yet bedewed Calvary, the Roman armies surrounded the city; and after a siege the most cruel, and sufferings the most unparalleled that history records, Jerusalem was destroyed; its Temple given to the flames, its lofty towers dismantled, its walls razed to the ground, and not a stone was left upon a stone to tell where it had once stood. The Roman general tried hard to save the Temple, but declared that its destruction, and that of the whole city, was clearly the work of the Most High; for his arms and forces had been insufficient to overcome such impregnable fortifications.

Not alone by the exact fulfilment of all that had been written concerning the Messiah, and by His own prophecies, then, and since luminously verified, but by the performance of miracles, and by the visible testimony of nature, even in the midst of what, to human eyes, might seem the season of His weakness and confusion, did Jesus Christ proclaim His eternal power and divinity. In His passion, He was comforted by an Angel sent from heaven in answer to His prayer of resignation to the will of His Father. On the first approach of the soldiers sent to apprehend Him, they fell prostrate before Him, overcome by the majesty of His bearing, and probably, too, by the consciousness of the iniquity of their errand. He restored the ear of Malchus, which Peter in his hot indignation had cut off. There was darkness over the earth from the sixth to the ninth hour; and whether this was confined to the land of Judea, or extended over the whole globe, the occurrence was equally prodigious, and equally the attestation of nature suiting itself to and abhorring the black deed of Deicide. When the God of nature suffered, no wonder that even inanimate nature by the power of its Creator, expressed its horror at the crime perpetrated by man, His free and noblest being. The creation awaiting for its redemption, according to the mind of St. Paul, could not fail to manifest its sense of the value and plan of that Divinely-wrought deliverance. The earth shook, the rocks were rent, the graves were opened, the dead arose and appeared to many. The veil which separated the holy of holies from the body of the Temple, was rent in twain from top to bottom, thus signifying the end of the Old Law with its types and symbols, and the removal of all obstacles that stood between the creature and his Creator, hindering his approach to Him. The centurion who stood by the Cross, struck by all that he saw and heard, exclaimed, "This, truly, was the Son of God." Those others also who stood by during the Crucifixion returned, striking their breasts, uttering the same Divinely-infused faith. The two thieves who were executed on either hand, may well be taken as types of the predestination which exists in God's eternal counsels. His life and death were, indeed, ordained for the fall and rise of many in Israel. To the penitent thief was given pardon and the promise of glory: the impenitent, who with the executioners reviled the Saviour of men, died in his blasphemy and impenitence.

In this act of forgiving sin, and promising paradise, Jesus Christ, with His dying breath, claims the power which during life He had claimed and wrought miracles to establish; and shows unmistakably His consciousness of the truth of His divinity. At the same time, He proclaims the reality of His sufferings, by the cry, "Lord God! why hast thou forsaken Me?" thereby indicating the withdrawal, by his own act, or the suspension or retirement, in some manner, of His divinity. Having thus, for the last time, proclaimed His divinity by the exercise of God's prerogative, and His humanity by the declaration of the reality of His sufferings, He seals the truth by commending with the utmost confidence His soul into the hands of His Father, and gives up His Spirit.

St. Paul had sounded the depth of the philosophy of the passion and death of Christ when he declared that he gloried in the Cross of Christ: "God forbid that I should glory in aught else, save the Cross of the Lord Jesus Christ." "For seeing, that in the wisdom of God the world, by wisdom, knew not God; it pleased God by the foolishness of preaching to save those who believe. For both the Jews ask for signs, and the Greeks seek after wisdom: but we preach Christ crucified: to the Jews indeed a stumbling-block, and to the Gentiles foolishness; but to those who are called, Jews and Greeks, Christ the power of God, and the wisdom of God: for the foolishness of God is wiser than men: and the weakness of God is stronger than men."

In entire harmony with this Divinely-ordained economy disclosed in the passion and death of Christ for the world's salvation, was the means elected to continue and perpetuate it among men. "But the foolish things of the world hath God chosen, to confound the wise: and the weak things of the world hath God chosen, to confound the strong: and the base things of the world, and the things which are despised, hath God chosen, and the things that are not, that He might bring to naught those things which are: that no flesh may glory in His sight." Such is "the wisdom of God in a mystery" "which none of the princes of this world knew; for if they had known it, they would not have crucified the Lord of Glory," and which, under the superintending providence of God, has been ordained for the world's redemption. Its weakness is its power, its shame is its glory, its triumph is the victory of God, "that no flesh may glory in His sight." "This is the victory that overcometh the world, our Faith."

Has He succeeded? The disclosures of the last day will make it known. There can be no doubt of it. There may be those who still refuse to believe in Him; there are those who would not hearken to Him even if He returned to earth. "No one can come to the Son save the Father draw him." Faith is not the gift of flesh and blood; it is the gift of the Eternal Father. "The Cross is to all that perish, foolishness; but to those who are saved, the power of God." Yes, Jesus has triumphed. "Fear not, little flock, for I have overcome the world." The power manifested in the Crucifixion of Christ has been manifested ever since wherever Christ crucified has been preached. The Cross has overcome the world: from it has gone forth a virtue, and an influence, and a grace, which has more than matched and overcome the maxims and wisdom and power of the world.

In His passion, He was charged with aspiring to be king: but He has become the King of an empire, of which the loftiest ambition or the most aspiring human pride never dreamt: the Spiritual Kingdom of souls and consciences. In derision, a sceptre was put into His hands: that sceptre has become the emblem of an authority, before which pales authority, the most despotic of human power. In mockery, He was crowned with thorns: that thorn-crown has blossomed into a diadem of glory, before which fades the lustre of all human thrones and dynasties. In ignominy, He was nailed to a cross: that Cross has become His everlasting Throne; as inseparable from Him, as the humanity which was nailed to it, is inseparable from His divinity. That sign shall be in heaven, when He will come to judge the living and the dead.

The mysteries and the truths which we have been considering are, at once, the loftiest that can engage the human mind, and the most necessary to shape wisely our lives. May, then, the great lessons of the Cross be fruitful in our souls; may they reap more than a transient emotion; may their effect be abundant and abiding, showing itself in changed thoughts, and a renewed life; may they ever be with us to fill our souls, and to direct our actions, that we may so live this life as to be made partakers of the next; may they be with us in the day of our death as the only source of our consolation, the only assurance of our salvation. May we, to-day, die to our sins, in image of His death, that we may rise with Him three days hence, in image of His resurrection, to a new life which purity, innocence, charity, patience, justice, temperance, and every kind of Christian virtue may illustrate; which will be a pledge and foretaste of the future life which Christ has purchased for us by His sufferings and death.

THE EXISTENCE OF HELL.

As, then, cockle is gathered up, and burnt in the fire, so will it be at the end of the world. The Son of Man will send His angels, and they shall gather out of His kingdom all scandals, and those who work iniquity; and cast them into the furnace of fire; there shall be weeping and gnashing of teeth.—St. Matt. xiii. 40-42.

And fire came down from God out of heaven and consumed them; and the devil who seduced them was cast into the lake of fire and brimstone, where both the beast and the false prophet shall be tormented day and night forever and ever.—Apoc. xx. 9-10.

GOD has established a moral law in the world. It is manifested to us by our conscience, which is the voice of God speaking in our hearts. Every law presupposes a legislator. The moral law can emanate from Him alone Who is at once the Maker of man's moral nature and the Source of morality. It is essential to the very idea of law that it have some sanction or penalty to secure its enforcement: hence no human law is made without a penalty upon those who refuse it obedience. What human wisdom has found necessary for laws ordained for the welfare of human society, Divine wisdom has established to secure the observance of the moral law. Yet Divine wisdom goes farther; and not content with punishment for the violation, also assigns rewards for the faithful observance, of its laws.

We do not find this sanction of the moral law in this world. Hence we must look for it in the next. We see that such rewards as this world affords, are, for the most part, enjoyed by those who would have least claim to them on the ground of their faithful observance of the moral law; and those who might claim them on this score, are, for the most part, deprived of them, and compelled frequently to pass life, it may be, in destitution and suffering. God would be indifferent to virtue and vice, if there were no future rewards or punishments. The cause of virtue must necessarily be His cause, and the virtuous His friends. Vice and its votaries can have no claim upon Him. Few are disposed to call in question the existence of heaven. No one is inclined to doubt whatever he desires, or whatever will yield him happiness. His misgivings begin when required to believe what may be repugnant to his feelings, and to his notions of what an Infinite being should do. Yet, if there is a heaven, there must be a hell; the one argues the existence of the other. If all the wicked, no less than the good, are to enter heaven, there is no reward, and there is no essential difference between virtue and vice. If the good are to be rewarded, the wicked are to be punished. Exclusion from heaven would itself be a hell. As the good are to be rewarded, positively, with felicity far beyond that to which they may lay any rightful claim; so the wicked are to be punished, not only negatively, by the deprivation of this reward, but also positively, by the infliction of punishment which will bear a just

THE EXISTENCE OF HELL. 419

proportion to the malice of sin, and the moral disorder which they have caused in the world.

The pursuit of virtue is arduous and difficult. It is beset with obstacles. Man is prone to vice. The lust of his heart is to be slackened and overcome. External temptations are to be vanquished or shunned. Continual vigilance and effort are the price of virtue. After years of innocence, vice may obtain the mastery. Yet virtue is necessary to the salvation of every man. There must, therefore, be an inducement to its practice and a compensation for the sacrifices it calls for. There must be a deterrent and dissuasive from vice. Grief and pain and anguish proportionate to the offence, should be the portion of those who have sought the unhallowed delights of sin; punishment proportionate should be the wages of the sinner.

As it belongs to God to ascribe sanctions to His law, it is His right to ordain such as He may deem sufficient or necessary. In this, He will act as the universal Ruler and Disposer of all things. He will consider not merely the means that may be necessary to the observance of His law, but also, what may conduce to His final purpose in the creation of the world. He will ordain means compatible with the freedom of the human will, and the economy upon which He has been pleased to place the salvation of man. According to this sense, whatever means or sanction He ordains will be absolutely sufficient, although man may still be at liberty, in the exercise of free will, to contemn it. The only means absolutely sufficient, at once, to allure to virtue and to overcome vice, is perpetual happiness for the one, and perpetual pain for the other. Any retribution short of this, would be insufficient. Although even this may seem insufficient to many, yet it is owing to their perversity, which leads them to try to reconcile sin with salvation, and the commission of sin, with the prospect of future pardon. No one deliberately and irrecoverably abandons the hope of salvation. The retributions of the future life would be insufficient, only where one could knowingly abandon them for something else. The sanction with which God has confirmed the moral law, is absolutely sufficient, whatever man in the freedom of his will, may do. If so many in their blindness, shut their eyes to the eternal character of future rewards and punishments, and give themselves to the gratification of sin with the hope of some time rising from it, how would it be if the future retributions were anything short of eternal? If the eternal scarcely holds man to his duty, how little observance of the moral law would there be, if there was any hope of future alleviation or pardon? Eternal sanction is alone sufficient. If there was a limit to future punishment or reward, there would be, in a manner, some excuse for the sinner's infidelity. Future hope, relaxing his obligations, would extenuate his guilt. Nor could the offence be without limit, whose punishment was one day to end.

It belongs to God to declare when the retributions which are the sanction of the moral law, shall take place. Naturally, we should look for them when the law itself will cease; with the death of the individual, and the termination of human society. God is, assuredly, free to make the period of probation, that of human life. There is no reason why it should not expire then as at any remote period in the future. There is fully as much reason why we should experience reward and punishment after the years of this life, be they few or many, as after uncounted ages. Nor can it be said that man has a right to a longer time. It is for the Creator to declare the term of the creature's probation. God's omniscience can perceive that the shortest span of life suffices for this, as much as the longest. He who has no right to time at all, has no right to its farther instalments. He who has no right to sin at all, has no right to sin for a longer time. In the exercise of free will man should follow the light of his intellect; but this teaches him that sin is the greatest of disorders and therefore to be avoided at every sacrifice. To sin, consequently, is to abuse the freedom of the will. How long this abuse shall continue, it belongs to God to declare and not to the sinner. He who is justly condemned for his first offence, has no right to opportunity to repeat it. Sin has no right to dictate terms to God and to demand a longer impunity, a broader field, or a more lengthened opportunity. The creature has no right to sin, and sin has no claim upon the sinner, and neither has any claim upon God. He could, in justice, have annihilated both in the act of the very first sin. Sin, accordingly, has no claim that the period of transgression be prolonged.

God, then, can decree the hour of death to be the hour of retribution.

They who question the existence of hell, fail to understand the nature and enormity of sin, and the infinite perfections and attributes of the Godhead. The sinner, as a creature, belongs to God, as his Creator, by every title. Over him, God has the most indefeasible right and dominion; to God, the creature is bound, by the most inalienable duty and subjection. From God the creature came as from his cause. To Him he is bound to return according to his nature, in the use of free will, as to his final end. To hold him to this duty, God has disclosed the retributions of the future life, alluring free-will by the prospect of eternal happiness, intimidating it by the assurance of everlasting suffering. The sinner spurns this lofty economy, renounces his God, forsakes his supernatural destiny, sacrifices heaven, embraces hell, and makes himself a slave of sin. Besides, when the creature sins, he places himself in conflict with God's order, and creates an irreparable confusion. It could never be in his power to restore the order he perverts, and reinstate himself in God's favor by his own unaided strength. Behold the grievous and irremediable nature of sin. This nature shows the necessity of hell as its just punishment; so great a disorder, and perversion of God's law and providence, should be repaired by a condign satisfaction. Sin's punishment should be proportioned to sin's malice.

I hear it said that there is no proportion between eternal punishment and sin, the work of a moment. But, what is there in sin, that for a moment of it, the sinner should contemn God? If man for a moment's gratification sacrifices God forever, why should not God give him his choice? If for a moment's sin man sacrifices an eternal good, what injustice if for the same sin God inflicts an eternal punishment? Man is free to sin and to abandon God forever; God is bound to exert justice and to cast away forever the sinner. The violation of the supreme dominion of the Creator over the creature, and of the correlative absolute duty of the creature to the Creator, can never be measured by the duration of the act. Its intrinsic malice is only exhausted by an eternal expiation. The malice of sin is indestructible and inexpiable. Eternity itself cannot atone for it. In itself, sin is unpardonable; once committed, it is an everlasting evil. It is the essential malignity, not the length of the act, of sin that is the measure of determining its nature. The civil law does not count the length of the act of violation, but the act itself as an affront to the majesty of the law, as an injury to the state, involved therein. Murder may be but the work of a moment, yet the law does not hesitate to punish it with death;—a punishment as infinite as human wisdom and power can execute; infinite, in a sense, absolutely, inasmuch as it may deprive the victim of salvation, by depriving him of further opportunity. It consigns him to death; it may be an everlasting death, for all the law cares; it never stops to inquire whether he will rise to life again in the next world. It is an infinite punishment because it takes away a life which it can never restore. Death, as a punishment, is a fit image of eternal reprobation. It is as infinite as man can inflict, human power can go no further. Thus, the civil law does not hesitate to visit the most condign suffering, the most revolting torture, even loss of life for that offence which is but the work of a moment. Why cannot God do the same for sin, which although momentary is yet essential contempt for His Divine Majesty? which is the wilful perversion of the order which His wisdom has established, which is the perfidy involved in the rebellion of the creature against the Creator, which is the abuse of free will, leading to forfeiture of heaven and entailment of hell. If man can justly for the good of temporal society cause death, cannot God inflict eternal punishment, as the sanction of His law, for the government of His eternal kingdom? Cannot God restrict the time of pardon to this life, and decree that reward and punishment shall be measured out, when this life, as the time of probation, shall cease?

God is infinite perfection and sanctity. Before His unblemished majesty the angels are not pure. To His all-seeing eye the heart of the purest is not without stain. In the light of His holiness and glory, the angels, with unceasing praise, proclaim the perfection of His nature. Nothing stained can stand before His unsullied purity. No defilement can co-exist with His absolute perfection. No sin can enter heaven. Darkness cannot subsist with light. Neither sin nor the sinner can be united to God. The moment mortal sin is committed, there is separation between God and the soul. This separation is in itself absolute and eternal. The interval that divides extremes the farthest apart, is small, compared with this separation. The sinner becomes the enemy of God. His state is that of damnation. The grace which united the soul to God and made it live in Him, passed out when mortal sin entered. Unless by repentance, the soul remains forever in that forlorn condition. It needs no intervention on the part of God to damn that soul; it would rather be needed to save it. It only remains that the sinner's vital breath may cease, that the cord of life be broken, for him to pass naturally to his proper place. Just as a man tied or fastened to some height needs but that what secures him should give way, to fall to the earth, so the sinner needs but that he pass from life to death, to meet his eternal doom. And as in the first case the man would need a suspension of the laws of nature to save him from falling, so would the sinner need the suspension of God's laws and His own direct interposition to rescue him from hell. Death makes no change; it only seals and confirms forever what has been done. At the end of life the sinner only enters upon a new form of the same damnation, he begins to suffer the punishment that belongs to it. The union of the soul with God, which constitutes salvation, unless effected in this life is lost forevermore. The disunion, which constitutes damnation, caused in this life and persevered in till death, subsists forever. This separation from God, wrought here below and sealed by death, is the essential misery of the damned; and even without any pain of sense would by itself be a hell. Nothing else is required to make the soul supremely and forever miserable. The existence of hell, then, flows as an intrinsic necessity from the nature of God, and the undying hate with which He must ever pursue sin. It is the just vengeance of God upon the opposition and affront which sin offers to His essential holiness. Sin must suffer the condign punishment which His inscrutable counsels have declared against its black and mysterious nature. Hell is the abode of this punishment. During life the sinner contemned the mercy of God. During eternity he shall forever proclaim His justice.

It has always been the universal persuasion of mankind that this life is one of probation, and that after it comes retribution. This belief has also induced the conviction that pardon for sin is restricted to this life, and that the manner of life decides the eternal doom. While here, we may merit or demerit. But in the life that begins at death, we must expect only reward or punishment,—that then there is no longer pardon, that the sentence uttered at death settles the eternal destiny. This belief so universal in its extent, finding acceptance among every people of the most different character and kind, coming down through all ages from the origin of man, and so familiar to, and approved by, the conscience of every one, can only be accounted the inborn conviction of his rational nature, and the result of the primary dictates of his intelligence. Such human sense, in every matter, is held to be an unfailing source of truth and one of the criteria of certainty. Whatever has such authority in its favor, must be esteemed true. God alone could have been its Author. He alone planted it in the human heart.

The moral law, of which the retributions of the future are the inexorable sanctions, was imposed upon man, as such : as a being made up of soul— gifted with free will and the option of good or evil—and of a body subject to lust and passion, and therefore fit subject upon which the will, exercising its freedom, can by its control, attain to virtue and its reward, or by its license, become guilty of sin and of its wages. When, then, man ceases to exist, the moral law for him should cease and retribution should naturally come. He is no longer the being capable of vice and virtue, to whom the moral law as a test and restraint was given. After the labor should come the wages. His life as man is at an end. It is true that his body will rise again, but it will arise supernaturally endowed—glorified and immortal, no longer subject to passion and prone to sin, but a new creature ; the soul no longer on probation, no longer in peril by its freedom of sin, but confirmed forever in God's grace. They will begin a new life, and develop new activities wholly different in character and object from that of this. They will be no longer capable of virtue and vice. If there was pardon in the future life for sin done in this, it should be given immediately after death ; not in the untold ages of eternity. For, man at the time of death is what he shall ever be. No change will take place in him which could induce God to grant the pardon, after ages, which he refuses at death.

The sanctions of the moral law are abundantly sufficient to hold man to virtue and to deter him from vice. There is no temptation however great that cannot be overcome by the fear of hell or the hope of heaven; there is nothing that sin and the world can afford, that, for a moment, can be preferred to God and the eternal happiness of the soul. It is only reflection that is needed to enable them to exert their unyielding force and efficacy. Yet, such is the freedom of the will, and the perversity of the heart, that most men are unrestrained by eternal retribution and give way to sin. How would it be, if there was any pardon or hope, that, in the remote ages of the future, there would be prospect of forgiveness? How would it be if men could but induce the hope, that, at the hour of death, a few years hence, there would be no retribution? The sanctions of the moral law would fail. If, now, with absolute assurance of eternal punishment and eternal reward, with absolute security of no forgiveness after death, and all this but a few years hence, men are not deterred from sin, how would it be if death brought no punishment, or if the remotest future afforded the faintest hope? If the soul of the sinner be such an incipient hell, if human society be but a prelude of hell, in spite of the dread future alternatives which we know and which should be restraints, into what a hell would both be turned, if these retributions were withdrawn, or even weakened by doubt?

If a subject rises in rebellion against his government, especially a just one, and if a period is assigned within which he must return to his loyalty or suffer the penalty of death; who is to be blamed if he, persisting in his crime, suffers the punishment of the law? is it the law, or the law's leniency, or the rebel's contumacy? is not his death to be ascribed to himself, as he had it in his option to avoid it? If a great multitude rise against a beneficent government, and a time is allotted within which by a return to obedience and loyalty they are pardoned, or, continuing in rebellion, they are slaughtered or decimated; who is responsible for the carnage? Who will hesitate to attribute it to their neglect of the proffered pardon? If, to reduce an individual, or even a multitude to the observance of law, confiscation of goods and forfeiture of rights are threatened; who will censure or condemn, if the threat is executed on their failure to fulfil the required condition?

History is full of such instances. The wisest men and legislators have not condemned them. The accumulated wisdom and experience of mankind have justified them. Can we deny to God the right we claim for man? Can that be folly or cruelty in God which is wisdom and leniency in man? Can that be condemned in God which is lauded in man? If man is free to employ such measures for human government, can God's wisdom be impeached for employing man's own instruments for the Divine government? Cannot God chastise individuals or human society for rising against the mildest and most lenient government, which He by His providence has established to secure the end of our creation, with the punishment which is not more infinite for Him, than those ordained by human law are for man? Exile and forfeiture of goods are among the most grievous penalties of human law. Cannot God sanction His law by expatriation from heaven and forfeiture of eternal goods? Death is as infinite a punishment as man can devise. Cannot God inflict a punishment as infinite, proportionate to His infinite nature? Unless, then, we are prepared to say that what the wisdom of mankind has declared wise and necessary for human society, is folly and unnecessary for the moral government of men, we must conclude that God can decree punishments and rewards after death.

If, to protect his life and property, one should cause a great chasm to be dug around his estate, so steep and deep and precipitous as to be sure and swift destruction to the invader; who would blame him, so protected, if his enemy, in mad fury, and with full knowledge of his peril, rushing to assail him, should fall into this gulf and be forever lost? Cannot God safeguard His majesty and name against rebellious creatures by surrounding His throne with similar bulwark, and forbidding them, at their eternal peril, to assail Him? If a great city protects itself, as has been frequently done, by a vast trench or circumvallation into which an invading army falling is destroyed; who will question the wisdom or justice of such a fortification? Who will fail to ascribe the great destruction, not to the city so defended, but to those carrying on the invasion? Cannot Divine wisdom protect the City of God by causing to be sunk the deep pit filled with torture and everlasting misery? Whose fault is it if myriads of men, in their wilful passion and blind folly rushing to assail the heavenly city, stumble into this bottomless gulf and are lost forever?

No sane person will deny that God can assign a period after which there shall be no longer pardon for sin. No one will claim that the creature has a right to sin forever. No one will affirm that forgiveness must never be denied in order that license for sin may reign forever. Have men a right that God should never refuse them pardon? If God is not bound to forgive man even once, no one will dream that He is bound to forgive him forever. To maintain a proposition so absurd, would be to say that the creature and his passions are greater than God and His law; that the violation of law is more sacred than its observance; that virtue is a delusion, that the moral law does not exist, that sin is the normal rule which alone should subsist; that the freedom of sin is more inviolable than the obligations of virtue; in fact, that there is no such thing as virtue, and that there is no God. Unless we are prepared for such absurdities, we must say that God can decree a limit to human probation and a period to pardon.

If God can do this, He is as free to declare it to

be now, or at the hour of death, as at any indefinite time in the future: as free to declare it to be after the short years of this life, as after ten million or any other period in the life to come. Every objection that the individual or society could urge against the execution of such a decree at the end of life, could be urged against it after any indefinite period, however long, in the future. Such a vast period of delay would afford as little time to the individual, or to the society of that time, as the few years of life afford to the individual, or to society of to-day. Such a duration of sin might well prescribe against virtue. Besides, it could not benefit the individuals who should have died before it came. They would still be confined to their few years of life. No one claims that individual human life should be prolonged to that indefinite period. Even then the time of life would be as short for salvation, sin as pleasant, conversion as difficult, God as far removed, the idea of God inflicting eternal punishment as incredible, the arguments pro and con, the same as now, to the men and women who would be then alive. The past would seem to them as short as the past now does to us. The career of men would appear as suddenly checked then, as it now appears after the course of this supposed short span of life. As, then, God is free to assign a limit to probation and pardon, and to declare there shall be no forgiveness after this limit, He is free to declare that limit to be when the soul leaves the body at death. What He can do later, He can do sooner. What He can do

THE EXISTENCE OF HELL. 433

after the first sin, He can do after a life of many sins.

Ponder carefully some of the passages of Holy Scripture, in which the existence of hell is plainly taught. There is no truth disclosed by Divine revelation more unmistakably or frequently. If the words that I shall quote do not establish the fact of eternal punishment, tell me what can their meaning be? St. Paul to the Romans ii. 4-6: "Or dost thou despise the riches of His goodness and patience and long-suffering! Dost thou not know, that the benignity of God leadeth thee to penance? But, after thy hardness and impenitent heart, thou treasurest up for thyself wrath on the day of wrath, and revelation of the just judgment of God, Who will render to every man according to his works." St. John v. 28, 29: "Wonder not at this, for the hour cometh in which all that are in the graves shall hear the voice of the Son of God. And they who have done good shall come forth unto the resurrection of life; but they who have done evil, unto the resurrection of judgment." Matt. x. 28: "And fear not those who kill the body, and cannot kill the soul; but rather fear Him who can destroy both body and soul in hell." Mark ix. 42-47: "And if thy hand scandalize thee, cut it off: it is better for thee to enter into life maimed, than having two hands to go into hell, into unquenchable fire, where their worm dieth not, and the fire is not extinguished; and if thy foot scandalize thee, cut it off: it is better for thee to enter lame into life than having two feet, to be cast into hell, into unquenchable fire, where their worm dieth not and the fire is not extinguished. And if thine eye scandalize thee, pluck it out: it is better for thee with one eye to enter into the kingdom of God, than having two eyes to be cast into hell fire: where their worm dieth not, and the fire is not extinguished. St. Paul, II. Cor. v. 10: "For we must all be manifested before the judgment-seat of Christ, that every one may receive the proper things of the body, according as he hath done, whether good or evil." Matt. xiii. 49, 50: "So shall it be at the end of the world. The Angels will go out and separate the wicked from among the just, and cast them into the furnace of fire; there shall be wailing and gnashing of teeth." St. Paul, II. Thess. i. 7, 8: "And to you, who are afflicted, rest with us when the Lord Jesus shall be revealed from heaven, with his mighty Angels in flaming fire, taking vengeance on those who know not God, and on those who obey not the Gospel of our Lord Jesus Christ." Rev. xiv. 10: "He also shall drink of the wine of the wrath of God, which is mingled with pure wine in the cup of his wrath, and he shall be tormented with fire and brimstone in the sight of the holy Angels, and in the sight of the Lamb." Matt. viii. 12: "But the children of the kingdom shall be cast out into utter darkness; there shall be wailing and gnashing of teeth." Luke xiii. 28: "There will be wailing and gnashing of teeth; when ye shall see Abraham and Isaac and Jacob and all the prophets in the kingdom of God, and you yourselves cast out." Isaiah lxvi. 24: "And they shall go out and see the carcasses of the men that have transgressed against me; their worm shall not die, and their fire shall not be quenched; and they shall be a loathsome sight to all flesh." Matt. xxv. 41: "Then he will say to those also on his left hand: Depart from me ye cursed into the everlasting fire, which was prepared for the devil and his angels." St. Paul, II. Thess. i. 9: "Who shall be punished with everlasting destruction from the presence of the Lord, and from the glory of his power." Matt. xiii. 40-42: "As then, cockle is gathered up and burned in the fire, so will it be at the end of this world. The Son of Man will send His Angels, and they shall gather out of His kingdom all scandals, and those who work iniquity: and cast them into the furnace of fire: there shall be wailing and gnashing of teeth." Rev. xx. 10: "And the devil, who seduced them, was cast into the lake of fire and brimstone, where both the beast and the false prophet shall be tormented day and night forever and ever."

Consider the goodness of God as shown in nature, and in man: in his rare endowments and supernatural destiny. Behold it in mere matter, seemingly dead, yet alive with fertility for his use and comfort; behold it in animal nature, and in the varied forms of physical life; all this for man: what a claim upon our love! Reflect upon the wondrous goodness of God as shown in the mystery of the Incarnation. What it was for the Infinitely Good and Eternal Being, our Lord and Maker, and the Creator of all things, to have stooped to our condition, and become man out of very goodness: to save us from sin, and to die that we might live. Ask yourselves how great is the claim which all this display of goodness exerts upon our service and our love; how great must not be our punishment if we refuse it? In view of the gratitude and love which we owe to our Lord and Maker for His infinite goodness, as shown in nature, and in the supernatural order, especially, in the amazing fact of the Incarnation, we cannot be surprised that eternal punishment is the alternative, if this goodness is ignored or contemned; it is the result of Divine justice. Infinite goodness calls for infinite love; infinite goodness despised, calls for infinite wrath to be inflicted. Divine patience abused, calls for the manifestation of the just judgment of God. "Or dost thou despise the riches of His goodness and patience and long-suffering? Dost thou not know that the benignity of God leadeth thee to penance? But, after thy hardness and impenitent heart, thou treasurest up for thyself wrath on the day of wrath, and revelation of the just judgment of God, Who will render to every man according to his works." (St. Paul to Romans, chap. ii. 4–6.)

Call to mind the infinite price that has been paid for our Redemption, and calculate the infinite evil that must be, from which such Redemption has saved us. The incarnation and death of Jesus Christ was the infinite ransom of our rescue from sin and hell. When we consider mortal sin, with its boundless malice, as an affront offered to a God of Infinite Majesty, and its wages, hell, with its eternal duration, as the evils from which that Incarnation was to save us, we are not surprised, at least, after faith has taught us the fact, that God should make such an Atonement. To rescue an immortal being from endless torture was a purpose worthy of the incarnation and death of the Son of God: He knew the value of human souls; He knew the infinite punishment that was in store for them; and that He alone by His Infinite Atonement could redeem them. The existence of hell renders credible the Incarnation; the Incarnation makes manifest the existence of eternal torture. An infinite price implies an object worthy of it, or an infinite debt to be discharged. All the souls of men, all the sacrifices that even Angelic nature could make, would not have been sufficient to atone for sin and to save man from hell. Nothing finite could compensate the Infinite Majesty of God, outraged by sin. Nothing finite could be an expiation for the punishment of eternal guilt. In Christ there was an eternal redemption, an eternal justice, an eternal sacrifice and priesthood, by whose efficacy "He can forever save those who through Him approach to God, since He always liveth to make intercession for us," and upon whom the sentence of eternal reprobation has not yet been uttered.

In the incarnation and death of Christ, as the price of our redemption, we behold at once the boundless nature of sin, the eternal duration of its punishment, and the Infinite Sacrifice which was necessary to save those who would apply it to their souls. But to the damned, this Infinite Atonement can no longer be applied. During the time of probation they had it at their command; to them it was an abundant salvation, but now the day of retribution has come; they have been cast out from the city of God, to perpetual exile and unceasing torture; they can no longer benefit by the blood of the Immaculate Lamb, Which during life they contemned, and Whose atonement for them, by their impenitence, they made void. They who decline infinite love, court eternal anger; eternal punishment is the retribution of infinite love despised. The blood of Christ was never meant in God's counsels to reach or rescue or relieve the damned; it was meant to anticipate their damnation and to save them from it. If it was the purpose of God ever to apply it to the souls of the lost, that blood had been equally efficacious to have saved them from hell and to have blotted out their sins before the eternal curse was pronounced upon them. They are no longer capable of the application of that Sacred Blood, because of their state of eternal reprobation, in which they are forever dead to God, and where their wills are confirmed forevermore in iniquity.

www.ingramcontent.com/pod-product-compliance
Lightning Source LLC
Chambersburg PA
CBHW021415300426
44114CB00010B/509